FROM DESERT STORM TO IRAQI FREEDOM:

ONE SOLDIER'S STORY

by

ERICK W. NASON

Bloomington, IN Milton Keynes, UK

authorHOUSE

AuthorHouse™
1663 Liberty Drive, Suite 200
Bloomington, IN 47403
www.authorhouse.com
Phone: 1-800-839-8640

AuthorHouse™ UK Ltd.
500 Avebury Boulevard
Central Milton Keynes, MK9 2BE
www.authorhouse.co.uk
Phone: 08001974150

First published by AuthorHouse 3/8/2006

ISBN: 1-4259-1887-5 (e)
ISBN: 1-4259-1886-7 (sc)

Library of Congress Control Number: 2006901973

Printed in the United States of America
Bloomington, Indiana

This book is printed on acid-free paper.

Contents

PREFACE

This is the story of a single soldier, one of many who have served in Iraq. It is my intent to write about my experiences while serving in Southwest Asia and provide a point of view based on what I learned in different operations and situations in Iraq. My first exposure was during Operation Desert Storm as a member of a Special Forces Operational Detachment. My last time in Iraq was as a member of a combined and joint staff, looking at the war from the middle-top, versus the bottom of the food chain. In a sense, I have been part of the ongoing history that is the conflict of Iraq, a very small part, but a part just the same. I have seen the country transformed and witnessed the history being made. This is the account of what I actually witnessed, with the intent to provide another side of the story to confirm or deny what was presented in the news media. Unfortunately, sometimes the details of these events are deleted or ignored due to the political climate of the time or the fact that the regular things soldiers do over in Iraq wouldn't make the press because the stories wouldn't be dramatic enough to grab headlines. With the advancement of technology and the ability to e-mail letters home during my last tour in Iraq, I was able to let my family know (within the security parameters, of course) what was actually going on. I wrote them stories about the brave and dedicated work of the soldiers serving in Iraq that were being left out of the evening news. Someone commented to me that I should write about what I saw, and thus this book was born.

My other intent with this book is to provide an unbiased look at the events as they occurred in Iraq. As a student of military history, I have been taught to look at history from an impartial point of view. I have seen what the lack of information can do to those who only get their information from the newspapers or television shows. Unfortunately, sometimes information is left out or washed over. This book is intended to allow the reader to understand what one soldier saw and experienced while serving in the Iraqi Theater of Operations. Granted, I will interject my own views or opinions, but I will attempt to approach this in an unbiased way and present the facts as I saw them on the ground.

As most of us veterans grow older, the details of what we experienced over in Iraq will begin to fade. If not preserved, who will read of our experiences and learn from them, how our stories will be told. During Desert Storm and Provide Comfort, I did not keep a journal of my experiences. When I deployed on Operation Iraqi Freedom, I began a journal to record my feelings and experiences in case I wanted to write a book. I continued my journal when I returned for Iraqi Freedom II. Therefore, the descriptions of what occurred during Operations Iraqi Freedom and Iraqi Freedom II will be more detailed, because they are fresher in my memory and I have the help of my journals.

I especially want to shed some light on what was experienced by us soldiers in the Special Operations community. Granted, due to the classified nature of our operations, I cannot go into any great detail on techniques and procedures. Being one of the "quiet professionals," special operations soldiers do not talk about what we do, nor are we normally seen on the news or in documentaries. I hope this book will shed some light into our normally dark and unknown world and will let people know about all of the great work and sacrifices the men and women of the Special Operation forces serving in Iraq accomplished with little or no recognition.

DEDICATION

I would like to dedicate this book to all of those who have served and will probably serve again in the Iraqi Theater of Operations – to all of the men and women, on active duty in all branches of the armed service, in the reserves and in the National Guard, to all those who came together to usher in a new period of democracy in Iraq. I would especially like to dedicate this to the family and friends of those who have made the ultimate sacrifice. To those who are serving and to those who may serve in the future, I say, stay the course, even when it seems nothing is going your way.

I also have some personal dedications. I would like to dedicate this book to my wife Karin and to my daughter, Samantha. Karin had to endure years of my beeper going off in the middle of the night and with my deploying to undisclosed locations for an unknown period of time. It has been said that military spouse is the hardest job in the military. My wife endured through the long separations while I was in Iraq. For my daughter, the early years of her life were not as difficult as the recent deployments. Samantha was now old enough to understand why I was gone. To make the matter somewhat worse, it always seems that I deploy on or about the time of her birthday. She also endured my absence through her baseball and soccer games and her school award ceremonies. The spouse has it tough. So does the military child. Sammy showed that she was tough as nails, hanging in there through the long months of my deployments.

I also would like to dedicate this to the members of my family, who have endured my twenty years in Special Operations. They realized that if there were a trouble spot somewhere in the world, I would more than likely be close by. I come from a large and unique family, literally split down the middle on political views. This has allowed for some interesting discussions concerning politics and current events. Though some of my family members may disagree with decisions made by our government, they have supported me and have also endured my times in hostile environments. It is for this reason that I am forever grateful for my family, and I thank them for their support. I would especially like to thank my stepmother, Sheila, who volunteered to edit this book for me.

Finally, I would like to dedicate this book to the families and the memory of Master Sergeant Richard Lee Ferguson and Major Paul R. Syverson III. Master Sergeant Ferguson, known to some of us as "Ferg," was killed in the line of duty on March 30, 2004. I had the pleasure and honor of serving with him in Germany with the 1st Battalion, 10th Special Forces Group and at Group Headquarters itself in Colorado Springs. I had seen him and spoken to him briefly a week before his untimely death, when his convoy stopped at our camp outside of Baghdad. He was a great person to know and will be sorely missed. Major Paul Syverson from the 5th Special Forces Group was also killed in the line of duty. I had the honor of knowing him and working with him in our Joint Operations Center in Iraq. Both of these men didn't have to be there, but they volunteered to do so. Both were "Quiet Professionals" of the Special Forces and heroes all.

List of Maps

CHAPTER 1

GROWING UP

Perhaps one of the mysteries of my life is why have I always been fascinated with the military, and military history. There is no real explanation for why I always wanted to be in the military, I could say that wanting to be a soldier was in my blood, influenced perhaps by where I was born and raised. I was born in the City of Glens Falls in upstate New York, just south of Lake George. This region played a key role in our nation's history from the early Colonial Days, including the French and Indian War and the American Revolution. Growing up with James Fennimore Cooper's "Last of the Mohicans" and visiting the places mentioned in the book as well as the following movies. My ancestors have served in just about every major conflict, including the French and Indian wars, the American Revolution, the War of 1812, and so on.

A fascination with the military did come with a small price; my mother was not very thrilled at my interest. This may be due to Vietnam just ending and my uncle who had served with the Marines there. As far back as the 3rd grade, my teacher, Mrs. Shanahan, explained to my mother that "the world will always need good soldiers, and Erick will grow up to be one of those good soldiers!" It was not what my mom wanted to hear, but she continued to watch me pursue my interests. As a senior at Glens Falls High School, I was torn between going to college or with joining the military. At the age of 17, I had tried to join the delayed entry program so I can guarantee my choice of assignment. I wanted to join the Special Forces, but at this time the Special Forces no longer took fresh recruits from the streets. I settled on the next best thing by volunteering for the Airborne Rangers. Even after the recruiter drove up to where I lived and talked to my mother about the delayed entry program, I could see my mom had made up her mind, and there was no way she would give permission to sign up.

After looking at colleges, I honestly felt there was no way my parents could afford a third person in college. My stepbrother and twin sister having being accepted to attend colleges. If I joined the Army, I could earn my own college money and would not have to rely on them. It would be later in my career that my dad told me he could have paid for my college. It made no difference. I felt better that I had earned my college money rather than relying on my family. Waiting for a few days after my eighteenth birthday, I signed my enlistment papers and joined the Army. Needless to say, my family was not altogether pleased at my decision.

After I spent one last summer at our family camp in Maine, I entered the Army at Fort Benning, Georgia, the home of the Infantry. There I would spend the next thirteen weeks becoming a basic infantry soldier. Where most volunteers today join the service to earn the college money, I had joined wanting to see combat. The college money I would earn with the G.I. Bill would be great, but I wanted to face the ultimate challenge of leading men in combat. I volunteered for the Rangers, believing with them was the best chance of seeing combat. Upon graduation, it was a quick bus ride over to the other side of Fort Benning where I would spend the next three weeks learning to jump (or more correctly, to fall) from perfectly good flying aircraft at the Army Airborne School. No sooner had I graduated from that school than I literally ran to my next phase of training, the Ranger Indoctrination Program. One of the instructors met us at the Airborne School. After we loaded our duffel bags onto a truck, the instructor organized us into a formation, and we ran the mile or so down the road to the 75th Ranger Regiment Indoctrination Center. There I learned the basics of what I would be expected to do as a Ranger. By December of 1985, I had earned my coveted black beret and was assigned to the 2nd battalion, 75th Ranger Regiment at Fort Lewis, Washington.

While a Ranger at Fort Lewis, I began to learn the tradecraft of the Rangers, to include small unit actions such as raids, ambushes and reconnaissance missions. I also was exposed to a mission set that I would become more familiar with later on with my career, Combat Search and Rescue (CSAR). My primary job was as a 90-

mm recoilless rifle gunner, then as a fire team leader once I made sergeant. After two years as a Ranger, I began to consider volunteering for Special Forces. In 1987, the Ranger Regimental Sergeants-Major spoke to us sergeants at Fort Lewis. He said in simplest terms that the Rangers were no longer to be Special Operators, but the best light infantry in the world! No longer would we attend specialized schools such as the Military Freefall or Sniper School, but we would concentrate on our professional development, jumpmaster, and Ranger schools. This did not sit well with me, for I had volunteered to be a Ranger because they conducted special operations. I made up my mind right there and then to volunteer for Special Forces training, and was accepted as one of the first students to attend the Special Forces Selection and Assessment program, a program designed to weed out those who were not ready to be Special Forces soldiers.

Prior to the creation of the Selection and Assessment program, anyone could volunteer to join the Special Forces. During the process of the training, the students would be weeded out. The new Selection and Assessment program was designed to get the qualified candidates a head of time prior to arriving for training. This allowed the instructors to focus more on the training during the first phase of the qualification course. The Special Forces Selection and Assessment (SFAS) program was a three week course designed to test Special Forces candidates in both physical as well as mental challenges while the whole time being evaluated by the cadre. Four hundred of us began the selection course, and only one hundred of us were accepted for Special Forces training. After returning to my unit to out process, I arrived at Fort Bragg, North Carolina in November of 1987 to begin the Special Forces Qualification Course. This was six months of intense training as I pursued the goal of becoming a Special Forces Weapons Sergeant.

Let me provide at this point a quick description of the different Special Operations forces within the United States Military. In the Army, there are four different types of forces. The Rangers are in simplest terms, commandoes. They are experts on light infantry tactics such as raids, ambushes, and reconnaissance and are identified by their tan berets. (It used to be black until the Army made the black beret the official headgear of everyone in the Army, including the National Guard and the Reserves) The Special Forces, or "Green

Berets," are experts in unconventional warfare and training partisans or guerrillas. The 160th Special Operations Aviation Regiment (SOAR), the "Night Stalkers," who fly specialized helicopters made famous in the movie, "Blackhawk Down." The fourth unit would be Delta, but I will not go into any further details about that unit, other than saying they are the premiere counter-terrorist unit of the United States.

The Navy has commandoes as well, known as the SEALs, which stand for Sea, Air and Land. Navy SEALs operate along beaches or rivers, conducting Special Operations as well as interdicting naval or civilian vessels. They can parachute in, either from static-line or free fall, swim in under or on the ocean, or operate on the ground using small unit tactics. To support them, the Navy has Special Boat Units that operate specially equipped vessels and small boats, as well as specially modified submarines.

The Air Force has Special Tactics Squadrons composed of their Pararescuemen and Combat Control Teams. Additionally, the Air Force has Special Operation Squadrons that fly specially equipped C-130 transport aircraft (the MC-130 Combat Talon II, MC-130P Combat Shadow Tankers, and the AC-130 Specter Gunships) and the MH-53 Pave Low III helicopters. All of these units belong to the United States Special Operations Command at Fort Bragg, North Carolina.

The Special Forces Qualification course was broken down into three phases. In the first phase of training, students learned small unit tactics (patrolling, raids and ambushes) and land navigation. The second phase involved skill-specific tasks, for me meant weapons. That meant students learned everything there is to know about small arms, ranging from pistols, to rifles, to submachine guns, to machine guns and assault rifles, as well as mortars, anti-armor weapons, and air defense weapons. The training covered both American/NATO weapons and the weapons of the former Warsaw Pact. The third and final phase was the culminating unconventional warfare exercise known as Robin Sage. It was here that all of the specific Military Occupational Specialties (MOS) of the Special Forces (18A-SF Officers, 18B-Weapons, 18C-Engineer, 18D-Medic, 18E-Communications, and sometimes 180A-SF Warrant Officers) were combined into student operational detachments. These teams infiltrated and linked up with "guerrilla fighters," assessed them, and trained them in unconventional warfare tactics. Then the student advisors led these guerrillas in combat operations. Once all of this training was successfully completed, I earned my coveted green beret.

Normally, following the qualification course, new SF soldiers would have attended language school. However, being one of five who were assigned to the 1st battalion, 10th Special Forces Group stationed in Bad Tolz, Germany, I would learn German there. When my class graduated, the 3rd Special Forces Group was reactivated at Fort Bragg. To provide a battalion for the new group, the 5th Special Forces gave up the personnel. The majority of my graduating class was assigned to the 5th Special Forces while a very small number were assigned to other groups.

For the most part, each Special Forces Group is organized along the same line. There is a group headquarters along with supporting companies, and three battalions. The 10th Special Forces Group Headquarters was at Fort Devans, Massachusetts with the second and third battalions. The first battalion was forward deployed in Germany. In April of 1988, I arrived at my new assignment in the picturesque Bavarian Town of Bad Tolz, and Flint Kaserne, home of the 1st battalion, 10th SFG. When the group was first formed back in 1954, all three battalions were either stationed in Flint Kaserne or over at Prinz Heinrick Kaserne, in Lenggries. Now only the first battalion remained. Bad Tolz is located south of Munich, near the border with Austria, and north of the tourist city of Garmish-Parten-kirchen.

Flint Kaserne had an interesting past. It had been built under Adolf Hitler's orders as one of the three Waffen-SS Officers Academies. During World War II, it was captured as a war prize and was once commanded by General George S. Patton. The name "Flint" was given to the kaserne for Patton's friend, General Flint who had been killed nearby during the fighting. Patton commented that Flint Kaserne was perhaps the best example of how to build a base. The main building was a large square structure with connecting corridors and four large gates. There were tunnels that connected the officers' and sergeant's houses to the main building. The basement itself went down for three levels, but it was flooded before the Americans arrived during the war and was closed off for safety reasons. Flint

Kaserne sat on a high plain, with a panoramic view of the snow-capped Austrian mountains off in the distance. This was going to be my new home.

My first assignment was to a regular team or also known in our slang as a "ruck" team in Company C, meaning that the detachment was not specialized in the sense of being either a free-fall or a scuba detachment. During this period of time, the battalion was not heavily involved in world-wide deployments. The biggest event for the unit was the unconventional warfare exercise known as "Osprey." As luck would have it, the team I was assigned to would be one of the guerrilla teams selected for that year. Normally, the exercise splits our three companies into three specific tasks. Our company would lead and train the partisans, another company would train and lead the security forces (known as Foreign Internal Defense), and the third company would conduct direct action or strategic reconnaissance missions.

When later in my career I was asked about what I did in Germany from younger soldiers, I would normally get some funny looks from them. It was hard for them to understand that I trained and prepared incase the Warsaw Pact invaded Germany and we would conduct unconventional warfare against them. They replied that the Soviets are our allies, and I had to explain that back when I was stationed in Germany, they were not. Having not served in Europe during the Cold War, it's understandable to their confusion. On my detachment, we emphasized knowing each other's skills. We were all cross-trained and spent one day a week training each other on the team. This was so we could split up the team and not be short on skills. I concentrated on learning the job of the junior medic for the team, since we had only one instead of the normal two. We had three weapons sergeants, so I was a free agent to be used as necessary. We all learned Morse code, and we all worked on our German. All of this training would become essential in the near future, but that was unknown to me then. The world was relatively quiet, but that would soon change.

A Special Forces Group is normally composed of a headquarters and three battalions. Normally, each group has around 800 personnel assigned to it. For the most part, it's all men, except for headquarters, where some women serve in the rigger (pack parachutes), supply, or military intelligence sections. The battalions are considered combat arms units, so there are no women assigned to them. In the Group Headquarters, there are the Group Support Company and the Headquarters Support Company. The headquarters is referred to as the "C-Team." These are where the support personnel who run the day to day activities are located. Within the battalions, there are three Special Forces companies and a Headquarters and Headquarters Company. Each battalion has approximately 250 men assigned. Each Special Forces Company has a headquarters, known as the "B-Team" and up to six "A-Teams" or detachments. These are the classic 12-man Special Forces A-Teams (not the A-Team television show), and the B-team is slightly larger due to its administrative duties.

The world seemed to start coming apart at the seams in 1989, when the Berlin Wall came down. Our company had received a new mission of becoming the European Commander's (EUCOM) Special Operations Contingency Force, and I was attending the Special Forces Advance Reconnaissance and Exploitation Course (SFARTEC) at the Special Forces Advanced Urban Warfare School at Fort Bragg when I learned the news. The Cold War had come to an end, and our mission shifted away from leading and training guerrillas to performing contingency operations. In 1990, I attended the Special Operations Target Interdiction Course (SOTIC), the Special Forces Sniper School. At SFARTEAC, I learned special skills similar to those used by Police SWAT teams in an urban environment. SOTIC taught me to be a sniper, able to place a precise shot with a high-powered rifle.

In August of 1990, Saddam Hussein's Republican Guard and mechanized forces invaded his neighbor, Kuwait. As the United States began mobilizing forces to defend Saudi Arabia in what would become known as Operation Desert Shield, we in Bad Tolz learned of our new mission.

CHAPTER 2

OPERATION DESERT SHIELD/ DESERT STORM

For the last couple of years, my assignment with the 1st battalion had been interesting, but quiet. With the invasion of Kuwait, we began to train for our new mission specialty, Combat Search and Rescue (CSAR). Granted, we had not (to my knowledge) received any specific orders to deploy. Being the EUCOM Commander's Special Operation Contingency Force, with Brigadier General Richard Potter in command at that time, and he wanted us to be prepared in case we were needed. Taking the lead on our training was the detachment's warrant officer, Mike Dozier, who had to be the most knowledgeable man I had ever met.

Mike Dozier was one of the "old school" Special Forces Warrant Officers, having served as an enlisted Special Forces soldier before becoming a warrant officer. Mike always impressed, beginning on the first day I arrived on the team. When I arrived, he sat me down and started to go over what was expected on the team. What really stood out was when he said, "Don't get into bad habits. You better have tough skin, for if you're down you're going to get kicked." After a pregnant pause as he looked me over, he added, "from now on, your nickname is Aag." Aag was a comic strip character, a caveman who was very strong. During one of training events with a German Mountain unit, Mike gave an excellent lesson to one of the Germans first sergeants on our weapon-cleaning solvents. Mike speaks excellent German, but his simulation of the "eating" process of the solvent with crossed-eyes and over-exaggerated chewing motion was a sight to see that I remember vividly. It definitely got the point across.

We began by developing tactics that would become our standard operating procedures, and each man in the detachment learned them inside and out. After developing our tactics, we began to rehearse them in the mountains and fields of Southern Bavaria. Our cross-training continued with more of a sense of urgency and more details. However, even though Bad Tolz was a nice area to train in, it did not come close to what the terrain would be if we were deployed to Iraq. Our company flew to a small island on the west coast of Scotland, where at the time; the Naval Special Warfare Unit #2 (SEAL) platoon is was stationed, for further training. Granted, the terrain was open and rolling, similar to Iraq, but there the similarity ended. This area of Scotland was full of moors (swamps) and wet. It was here that I did, in fact, witness Scottish rain coming down horizontally. The open terrain did, however, allow us to work out our procedures in a location where everyone could see what we were doing. Perhaps the most beneficial part of the training was working with the Special Tactics Team including the Combat Controller Teams (CCT), and Pararescuemen (PJs), who would be working with us in Iraq. CCTs are Air Force personnel specially trained to set up hasty airfields and control aircraft. Pararescuemen are the Air Force rescue specialists, trained to recover downed airmen and provide life-saving care. They are as comparable to our 18-D Special Forces Medics when it comes to medicine.

Additionally, we worked extensively with the Air Force's 352nd Special Operations Group (SOG) and their large MH-53 Pave Low Helicopters of the 21st Special Operations Squadron (SOS). These would be the aircraft we would use in case we had to conduct recovery missions. The MH-53 is a modified version of the "Super Jolly" from the Vietnam War and the CH-53 Sea Stallion of the Marines. The aircraft was modified with additional radar, Forward Looking Infrared Radar (FLIR) systems, and threat avoidance equipment. Though the equipment and avionics were new, one of the aircraft was built on the frame of a helicopter that had been used during the famous Son Tay Raid of the Vietnam War.

This training was very advantageous to us, because we were able to work with the very personnel and aircraft that we would deploy with. We were able to learn about each other, and we developed a close bond. I worked mostly with Captain Harding's aircraft and crew (unfortunately I never learned Captain Harding's first name). I was always impressed with Captain Harding; for a short man of small stature, he could really fly that large helicopter. He flew it almost like a fighter, and that made my confidence in him grow. My team was sure that if we got into trouble, he would get us out. Our part of the CSAR team's mission was to provide the ground security and, in case of enemy contact, the firepower to keep the enemy off and protect the Air Force PJs who were charged with securing the downed pilot. We all trained to do each other's jobs, in case one or both of the PJs or the CCT was injured. We practiced search patterns in case we had to look for a pilot, even in the desert.

As the training continued, we practiced every conceivable event and contingency that might occur. This included infiltration techniques, including the use of the Fast Rope. With this technique, the helicopter hovers while a single rope, approximately four inches thick, is kicked out to the ground. The rope is made of a special fiber that allows the soldier to grip it and slide down, like a fireman's pole. Due to my stature, I normally led the team down the rope, both because I was supposed to straighten it out and because no one wanted me to land on top of them. Additionally, we rehearsed and practiced the alternate means of exfiltrating, climbing a cable ladder up to the aircraft. Again, due to my stature, I anchored the ladder as my team climbed, rucksack, weapons, and all. The big challenge to climbing the ladder is getting a good footing on an approximately foot-and-a-half rung while fighting the strong downward rotor wash of the helicopter.

Additionally, we learned everything we could about the aircraft and how to get the aircrew out if we went down. This included destruction procedures after getting the pilots out. We also practiced using the aircraft machine guns, both the .50 caliber at the rear and the 7.62-mm mini-guns on the sides.

After we trained in Scotland, we moved down to the Stanford Training Area, northeast of London, to conduct live-fire training. Here we were able to work out our Standard Operating Procedures (SOPs) and battle drills, utilizing live fire exercises. Training with blanks allows the soldier to get the mechanics down, but live fire gets you tuned to what to expect for real and forces you to concentrate on safety. We practiced everything we could, from two-man movement drills to maneuvers involving the whole detachment, including anti-armor weapons and demolitions training. This concept is called, "Train as you fight," which means becoming accustomed to the sight and sound of what fighting will actually be like. This was perhaps the best training I went through in preparation for the possibility of a deployment.

Returning to Bad Tolz, we continued to train, and enjoyed the holidays with our families. In January of 1991, our company was alerted, and the whole company loaded up on buses and moved to the departure airfield outside of Munich. Waiting there for us was a gigantic C-5 Galaxy transport plane, our ride to the theater of operations. We loaded our equipment which was being transported in six-ton vans and climbed aboard. Having our own vans made moving our equipment easier. Normally, our equipment would be loaded on metal pallets, and then loaded on the aircraft. Once the aircraft and the equipment arrived at the destination, you had to wait for a fork-lift to arrive and unload the equipment. Now, we could just unchain the vans and drive off. The vans were parked on the main deck while we climbed up a thin stairway to the second deck where passengers rode. Soon we were on our way to our next stop, Incirlik Air Base, in Turkey.

It was a bright and sunny day when we arrived at the American Air Base at Incirlik. People have joked, "What if you had a war and no one showed up?" In Incirlik, we were faced with a similar problem. "Who are you guys and what are you doing here?" was asked of us when we got off the plane. We explained we were here to support Desert Shield, but no one seemed to have known that we were coming. That didn't faze any of us, because such mix-ups had happened before. After waiting for a bit, we were moved to where we would be quartered in the base housing area, which we believed was in the process of being renovated. Most of the family members had been evacuated back to the United States before we arrived. All of the teams from the company received their own houses. My team of 15 men occupied a single-story, four-bedroom house. Our team was a "non- standard" team so more men were assigned to it. After becoming the EUCOM (European Command) Commander's Contingency Force, our team became specialized. Instead of being a normal "ruck team," we were a sniper/observer team that also specialized in collecting battlefield and urban reconnaissance. We had more men assigned due to operating in small, three-man sections for reconnaissance and sniper missions.

We fell back on our old training and began to prepare our house as a planning area. For security reasons, I helped our detachment's intelligence/operations sergeant, Ricky Williams, place newspapers over the windows. Sections of the house were set aside for planning, equipment areas, sleeping areas, and meeting areas. I roomed with two of my fellow weapons sergeants: Sergeant First Class (SFC) Todd Sowerby and Staff Sergeant (SSG) Lauren Sharp. Todd, the team's senior weapons sergeant, was on the team when I arrived. Lauren, who had gone through the Q-Course with me, was from Oregon, and somehow he had earned the nickname "sheep-herder." To this day, I don't know where it came from. The other Weapons Sergeant on the Team was SSG Roger Moore, who was in one of the other rooms. Roger had been the team's Junior Weapons Sergeant before Lauren and I showed up. Roger would be going about his business when out of the blue, we could hear him imitating Eddy Murphy in the movie "48 Hours," his voice rendering a loud "Roxanne" followed by a softer, "yeah baby."

The rest of our detachment was quartered in the other rooms. The leadership included the detachment commander, Captain (CPT) Christopher Perkins; the detachment warrant officer, Chief Warrant Officer 3 (CW/3) Shawn Driscoll; and the detachment team sergeant, Master Sergeant (MSG) Robert Spears. Before coming to Special Forces, Captain Perkins had been in a mechanized unit stationed in Germany. Shawn Driscoll, who was from Vermont, had replaced Mike Dozier who moved up to become the Company Operations Warrant Officer.

Bob Spears had been in the Army a long time, having served in Vietnam. When I joined the team, he commented that his dog tags were older than me. In fact, he could have been my father because of my young age. Such a relationship was genetically impossible, however, seeing we are about as opposite as it can get physically. He stands about five foot ten and weighs about 130 pounds, where I was six foot, two inches and 230 pounds. He told me that when he was on convoy duty in Vietnam, he managed to "liberate" some beer from the truck they were following, and they got a little buzzed. During one of the halts, he was fooling around with his grenade launcher and blew up a nearby hut. He was soon reassigned off convoy duty and became a door gunner in a UH-1 Huey transport helicopter. Bob had served in 1st Battalion of the 1st Special Forces Group on Okinawa, before coming to 10th Group.

Additionally, assisting in the operational planning were SFC John Simpson and SFC Ricky Williams. John Simpson became one of my closest friends and my sniper buddy. We were both fans of the movie "The Highlander" and would recite lines from it as we ruck-marched around Bavaria. With my nickname of Aag, John and I became known as the "Aag Brothers," and we maintained our reputation as good shooters who played really hard when we could. From time to time, I would go over to his house to smoke cigars, drink Gin and Gatorade (called wind calls), and watch "Black Adder." Ricky Williams could be considered a "Good Ole Boy" from Kentucky and was a big NASCAR fan. He had originally been assigned to the 5th Special Forces Group before coming to 10th Group.

Our engineer sergeants included SGT Lee Tomasic and SFC Glen McMurry. Lee had been on the team for awhile and was a really good engineer, who also enjoyed working with explosives. During our training in England, we spent a day on the demolitions range. Lee wanted to experiment with a charge that he had read about called, "The Perpetually Detonating Charge," which to me meant a sun, but I trusted he knew what he was doing and went about my tasks. After all of the charges had detonated, we found that Lee's experiment hadn't, and it was on fire. This meant the charge was really unstable. Lee had built it, so he had to clear it, which he did without any problems. Glen had the nickname of "Stumpy" and had also been on the team for a good while. He was our tour guide whenever we were in London, having spent some time there with his wife, who was from London. We had taken a day off from training and spent the day in London after riding the train into the city. We actually did some sight seeing, passing by Buckingham Palace real quick on our way to the Hard Rock Café, where we drank and worked on our cultural immersion training.

The detachment's medics were SSG Tony Hernandez and SSG Stan Shank. These two would take me under their wings and show me the ropes as I was cross-trained as a medic for the team. Stan had served with 7th Group over at Fort Bragg before coming to the 10th Group. Tony was like myself, a new member of the team, and he helped me a lot in my cross training. Tony was one of those quiet guys who sat back and watched what was going on, assessing everything. The detachment's communication sergeants included SSG Kevin Morse, SSG Dave Talarczyk, and SFC Dan McLean. Kevin had been on the team for a few months before we deployed, arriving just as the team began planning for a possible evacuation of American citizens from Liberia in early 1990. Dan had been on the team for awhile and was responsible for keeping all of our radios up and running. Dave Talarczyk was another new member to the team after we became a "non-standard" team. Our Air Force brothers were located in the main gym of the Air Force base, which was fine with us. With all of us in one house, it was already pretty tight with all of our gear included.

As we began to refine our plan on how we were going to configure the team for Combat Search and Rescue missions and work out any kinks in our SOPs, President George Bush drew his line in the sand, and the United Nations gave Saddam Hussein until January 15 to remove his forces from Kuwait. He refused, and what would become known as "Operation Desert Storm" began in the early morning hours of January 17, 1991. The majority of our team was fast asleep when the war started. The only way we knew for sure was that the war had begun was while Captain Perkins and John Simpson was over visiting our Air Force brothers in the gym. Being good Air Force folks, they had a television tuned to CNN. As Captain Perkins was speaking to the CCT's Team Leader, John looked over to what would become the famous night broadcast of the anti-aircraft fire over Baghdad. John went over and attempted to get Captain Perkins's attention. "Sir, you need to see this," John said. Captain Perkins continued talking and paid no attention. John really emphasized, "Sir, you really need to see this!" Captain Perkins looked over and saw the news report, and soon they were both heading back to our house.

We finally learned what was happening when the phone rang. In typical military fashion, the base overreacted. We were given the news that the war had started and we should get into our chemical protective suits! There was a fear that Saddam would launch one of his chemically armed SCUD missiles at our base. We took the news in stride; it was what we had been waiting for. Being the good Special Forces soldiers that we were, we obeyed the letter of the law, but allowed common sense to take over. We went back to our rooms, pulled out our Nuclear, Biological, and Chemical (NBC) protective garments and our protective gas masks, and promptly tried to get back to sleep. I knew in the next couple of hours we were going to start to be very busy.

A lot of thoughts were running through my head, and I assume my bunkmates were having the same feelings. As for my protective gear, I used it as a pillow. We all knew that Iraqi SCUD missiles did not have the range to hit us in Turkey. We also surmised that Saddam would not shoot his missiles at Turkey, a Muslim country. In the morning, we awoke and received our orders to pack our gear and head to the airfield. We were going to move to our next location. My good friend and sniper partner, John Simpson, had to remain behind to help push the company forward.

John quickly wrote down some bullet data and shooting technique data that we had been working on together, known as "negative-aiming." He wrote this down on an orange five by eight card and handed it to me. "In case you need it, "John said, "but if you get a confirmed kill before me, I'll kill you!" With those warm words, I loaded up my rucksack and prepared to go. I still carry that data card in my "deployment book" to this day. It has come in handy a few times in other places.

Our intelligence folks told us the area we were going into was a dirt strip near the Iraqi Border. There was nothing there except a single concrete building. We packed accordingly, believing we were heading for a cold, rustic environment. Being a cold-weather-orientated unit, we knew what to expect. Then the medics showed up with vials of clear liquid with a white sticky label on it. As we were lined up to receive the injections, we found out it was Anthrax serum, in case we were hit by biological weapons. Between the intelligence of where we were going and the Anthrax shot, we were ready. I kept thinking, "Here we go. A lonely dirt strip in the middle of nowhere, ready to go to war!"

The team loaded up on trucks and was driven out to the airfield. Our team would be going first, with the rest of the company following in a couple of days. Since the war had started, the activity around the airfield had dramatically increased, with fighters and attack aircraft taking off regularly. We found ourselves a comfortable spot on a grassy section near a parking lot and began our wait. One of the oldest institutions in the military is the dreaded "hurry up and wait." This was what was happening to us at that very moment, and it would continue to plague us throughout the time I served in and around Iraq. We had been awakened early, and we had gotten ready to get out to the airfield as soon as we could. Now we began a wait that would take all day. We just didn't know it yet. We made ourselves as comfortable as we could and did whatever we could to pass the time. I doubled checked my equipment and cleaned my M24 sniper rifle, my M9 pistol, and my M4 carbine. As I was cleaning my sniper rifle, an Air Force technician, who was walking by, stopped. He looked over at me and asked, "Are you a sniper?" I nodded that I was, and he smiled and said, "Get a few for me!" With a big smile and enthusiastic thumbs up, the airman was off to wherever he was going.

As we waited, we watched the Air Force folks unload one of the 352nd SOG's MH-53s from the bowels of a C-5 Galaxy. They pulled the aircraft into one of the hangars and begin to reassemble it, almost like a large model kit. How long were we waiting there? Not only did they finish putting the helicopter back together, but we actually watched them test fly it! Still we waited, and soon the sun began to set.

Then we received word to load up and head out to the waiting aircraft. Sitting on the tarmac was one of the 352nd SOG's MC-130 aircraft, a standard C-130 transport that has been modified to support Special Operations. As we began to load, the EUCOM Deputy Commander, Colonel Getty, came out, wished us luck, and talked with Captain Perkins. After the aircraft was loaded, we took off into the night sky and were on our way. It was not a long flight, and soon we were given the warning that we are beginning the descent to the airfield. As we began to flare for the landing, I looked out of the window and saw landing lights flashing past. "That's odd," I thought to myself. "I guess it isn't as rustic as we were told." The intelligence section was slightly off on their assessment.

The team was driven over to where we would be quartered in the dark, and I was unable to see where we were. Our new home was a cold, concrete ammunition storage bunker. The bunker had lights though, and we made ourselves a place to sleep. The following day, we looked around our new surroundings. We were located on a modern Turkish Air Force Base and were residing in their ammunition storage area. Our team was not alone; an Air Force Engineer element was on the base as well. They were here to begin building the tent city which would become our base camp.

With no immediate taskings, we decided to give them a hand to help kill time. The Air Force guys had no idea who we were, but they readily accepted our help. When we deployed, we continued the Cold War practice of deploying in sterile uniforms. That is, on our Battle Dress Uniforms (BDUs), all we had was our name tape, U.S. Army tape, and our rank. No unit identification or patches. For the most part, any time a Special Forces unit went anywhere, it was considered sensitive. Therefore, we never "advertised" who we were by wearing our berets or unit patches on deployments. Now with something to do (and a chance to get out of that cold bunker), we happily went off to work, building the wooden floors for the tents. The first floors we built were for ourselves, and we soon moved out of the bunker and into our new home.

The base itself was situated in a large open valley, surrounded by low hills and mountains. There was a town located southwest of the base, just past the perimeter fence. There was very little vegetation to look at, just flat open and rolling terrain with some scattered bushes or small trees. There was a single three-story building on this base which served as a barracks (I believe). The rest of the base was scattered with small, single-story buildings. The NATO star symbol could be seen on all of the buildings and the bunkers, showing this base was also a NATO base. There was no American facility built to feed us yet, so we ate local Turkish food that was catered for us until our dining facility was up and running. We spent the next week or so building the floors and tents for the new camp. Our identity remained unknown until one of the Air Force engineers injured his hand. I took him inside our tent to clean up his injury, and his eyes went rather wide at what he saw. In our tightly packed tent were our equipment, rucksacks, and assorted weapons. As I pulled out my medical bag, he stared at my sniper rifle, and then at the machine guns. (We had deployed with HK-21s instead of the common M-60s). His eyes became even bigger when I opened the medical bag and began removing some of the surgical items and IVs. As I cleaned up his hand, he asked who we were, and I promptly replied, engineers. He stared at me in disbelief and stated he never saw engineers with all that stuff. I calmly replied we were combat engineers and finished dressing his hand.

The secret was out when the rest of the company arrived after about a week and word quickly spread through the Air Force personnel that Special Forces had arrived. We continued to help construct the camp and get our portion set up. Eventually we found out the place where we were at was called "Batman," and we all snickered. Believing it to be a codename, like Gotham City or the Joker, but we came to find out the real name of the place was in fact, Batman. Since we had no shower facilities built yet, in good Special Forces tradition, we improvised. Securing an empty ammunition can, we placed it on top of the tent's heating stove and warmed the water. Once the water was hot, we went outside and gave ourselves a quick wash up.

Once we had our camp set up, we began our rotation cycle of three days. First, a day was spent training, rehearsals, and preparing and testing our equipment. The next day, we stood Combat Search and Rescue alert at the airfield, and the third day we stood down. We had broken down the team into two split teams, one of seven and one of eight respectively. Within those split teams, we broke ourselves down into smaller, three-man elements.

Once the helicopters arrived, we continued to refine and train, rehearsing our mission in the surrounding countryside. There was a small range complex on one side of the airfield that we used to maintain our weapons proficiency and conduct live-fire rehearsals. The range itself was nothing really to look at, an open space with a berm topped by empty barrels at the end and along the sides. During our off days, we were not really off. We spent that time doing equipment and weapons maintenance, physical training, and other tasks. One of these was to construct air raid shelters in case the base was attacked by Iraqi SCUDS. The SCUD was an old Soviet built, medium range, tactical missile that had been sold to the Iraqis. The

Iraqis had modified their own version of the SCUD for longer range at the expense of accuracy, and could be equipped with chemical warheads. The bunkers were dug about ten to twelve feet deep, and the dirt dug from the hole was used to fill sand bags. The sand bags were layered on top of the bunker about four feet thick. We received advice from our team sergeant, Bob Spears, who had served in Vietnam, along with Chief Warrant Officer Jimmy Spoo, who had also served at Khe San, Vietnam, as a Marine. They gave pointers on the construction and told us tales of their bunkers. As we dug the bunkers, the Air Force "Prime Beef" team, the support folks who would build and run the camp, arrived and sat around watching us construct. The image of them sitting in their lawn chairs and watching us would come back to haunt them in a couple of days.

During one of our training days, we became unwitting participants in a deception planned against the Iraqis. We were told to conduct radio training around the tent area. We were to train on all of our different radio systems, but the catch was, our company commander told us to do it unsecured. Military radios have a device which prevents an enemy force from hearing what you are transmitting. However, speaking in the "clear" which meant without the secure device, the Iraqis would hear everything we transmitted. Still not really clear why, we all moved off to different spots on the compound and began our radio training, especially our High frequency (HF) radios, practicing Morse code and voice transmissions. What we were not told, was intelligence knew the Iraqis were listening to us. All of a sudden, the Iraqis began to hear multiple transmissions coming from Turkey. The Iraqis must have thought we had secretly moved an invasion force to just north of Iraq. Not knowing if this was true or not, the Iraqi High Command shifted some of their brigades north of Baghdad to counter this potential threat. These divisions would not be engaging US and coalition forces, and perhaps this deception saved a number of lives in the long run.

We had rehearsed what we would do in case of an attack, either from a SCUD or an air attack. The difference between a drill and the real thing was that a large red flag would be hoisted near the Turkish control tower for the real thing. A few days after we completed our bunkers, the air raid siren began to wail. I looked up and sure enough, the red flag was up, and Turkish F-5 and F-104 fighters were launching. I quickly ran to my tent, picked up my medical bag, helmet, and protective mask and suit, and moved to the bunkers. As I arrived, I was watching our Air Force Prime Beef personnel being politely but firmly removed from our bunkers and directed to the nearest stream ditch about a hundred meters away.

As everyone climbed inside the bunker, I sat on top with my helmet on, staring up into the crisp, blue sky. When asked what I was doing, I replied I wanted to see the air defense batteries open fire. I had observed that the base was ringed with Rapier missile systems and 30-mm anti-aircraft cannons. If this was an attack, I wanted to see the fireworks. After not seeing anything for several minutes, I observed three Belgium Mirages land on the airfield. One of the three Belgium aircraft had been damaged, and they diverted to our base. Unfortunately, the Iraqis also flew the same type of aircraft, and the base thought it was an attack. Though nothing happened, it was a great way to test our battle drill, not to mention the fact that it left an endearing thought with our Air Force Prime Beef brothers. They should have helped us instead of sitting there and watching us. Unfortunately, this would perhaps come back to haunt us later.

Perhaps one of the most memorable mornings I had occurred a few days later during the peak of the air offensive. The Coalition was striking targets in Iraq late at night and early in the morning during the period of darkness. The last run flew over our camp in the early morning. I woke up one day and stood outside my tent, having a cup of coffee. I heard the sound of jets and looked up into a clear, pristine blue sky. Then the jets and their contrails began to appear overhead, first singly, then in groups. Soon, the whole sky was filled with contrails as the jets passed overhead on their way back to Incirlik. I thought to myself, this must be what it was like during the Second World War when the British looked up to see the contrails of the bombers flying over. All of those contrails, pointing like long, white fingers towards Incirlik. It was a very impressive site to see, all of those fighters and attack aircraft filling the sky. That was a nice way to drink your coffee in the morning. Soon it became routine listening to the aircraft flying over, going to and returning from their missions in Iraq.

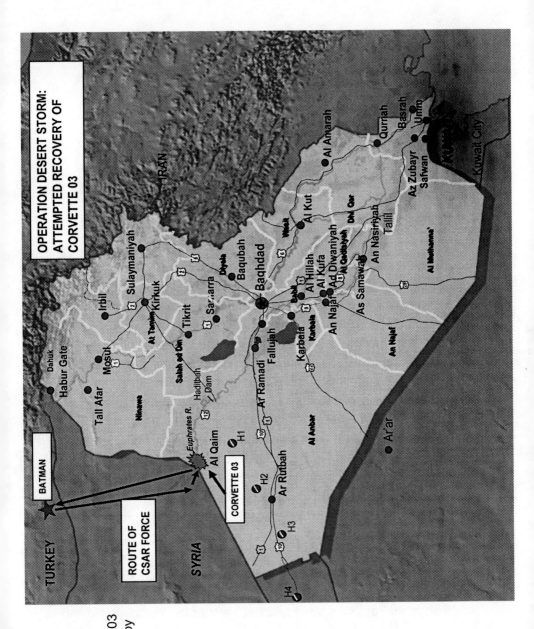

MAP 01: Location of Incirlik Air Base, Batman and the location of Corvette 03 and the route used by the recovery force.

CHAPTER 3

CSAR, CORVETTE 03 AND THE END OF THE WAR

Our six teams in the company, along with our headquarters, had been brought to this corner of Turkey to be available to rescue any downed airman who might become isolated in northern Iraq. For the most part, the southern portion of Iraq was well covered; our company was moved to Turkey to cover the northern portion. We soon became accustomed to the routine of preparing, standing alert, and then standing down. The night prior to going on our rotation as the alert crew, we made sure all of our equipment was ready and laid out. I carried an M4 carbine and an M79 grenade launcher, as well as an M9 pistol. We didn't have enough of the standard M203 grenade launchers to go around, so I carried the old M79 and a vest full of grenades. I carried a small backpack with survival and mission-essential equipment, such as my night vision goggles and extra ammunition. Some of us also carried a single bullet in our shirt pockets. This was intended to be our last resort if we were captured. We had been told what the Iraqis would do to us if they captured us and how we would be interrogated. Lauren, who had attended the SERE School at Fort Bragg, was adamant about not going through torture. I carried the bullet, but I wasn't sure if I would use it; I hoped not to be placed in that situation.

The following morning, we made our way over to the alert building where we would stand strip alert. Basically, strip alert meant that we as the duty crew for the day would be located next to the airstrip where our helicopters sat. Sometimes we broke up the monotony by walking instead of driving over to the airfield and carrying our backpacks and weapons to keep in shape. Once we arrived at the alert building, we placed our gear where we could get to it quickly. For the rest of the day, we stayed in that little room. The nice thing was, it had a television, and we watched CNN and kept abreast of what was happening in Iraq. After putting our equipment away, the first order of business was to receive the intelligence report for the day. My team which served as the security element, included Captain Perkins, Ricky Williams, Tony Hernandez, Lauren Sharp, Lee Tomasic, and Roger Moore, along with Lieutenant Maki and another Air Force Combat Controller whose name I can't recall went into a briefing room. Inside the room, everyone was assembled: the helicopter aircrews, the ground force (us), the CCT, and PJs. Like in old bomber movies from the Second World War, there was a large briefing map in the front of the room. The intelligence briefer climbed up on the stage and gave us the missions for the day. We learned where the targets were, which routes the aircraft would fly, and which routes they would use to exit Iraq. As this process became more like second nature, so did the briefings. We had an intelligence officer who appeared to be only sixteen years old. We gave him a hard time because he looked younger than everyone else. He responded by getting on the stage, giving his brief, and stating that he did in fact have a note from his mother to be there.

In addition to the briefing on the day's missions, we received updates on the air offensive and the enemy threat. After being there for a month, we had pretty much heard what the Iraqis had for a threat and were able to brief it back from memory. It got to the point that the intelligence officer would ask us to explain the characteristics and counter measures to a particular enemy surface-to-air missile. For example, if a SA-8 Soviet-built surface-to-air missile was able to lock on our helicopter with its guidance system, we would "pop flares and chaff (small pieces of aluminum foil [chaff] and small burning pieces of magnesium [flares] used to confuse a missile's tracking system) then hover the helicopter behind a building." Following the briefing, we returned to our little room and waited to see if anything happened. We did go out and conduct training when we could, as long as there was a means of recalling us. Sometimes we all went out, including the crew. The vast majority of the time, we sat, trained, and waited. It was frustrating, but, looking at the big picture, our lack of action was, in fact, quite good news. No pilots or crews had yet gone down.

Then, towards the end of January, it began to look as if we were going into action. While I was sitting strip alert, we received word that one of our aircraft, call sign "CORVETTE 03," had gone down in the Al-Qaim region of western Iraq. In this area on the western border between Iraq and Syria, there is a sharp bend in the country's outline. The aircrew of an F-15E Strike Eagle, Colonel David Eberly and Major Thomas Griffith, had been hit by two SA-2 Soviet-made surface-to-air missiles. Their ejection was monitored by a RC-135 RIVET JOINT reconnaissance aircraft and passed to higher head-quarters in Saudi Arabia. After receiving the information of the bail out, we began to plan in earnest. After receiving word of the ejec-tion, we had grabbed our gear and ran out to the helicopters. Unfor-tunately, we did not have the exact location of our pilots. Addition-ally, there was a problem getting there. Our helicopters did not have the range to get there and back without refueling, and there was a lot of hostile territory between us and the pilots. As we continued to plan, General Richard Potter and the senior members of the staff began negotiations for cross-border operations. This included con-ducting diplomatic coordination with both Turkey and Syria. Even though Syria was technically an ally and a member of the coalition, the Syrians did not want to have American helicopters flying over their territory. Turkey also made it difficult to cross its border and enter Iraq. The safest route for our aircraft would be to fly inside the Syrian border until close to the Sinjar region, and then enter from there. As the planning and negotiations continued, we were kept up-to-date on the pilot's location. We were told that signals were com-ing in from his survival radio, giving a good location for him.

After three days of negotiations, the Syrians agreed to allow us to fly through their border and make an attempt at the recovery. The plan called for the helicopters to make their entry at the same time that air strikes were going in. Hopefully, the Iraqi air defense radar would be watching the fighters and attack aircraft and not two, low-flying helicopters. As we prepared for the mission, it was decided that Roger Moore and Dan Mclean, from one helicopter, and I from the other would be taken off the mission and put on strip alert for the back-up team in case the primary team did not make it. The new primary team consisted of Captain Perkins and MSG Spears, who took our places, each being assigned to one of the helicopters respectively. Though I was not very happy about it, we returned to the ready room and watched the news.

However, the recovery team was in for a big surprise. The mission went well up to the point that the helicopters turned and made their approach across the border. To help cover their approach, the helicopters were flying below some strike missions against Iraqi targets along the border. They had only been across the border maybe five minutes when the threat warning went off in the aircraft. Iraqi air defense radars and missile tracking radars had targeted our aircraft. The pilots used countermeasures and turned quickly back as golf ball size tracers began to arch up and search the sky for them.

We found out later that the pilot had been captured, and the Iraqis might have set up what was known as a "SAM Trap." I believe they had taken either Colonel Eberly's or Major Griffith's survival radio and placed it in the middle of a circle of air defense artillery and surface-to-air missiles (SAM). As the recovery aircraft closed in on the survival radio's location, the Iraqis quickly turned on their radars and engaged the recovery force. Luckily for us, they didn't hit anything, and the aircraft returned safely to base.

This was one of those frustrating events, where politics and combat operations didn't mix. I have often wondered if we would have been able to recover the pilot if we had launched the day he went down instead of waiting for three days. I have also wondered if the Syrians finally allowed the mission to fly over Syria because they knew the Iraqis had captured the pilot. In any case, we were unable to recover him, and we went back to our normal three-day alert cycle.

The snubbing the Air Force Prime Beef personnel back during the air raid may have come back to haunt us. Once the rest of the Air Force personnel arrived, they needed more living space. We were told to pack our stuff and move further down the base and build ourselves a new camp. Our company just packed up and moved down the road. Along with giving us instructions to move, the Air Force headquarters folks selected a nice, low, swampy location for us. I guess payback can be a little rough. We took it in stride and began the construction of our new camp. The company had truckloads of gravel to level the place and get us above the groundwater. Then we laid the floors and erected the tents.

Once the camp was built, the next order of business was building air raid bunkers. However, this time we were ordered to build two firing positions at either end of the bunkers, which we would use in case we had to defend the camp. Once again, common sense made us skeptical. We wondered whom we would be defending against. Our camp was located inside a Turkish Air Force base; if the Iraqis attacked, they would have the whole Turkish garrison to deal with before they reached us.

With a vigorous "roger that," my team along with the other company's teams set to work on digging the new bunkers around the perimeter of our new compound. We no longer had sandbags, but we were supplied instead with large potato sacks. After filling them up and trying to lug the almost 80-pound sacks, we decided to fill them only halfway, making it easier to move them and place them on the bunker. We began to enjoy ourselves, and made it looked like we were wrestling with pigs as we hauled these sacks into position on the bunker. As one of my team mates "wrestled" the sack into position, the rest of us added the background noise of "oinks" and "squeals" while others cheered them on. It helped to break up the normally back-breaking chore of hauling sacks and building bunkers. There were two fighting positions on the ends of the bunker, as directed. We made sure we had interlocking fields of fire with the other bunkers on our left and right. One half of the team was housed in one tent; the other half was in the tent across from it, and the bunker was located in between on the perimeter.

My split team, including Captain Perkins, Tony, Lauren, Roger, Lee , Ricky, and Dan, organized our tent so it was functional, if not orderly, while our neighbors, the other half of the team, went out of their way to make theirs more livable. They actually took some of the sacks and made an entrance carpet, with a small sitting room. Then they had their personal areas. We felt they were just trying to get in "Better Tents and Living" magazine. Their carpet proved to be beneficial, however, especially when the rains came. Though we were north of Iraq, it rained heavily from time to time, as the season changed from winter to spring. We had to build a wooden walkway to our tents and the bunker, with an additional layer of sand bags in front of the bunker's entrance to keep the water out. Most of the time, we were wet and cold from the constant rain. As we walked across the camp, the mud caked to almost 4 inches under our boot soles, giving us the Herman Munster look. Then we had to scrape it all off before going inside the tents, to keep ahead of the growing muck. For the next month or so, we were at constant war with the mud to prevent it from getting into everything. Some of the guys clumped around to see how thick they could coat the bottom of their boots in mud. Dave Talarczyk came up with a brilliant idea. He used the big green Army-issued rubber boots to clump around in, and then took them off and entered his tent with clean boots. Soon this idea caught on, and everything from the regular green rubber over-boots to the black rubber boots used as part of our chemical protection gear was coming out to help us stay ahead of the mud.

The camp had grown, and soon some more amenities were added. A dining facility was built, and we were fed in a five-tent complex. A laundry facility, ran by the Air Force, was finally built. This, along with the shower, was probably the most important feature, as far as I was concerned. I attract dirt. I have always said that if I stood out in the middle of an open field, I would get dirty. Using only our improvised means of staying clean, I was dirty most of the time. From time to time I joked around that I was following a phrase from one of my favorite war movies, "The Cross of Iron": "The body's natural oil, when mixed with dirt, makes you waterproof!" I wanted to see if this was true or not, but my teammates probably would have disowned me because of the smell. Once the showers were up and running, I decided to forego my experiment and get cleaned up whenever I could. We couldn't take a shower every day, only at specified days to help control shower usage. To assist in my endeavors to remain clean, I had asked my wife to send me a small, kiddie pool to use as a bath tub. Unfortunately, the war ended before I received the pool to try it out.

In both of our team tents, we had one person on laundry duty. He gathered up the dirty clothes in laundry bags and took them to the laundry. Once the laundry was completed, he picked them up and brought them back to the tents.

A Morale, Welfare and Recreation (MWR) tent with books and magazines to read was also added. If the troops needed some store items, we gave a "shopping list" to our Air Force brothers who were flying over to Incirlik. This nearly got us in trouble when we decided to try an experiment in the camp. We were under the "no drinking rule" for the deployment, but Lee decided to take some fruit, add sugar and yeast, and see what kind of still we could build. We gave our Air Force brothers a shopping list for items "needed for our experiment" to be purchased at Incirlik. They came back with none of the stuff; I guess the authorities figured out what we were up to.

Eventually, a portable store in the form of a tractor trailer, arrived in camp, and we could purchase items there. We received care packages and letters from home, but they took a long time getting to us. Additionally, we received a standard package from MWR containing shaving supplies, soap, pens, paper, and snacks. Unfortunately, sometimes the M&Ms tasted like the washing soap that was also in the package. Jerry Zunnich, who was a member of our company, loved M&Ms and did not care that they tasted like soap. We all gave him ours.

In between alerts, we performed other jobs around the camp. Someone came up with the brilliant idea of turning our camp into a Vietnam-era Special Forces Camp. An officer told me and a couple of the other weapons sergeants to look at the feasibility of erecting a watch tower and mortar pits. We asked the officer, at what target would we fire the mortars at to level the base plates. With a mortar system, you had to fire a few rounds at the maximum propellant charge to make sure the base plate of the mortar was firmly sunk in the ground and would not move. Agreeing with us that the local Turkish farmers would probably not like having a mortar fired at them, the powers that be dropped the whole idea.

The other duty we all shared was burning our toilet wastes. Similar to what had been used in Vietnam, our outhouse had a half barrel drum under it to collect the waste, which was then mixed with diesel fuel and burned. This was an all-day event, to insure all of the waste was burned and the remaining ashes buried. Except for the smell, it was not a bad duty when the temperatures remained cold and wet.

To entertain ourselves, we built a volleyball court near our tent so we could play a few games. I improvised some sand bags and containers to use as weights for working out. One of our neighboring teams built their own SCUD Missile out of discarded items (small-scale version), which they mounted outside of their tent, aimed at Iraq. Before we had deployed to Iraq, most of our team members had been fans of a radio DJ known as "The Grease Man," who had his own style of humor. One of his better-known characters was a Vietnam Vet named "Sergeant Fury," who had some rather unique qualities and adventures. John Simpson made some tapes of his show, which aired on DC 101 from Washington D.C., and we listened to the tapes to get a good laugh.

Leslie "Less" Kush, the company medic had a video camera, and we spent a day recording video messages to our families back in Germany. It was something special we could do for our families to bridge the gap between us. Video letters are always better than the plain paper ones. During one of our range days, Dave Talarczyk brought a tape recorder with him to make a voice letter to his wife. He and I were positioned behind the berm to check targets once the shooting was complete. As the team fired, you could hear the snap and whiz of the bullets. With this in the background, he spoke into his tape recorder, sounding like he was under fire while taping the letter. Adding realistic sound effects to the "illusion," a Turkish jet flew over. I don't know if he ever sent it home or if he let his wife listen to it when he got back, but boy what a ham.

We still watched the news while we sat on strip alert, and we especially enjoyed the news conferences. The thing that impressed us most was how General Norman Swartzkopf stood his ground against the endless battery of questions from the reporters. He did not put up with frivolous questions or questions about operational activities that had the potential to compromise a mission. One of the daily briefings to the reporters still stands out in my memory. As he was about to move on, General Swartzkopf backed up and pointed out some symbols deep in Iraqi territory. Here, he pointed out, were Special Forces gathering intelligence on Iraqi operations.

Granted, it may have been a better idea not to mention it, seeing the Iraqis watched CNN as well, but at least he recognized what Special Forces were doing. Most of the time, we are ignored or never mentioned.

Except for the attempted recovery of Corvette 03, no other missions came our way. On one evening, our helicopter crew was going to fly a "wild weasel" mission along the Iraqi border. This means that our helicopter was going to fly along the border and see if it was targeted by Iraqi air defense radar. Once the Iraqis began tracking the helicopter, Air Force attack aircraft, F-4 "Wild Weasels," would go in to destroy the radar site. The crew was going to take one of us along to lead the air crew out if we were shot down and had to evade the Iraqis. By the luck of the draw (literally, we drew cards and I won), I was selected to go on the mission. During the briefing, the Turkish liaison officer told us flat out that we would not be allowed to fly the border. If we were to fly across the border, the Turkish air defense would shoot us down! Captain Harding stood up and told the liaison officer he did not have the technology to shoot us down, and we all left. But the possibility of that mission being flown was over, and we all went back to our tents.

There was a second recovery mission conducted in our theater of operations. An F-16 had been severely damaged on an air strike in Iraq. The pilot was able to nurse his crippled fighter over the Iraqi border, and he ejected near one of our other bases at Diyarabakir, Turkey. A truck from the base drove out and picked up the pilot and retuned him to base.

Our Air Force CCT teammates also were given a mission to recover or destroy a 2,000-pound bomb that was jettisoned from a damaged aircraft. They had to fly up into the mountains along the Iraqi/Turkish border. They came back, telling of deep snow and the difficulty of finding the bomb. I would have loved to have gone, so I could have said I had skied Iraq!

Our intelligence folks believed that they had detected Iraqi Special Forces operating near our camp. The Air Force attack aircraft were destroying all of the Iraqi air defense radar systems, so the Iraqis decided to keep their radars off until the last moment and then suddenly to turn them on. To assist them, we believed they had infiltrated Special Forces elements near us to watch for the aircraft flying over. The Air Force was using our camp as a navigation point, the air strikes beginning their run into Iraqi near or over our camp. The Iraqi Special Forces elements radioed back to their air defense command, letting them know that the aircraft were on their way so the radar operators would be ready. We had radio intercepts and believed we had pinpointed their locations through triangulation. We volunteered to go after them, but once again politics intervened. Our company operations officer informed us that the Turkish military would take care of the problem. The next day, we watched a flight of American-made Huey helicopters fly over, and about fifteen minutes later, fly back. That was the extent of the Turkish military operation.

On a sunny morning a few days later, John and I were cleaning our rifles outside of our tent. I was working on my sniper rifle when I heard a gunshot in the distance. Quickly putting my rifle into action, I took up a firing position, and John took up a supporting/spotting position just behind me. We actually saw the Iraqi fire a burst from his AK-style rifle into the air, and then he was turning away from us on a nearby hill. I was taking up the trigger slack to engage him when our company commander came out and told us not to shoot. Oh well! We watched him disappear over the hill and out of sight. Soon after this, our intelligence people began to lose track of the radio intercepts. Perhaps the Iraqi Special Forces had all returned to Iraq, and the gunshot was this guy's way of proving himself before he returned. As I was putting my rifle away, I was upset; but then, the more I thought about it, the more I realized that not shooting was the right thing to do. Technically, he didn't shoot directly at me; he was a target of opportunity, and was not really covered under our rules of engagement.

Our mission began to change about a week or so before February 24, 1991 when the ground offensive was launched against the Iraqi forces holding Kuwait. The Coalition had achieved air superiority, and the need for us to conduct CSAR operations began to dwindle. For some reason, our higher headquarters began to come up with some winners for plans, we assumed from watching too many "cool-guy" action movies. SCUD missiles were still the biggest threat, and the higher authority wanted them found. It was suggested that we infiltrate some of our teams by parachute on top of a ridge in the western desert to look for SCUDs. I looked at the map, which contained the Iraqis' order of battle and locations, and looked at the proposed landing sites. All along the top of the ridge were symbols depicting Iraqi air defense units. Pointing this out to one of our intelligence officers, I simply stated that I didn't believe the Air Force would want to over-fly these areas and drop us. Sometimes I wondered if the planners were looking at the same maps that we were.

That plan was scrapped, and a new one came up to take its place. An idea was hatched that a team would float down the Tigris and Euphrates Rivers on poncho rafts and take out some of the key bridges. Needless to say, in order for us to carry enough explosives to bring down a bridge, we would need a poncho raft the size of a destroyer; fortunately, this plan was quickly dropped.

The SCUD missile remained the chief threat, and a better and more realistic plan was developed. We would form "rat patrols" of jeeps to scour the countryside and look for the SCUDs. Personnel with experience in jeeps, which included me with my Ranger battalion experience, put our heads together to come up with a concept. The old Army jeep was small enough to fit inside one of the MH-53 helicopters and could be infiltrated by air instead of by driving across the border. The idea was simple: each jeep would have a sniper with a .50-caliber sniper rifle, a machine gun team, a stinger missile, and some extra gun fighters with mines and grenades. The jeep teams would look for the SCUD launchers. If the SCUDS were being transported along a road, they would be ambushed. If the SCUDS were found in a stationary position and being prepared to be launched, the sniper would take out the fuel cells within the missile (which was my job). The last resort was if we observed the missile being launched; the plan was to engage it with a stinger missile and attempt to bring it down. If all else failed, we were to radio the launch so the Patriot systems would be warned, based on the cardinal direction in which we observed the missile flying.

This plan actually looked like it was going to go forward as more of the specialized weapons and equipment were shipped to us. A real, no-kidding, rocket scientist brought us a blueprint of the

SCUD missile to show where exactly to place the round, if we had to engage the fuel cells within the missile. The bullet would punch a hole in the missile's fuel cell, draining the fuel and preventing it from launching. Also, the missile's fuel was toxic and would more than likely kill or incapacitate the ground crew if they were not in their protective gear. A few years later, I met a former East German SCUD commander, and I asked him about the information I had received about the fuel cell. He agreed that what I had been told by our intelligence folks was accurate. Imagine that, real intelligence that would have really worked!

Unfortunately this wouldn't matter at all, because on the morning of February 28, we were informed that the ground war was over. This came as a shock to all of us. We felt that the war couldn't be over. Granted, the Iraqi military had been forced out of Kuwait, but Saddam was still in power, and we really believed he was still a viable threat to the region. The majority of us in our camp believed we should have pushed into Baghdad and removed Saddam from power. However, the military had achieved both the military and political objectives for Operation Desert Storm. Military operations stopped and a cease-fire went into effect as terms were negotiated between the Iraqi military and our Coalition. For our company and the personnel at the camp, the war was over.

To celebrate, we had a big Bar-B-Q and picnic, along with some sporting events. I was walking over to the picnic with our team leader, Captain Perkins, and the CCT Team Leader, Lieutenant Mackie. My team leader sometimes started trouble that got me caught in the middle. It was a nice day, and I guess he decided to have a little fun with the Lieutenant. He started poking at him how I could beat him in wrestling. Lieutenant Mackie was an All-American in Football and Wrestling at the Air Force Academy. It was inevitable; the lieutenant and I ended up wrestling each other right there on the spot. Granted I had wrestled in high school and sometimes did it for fun while in the military, but not all the time. I was able to keep even with him, and it was all in good fun. We stopped wrestling, and he was amazed that I was able to keep up with him like I did. Even Captain Perkins was amazed that the lieutenant didn't wrap me up.

We went over and enjoyed the picnic and waited to see what would happen next.

For the next couple of weeks, we were busy getting ready to return home. Equipment was cleaned, inventoried, and packed. As the day for our return drew closer, the heating stoves were cleaned, and the tents broken down. I was assigned the chore of cleaning the stovepipes, probably because I was dirty most of the time (and perhaps because I was one of the lowest-ranking members on the team). By the second week in March, our team boarded a MC-130, and we returned once more to Incirlik Air Force Base. We spent a couple more days there waiting for transport back to Germany. While waiting, Tony worked out a deal in which I could help for half a day at the local clinic to practice my medical cross-training, while he went over to the dentist to practice there. It was good experience that helped to maintain some of my proficiency. Finally, on March 16, we boarded an Air Force C-9 and flew back to Germany. A color guard was waiting for us at the airfield, along with the battalion commander. We boarded buses and made our way back toward Bad Tolz. Approximately ten miles or so from Bad Tolz, the bus broke down. We said we were close enough that we could push the bus, but we ended up waiting until it was repaired. It was dark by the time we arrived at Flint Kaserne. We unloaded the bus, formed into our ranks, and marched into the kaserne to our waiting families. For us, Operation Desert Storm was over, but only for the time being.

"THE BUNKER" ODA 031 constructing their second air raid bunker at batman, Turkey during Desert Storm.

34

"THE CAMP IN BATMAN" C Company. 1/10th SFG's compound on Batman, Turkey during Desert Storm.

"THE CREW" CSAR team with Captain Harding's crew during Desert Storm. Left to right standing: PJ, Aircrew, PJ, Aircrew, Roger Moore, the Author, Aircrew (sitting on wing tank), aircrew, Lieutenant Maki, Captain Harding and Tony Hernandez. Kneeling left to right: Aircrew, Captain Perkings, Lauren Sharp, Lee Tomasic, Ricky Williams, and CCT.

"THE TEAM" ODA 031 during Operation Desert Storm: Front Two (L to R) Captain Perkings and MSG Bob Spears, L to R: Lee Tomasic, Kevin Morse, Lauren Sharp (sitting), and Dave Talarczyk (sitting). Standing rear row: Tony Hernandez, John Simpson, Ricky Williams, Dan McLean, Glen McMurry, Erick Nason, Shawn Driscol and Roger Moore. Kneeling middle are Todd Sowerby and Stan Shanks.

"WAR IS OVER" Captain Christopher Perkings, John Simpson, Lauren Sharp (rear row), the Author, and Shawn Driscol at war's end, Desert Storm in Batman, Turkey.

CHAPTER 4

OPERATION PROVIDE COMFORT: SINAT

While back in Germany, we went through our refit procedures and took some time off. We watched the news and saw how Saddam Hussein was crushing the Shi'ite and Kurdish rebellions in both the northern and southern regions of Iraq. These people were forced to evacuate their homes and to find shelter away from these brutal attacks. We began to watch more television broadcasts about the Kurdish refugees who were hiding in the northern mountains of Iraq. As we saw the suffering on the news, we began to wonder if we would become involved. Sure enough, we received our orders to prepare to move back to Incirlik. There was no train-up this time, just packing our gear and waiting for a time to be at the airfield. We said our good-byes, and after being home for just three weeks, we were on our way back to Incirlik. Instead of just our company, the whole battalion deployed as well as the rest of the group from the United States. During Operation Desert Storm, only our company had deployed, while the other two remained in Germany to pull security on the housing area and participate in the annual winter environmental training. The other two battalions of our Group were stationed at Fort Devans, Massachusetts. They were in the process of preparing to deploy and would link up with us in-country. All together, this would bring almost a thousand Special Forces soldiers to Turkey and Iraq, as well as the several thousand other nations provided for support to the United Nations for what would be called Operation Provide Comfort. We arrived at Incirlik Air Force Base to begin one of the longest sessions of hurry up and wait that I have ever experienced.

Instead of being housed in old quarters like before, our company was moved out to a large hangar in the middle of the airfield. This was going to be our home for a bit as our higher headquarters coordinated for our movement forward. We made ourselves as comfortable as we could and got settled in. Being out in the absolute, middle of the airfield, we had to either walk or ride a shuttle bus/van to go eat or use the gym or any of Incirlik's shopping facilities. I preferred walking to keep in shape, and I was in no rush to get anywhere. To make matters worse, we were restricted, having to remain near the hangar except for eating or working out. That meant no ranges or training areas; we had to do what we could around the immediate area. To help pass the time, we began playing the board game, "Axis and Allies." As part of our normal deployment equipment, each team brought a footlocker with items to entertain themselves. This included books, games, cards, footballs, baseballs, and stuff of that nature. Our games would sometimes last into the wee hours of the morning. We developed ways of keeping quiet, in order not to disturb our teammates. The box top was lined with a T-shirt, so the dice would make no noise. We talked in whispers and used flashlights for illumination.

Some of the fellows took this opportunity to become acclimated to the temperature by sitting out in the sun and working on their tans, sometimes totally nude. Most of the time, I sat and watched the aircraft land and take off, seeing all of the transports bringing in equipment that was going nowhere fast.

Some of our mail was still waiting for us, having been left behind when we returned to Germany at the end of Desert Storm. It was a nice surprise to be given mail as we waited and watched the news, seeing the plight of the Kurdish people in the northern mountains.

After about a week, we were told to prepare to move forward to the new base camp. Instead of flying, we would take a contracted Turkish bus to our new camp. This would be a ten-hour drive across Turkey. We loaded up at daybreak and started out on what would be an interesting trip. After only been on the road for less than an hour, when Ricky Williams (who was sitting in front of me) tried to close his window, which was stuck. The alternate bus driver, who was riding in the back of the bus with us, tried to fix the problem. He forced the window closed, which caused it to shatter into hundreds of tiny pieces. Luckily, I turned my head as the window exploded and the tiny shards that were caught in the breeze hit me in the side of the face or blew around me. Thanks to my reflexes, none of the glass got into my eyes. The driver just laughed, said something in his language, spat on the broken window frame, and crawled back up into his cubby hole and went to sleep. Ricky and I looked at each other, shrugged, and made ourselves as comfortable as possible.

After a few more hours on the road, our "buddy" the bus driver emerged from his cubby hole, carsick. He decided to throw up in the back stairwell of the bus, and then grabbed a bottle of water to wash most of his vomit from the steps and out under the door. I guess we were lucky to have a broken window so the breeze could push the vomit smell away from us. Halfway through the trip, the bus stopped at a gas station to fuel up, and some of my team members went inside to purchase some food and snacks. Ricky and I worked on washing the back stairs and cleaning out the mess as best as we could. Once the fueling was completed, we were on our way.

The remainder of the trip was uneventful, as we traveled along watching the Turkish countryside slide past us. We took a bathroom break a few hours later along the side of the road. It must have been an interesting sight for the Syrian border guards in their towers to see us get off our bus and relieve ourselves along the side of the road. We had no choice. It was where the bus driver had decided to stop, the area was all open, and we had to go. It must have been an interesting sight for the Syrian border guards. Towards evening, we arrived at the new base camp located near Silopi, Turkey, only about five miles from the Iraqi border.

The camp started out small, but grew steadily as more United Nations forces arrived. Luckily for us, most of the camp was already set up. At least we had a tent to sleep in, and the dining tent was already up. During Desert Storm, we had already endured the transition from winter to spring. Now, most of the rain that was common for that period was over, and the temperature was beginning to climb higher. Once again, this would be another example of hurry up and wait. The team settled down to wait out the final decision to allow us to go forward, which once again rested on our Turkish

39

allies. It was later learned that as we were prevented from going forward, the Turkish government charged us a "parking tax" for all of our vehicles. I guess after they got as much money as they wanted, they let us move on. The Turks knew they had us over a barrel. They were located north of Iraq, and we had to go through them to do our mission. Our leadership conducted what planning they could, and we rehearsed our SOPs and battle drills near our tents. Most of the time, we played volleyball, worked out, or visited the makeshift sellers' stalls outside the front gate. Soon, Great Britain, Canada, Holland, and other nations arrived, and the camp quickly grew. There was a contest to see who could raise the tallest improvised flag poles. Soon, multiple national flags flapped in the breeze across the camp. I believe it was an American flag set up by the Marines that stood the tallest.

It always seems that one of the last items to be built is the showers. Lee Tomasic brought a blow-up lounge-chair for floating in a swimming pool. He used it as an air mattress, as well as a bathtub. When our higher ups found out we were using the bottled water to bath in, we were instructed to find another water source. Most of us made sun tea by filling our water bottles with tea bags which we had brought, then placing them on top of the tent to cook in the sun. A road sign, similar to the one seen in the television show, "M.A.S.H.," was erected next to the dining tent. It quickly filled up with home towns and their respective distances away. We continued to play Axis and Allies as the days slowly marched by. C-130 transport aircraft were dropping food supplies to the Kurdish refugees in the mountains. The only problem was that the Kurds were trying to catch the several-thousand-pound pallets as they floated down on their parachutes. There were a few deaths because Kurds were crushed under the pallets. Additional reports stated that helicopters attempting to unload cargo were being rushed and overwhelmed by the refugees. This demonstrated how desperate the situation was becoming in the refugee camps, and yet we waited for permission to launch.

As we continued to wait, more of our forces arrived at the camp. The other two battalions of our group arrived, and the whole 10th Special Forces were now officially deployed. While in camp, I ran into old friends from the Ranger Battalion, Mike Hammer and Bill

Vogel who had been in the weapons platoon with me and were now themselves in Special Forces. The 24th Marine Expeditionary Unit (MEU) arrived with the helicopters, along with our brothers in the 21st Special Operations Squadron. The camp was now about a quarter of a mile wide by three miles long. The open field behind the camp was turned into a large helicopter landing zone for other nations' helicopters. Finally a shower was built. It was another asset of the shower, however, which briefly brought added relief. To supply water for the showers, a 2,000-gallon water blivet, or rubber bag, was filled. To me, this was the largest waterbed I had ever seen. The temperature was now hot enough to make sleeping difficult. So one evening, I grabbed my poncho liner, climbed out into the middle of the blivet, and slept quite soundly on the cool improvised waterbed. Unfortunately, others got the same idea, and one night we were discovered and ordered not to do it again. Oh well. It was good sleeping while it lasted.

Another thing that was helping pass the time was the local rumor mill and some of the nighttime "activities." It was inevitable that men and women who were stationed together would get lonely and hook up for nightly liaisons. One couple was found "liaising" between the tents, and was summarily charged. Another couple tried to do the same thing, but out in the open field where the helicopters landed. I guess they didn't realize that the helicopters were equipped with Forward Looking Infa-Red scopes and could see them in the tall grass in the dark. We had been wondering why the helicopters had been hovering or flying slowly around a certain spot in the landing field. This couple was also disciplined.

One of our MH-53 helicopters broke down at one of the refugee camps, and one of our detachments was sent out to secure the site. They sent back reports on the conditions and the desperate need for assistance for the refugees. Soon afterward, the Turkish authorities allowed us to begin operations. The 26th Marine Expeditionary Unit (MEU) was sent in to establish a forward operating base outside of the city of Zahko. We watched as the long lines of Marines walked out to the CH-53 Sea Stallions and CH-46 Sea Knights, supported by their AH-1 Super Marine Cobras, and then flew off toward the south and Iraq. I have always been impressed by the Cobra gunship, but this time there were air-to-air Sidewinder missiles hanging on their weapons pods. That was a very impressive sight to see. After the forward operating base was secured by the Marines, our detachments began to be sent out to the different refugee camps located within Turkey and stretching as far east as the Iranian border. Our detachment was going to be sent to a camp inside Iraq, helping the detachment that was already there. We all doubled-checked our equipment and packed our rucksacks for the mission. Everyone was going in heavy: each man's rucksack weighed between 100 and 130 pounds.

Everyone would have a specific job to do, but the big "money makers" on the team would be the medics and the engineers. The communication sergeants had an important mission in maintaining communication between the camps and our higher headquarters. The detachment leadership would assess and evaluate the refugees, and coordinate operations. The only ones with no real mission were the weapons sergeants. We were specifically told that under no circumstances were we to advise, instruct, or assist in any weapons or tactics, due to the political climate. Stan Shank and been assigned to Fort Bragg, and we were short a medic. I was assigned to fill the job as junior medic, while Tony Hernandez served as the senior medic. Except for a few changes, this was the same team that had served in Desert Storm. Captain Perkins had been reassigned, and Captain Patrick Gallagher had taken over. Todd Sowerby had remained behind to help the rear detachment. "Bunky" Burton was a new communications sergeant who was assigned to our team and would make this trip with us.

Helping the Kurdish people was a sticky situation politically for two reasons. In the first place, the United States had asked the Kurds and the Shi'ites to rise up against Saddam Hussein and his regime. Unfortunately, we did not send any support, and both the Kurds and Shi'ites were mauled by the Iraqi military, including being attacked with nerve and mustard gas. In the second place, the Turkish military were fighting Turkish Kurds and did not want them to be trained by us. Therefore, the weapons sergeants on the team were the designated "worker bees," or, like me, they used their cross-training.

We loaded up our equipment and boarded an MH-53 for the flight in. The helicopter had to make a quick stop at one of the large refugee camps inside Turkey before flying us to our camp. As we flew over, we could see the refugees' makeshift shelters all over the place, including on the sides of the mountain. The shelters formed a sea of different colors, mostly blue tarps that had been provided in the relief bundles from the U.N. After dropping off cargo and personnel at that camp, we flew across the border into Iraq and to our camp.

The MH-53 made its approach down a mountain valley and landed on the eastern side of the camp area, away from the camp itself. We quickly off-loaded our equipment and established a defense security perimeter. Bob Spears and Captain Gallagher headed toward the camp to make contact with the other team. We fell back on our unconventional warfare training, with the detachment's leadership making the initial contact as we stayed behind and prepared for anything.

The only thing I was not prepared for was the terrain. When you think of Iraq, you visualize the sand that is common in the western and southern half of the country. The north, however, looked like Colorado or the southwestern United States. The mountains were rugged and brownish in color, with green scrub vegetation and bushy trees. It was a warm and pleasant day as I looked around at our surroundings. The refugee camp was located in a high mountain valley, approximately fifteen miles inside Iraq. As we waited for the team leadership to return, we examined our landing zone. This had been the same landing zone in which the MH-53 had broken down with the team from Silopi coming out to secure it. The Kurds wanted the Americans to come back. So using several large cans of creamed corn that had been sent as part of the relief food bundles, they drew a big circle on the ground with a big "X" in the middle. Scattered around the perimeter were the large, rusted cans the creamed corn had come in. I guess the Kurds didn't like creamed corn (either). We named that landing zone "Corn LZ." I had to admit, that creamed corn worked great as a paint. I don't think it ever faded or washed away during our stay there.

As I scanned the area, I took in all the sights and sounds. The air smelled of grass and vegetation and felt warm, faint sounds of insects buzzing around. It was relatively quiet, except for the sound of helicopters off in the distance, which were bringing in supplies for the camp. Now and then, a UH-60 Blackhawk would fly by with a sling load of cargo hanging below it, then turn and head toward the main part of camp. After about an hour or so, we heard voices approaching our position, talking with each other in both English and Kurdish. Our leadership was coming back with MSG Victor "Vic" Allen, the team sergeant of the other detachment (the same team, in fact, that had come out there earlier to secure the helicopter), with some of his team, and a bunch of Kurds. Flying overhead was a slow-moving Blackhawk helicopter. Our leaders had convinced the air crew to fly up to get our heavy rucksacks and carry them down to the other side of the camp. An old rule of thumb warns never to allow the locals to carry your ruck, and I was not allowing them to grab mine. But I was told it was ok for them carry it to the helicopter, so I did. These two guys struggled to pick up my rucksack (which weighed close to 120 pounds) and gave me a funny look. They did manage to manhandle it/drag it over and load it into the helicopter. After our equipment was loaded, we began our trek down to our new base camp at the western end of the refugee camp. We followed a trail that snaked along a small stream through the valley floor and brought us into the refugee camp.

As our group of twelve SF and ten Kurds moved into the camp, Kurds with long sticks took up positions around us. These "Stick Boys" were responsible for keeping the Kurds from overwhelming us as we walked by. They carried long, slender sticks, thus earning their names. Normally these men were young, between sixteen and twenty-five years old. For the most part, Stick Boys were designated by the elders of the families, but a few were self-appointed in order to gain some prestige. As we made our way through the throngs of curious Kurds, we met one of the key family leaders, who would play an important part in our stay. I never learned his true name; we always referred to him as "The Teacher." He was a distinguished looking gentleman with gray hair and no beard, who carried himself with authority. He had been a schoolteacher back in Zahko. He spoke several languages, including Russian, Arabic, Kurdish, and English, which explains the nickname we chose for him. As we walked along, he learned that Ricky Williams, a former 5th Group member whose area of operation was the Middle East, spoke some Farsi. He and Ricky conversed for a little bit, and then the Teacher replied, "Ah, your Arabic isn't very good. Your grammar needs work." We chuckled among ourselves, delighted with our discovery that Teacher had a witty sense of humor.

We arrived at our new camp location, a small open plateau on the western outer edge of the camp, just below the plateau that was being used as the main helicopter landing zone (LZ). A single, medium-size military tent had been built, and there were a few small blue-domed tents provided by the United Nations. I found a comfortable spot, built myself a quick lean-to, and prepared my sleeping gear. As it turned to dusk, we talked to the other team to get a feel for the camp.

Later in the evening, we went off to bed, but it wouldn't be a quiet evening. Around two in the morning, I was awakened by some voices and loud moaning. Two Kurds were helping a third, who was bent over and moaning loudly. Working with the other medics, we figured out that he had a bad case of kidney stones and was in a great deal of pain. There was nothing we could do for him except gave him a morphine injection. Using hand signals, we explained that the closest hospital was over the mountain in Turkey. The two Kurds nodded their understanding, loaded their friend on a stretcher that we provided, and began to carry him over the mountain. The following morning, the stretcher was returned along with the blanket. The two Kurds had, in fact, carried him over the mountain to the hospital and had returned.

The Kurds were lining up at our tent for medical care as soon as the sun came up. I went to work inside our little clinic along with Tony and Keith Nease and Larry Halverson from the other team. I tried to maintain a log as we had been instructed in the Special Forces course, but Keith told me it was impossible to keep a log due to the large numbers of people showing up. Our tent was full of UNICEF and United Nation medical supplies, with the front quarter of the tent used as an examination room and the rear half for storage. It was a good experience working in the clinic, but I would soon have a new and different mission. A medic from the other team was assigned to walk through the camp and check on the various people there. He needed an extra hand, so I was given to him. We both carried full medical bags and began at first light to make our rounds through the camp. Though our camp was smaller in size when compared to the main camps in Turkey, it still took half a day to make one loop through. We estimated that there were about two to three thousand refugees in our camp, compared to the ten to twenty thousand refugees in the other camps. The camp may have been small, but it was necessary for us to conduct "house calls." Most of the refugees couldn't make it to the hospital site, so we brought medical care to them. After lunch, we reloaded our medical bags back at the base camp, and started out again for the afternoon loop.

The camp was broken into three sections, each belonging to a single family clan. Comparable to our Native American Indian clans as seen in the Iroquois Confederacy, Kurdish clans are extended families that make up a single clan with its own internal hierarchy. We walked up to a family area and asked if there was anything we could do. As soon as we sat down and opened our medical bags, the rest of the family members came out and sat around us. Then the sick or injured came or were pushed toward us, and we treated them. In one case, we were led into a makeshift tent, where a man's wife was gravely ill. As the other medic checked her, I provided assistance, passing him whatever he required from the medical bag. After we determined that she had to be evacuated, the husband nodded his understanding. He promptly covered her with a cloth and used her body as a table, where he began laying out some pita bread and tea, which had been cooking outside. This was an example of the cultural differences that I would have to become accustomed to. Kurdish people are very friendly, and they have very large families, some men with two or three wives and as many as twelve children. One of the hard things we in the Special Forces have to do is partake in local food or drink to build rapport with our hosts. As the tea was poured, they gave us bread spread with what we assumed to be a goat-milk yogurt. We ate and finished our tea, and after thanking the host, we continued on our rounds.

I grew to love the tea, called "Chai," that the Kurds made for us. In typical middle-eastern fashion, it was served very hot in small glasses with a lot of sugar. I believe it was this constant tea and sugar rush that helped me to move around the camp quickly. Unfortunately, whatever that yogurt stuff was, it put the medic I was working with down hard with some type of intestinal parasites or bug. I had a quick bout of dysentery, but he was reduced to staying in camp with severe diarrhea and vomiting. It was so serious that he had to be evacuated to a hospital for treatment, making me the default "house visiting doctor." Everyone else was now busy with their own jobs and it took all three medics to run the clinic. The rest of our group was either cleaning up the camp or running the landing zones where the helicopters brought in the food supplies.

I became accustomed to doing the roving sick call, getting to know the layout of the camp and meeting all of the various families, which started to become a daily routine. One of the large families I met was headed by a former officer in the Iraqi army, who had three wives, one of whom was his cousin. He also had about eight children running around his camp. Each family had constructed a tent, either out of materials they had brought with them or the blue tarps provided in the U.N. bundles. The living areas for the most part were clean and orderly, but there was a lot of garbage strewn around the camp proper. The women and young girls went to the stream that ran along the middle of the camp to gather water and to wash clothes. The children ran around the camp and played with each other, or shadowed us as we made our way through the camp. The men sat in groups, sipping tea, having discussions with each other, and observing us.

For the most part, I was treating minor injuries such as cuts and scrapes, and the occasional burn from the cooking fires. These refugees for the most part were from the city of Zahko and had absolutely no idea how to live in the woods. They lacked basic skills for staying healthy, like centralized garbage or washing clothes down stream versus up stream where it contaminated the drinking water. There was a single running stream through the center of the camp. The Kurds used this water for everything, from drinking, to cleaning and washing. The problem was they did what they needed at their spot, with no concern for the people downstream. We knew we had our work cut out for us if we were to make changes in the camp to improve their health. However, as the temperatures became warmer, I began to see more and more different type of ailments.

During this first week, I met the Peshmerga (meaning "ready to die") guerrilla fighters, the Kurdish soldiers who were fighting the Iraqis. One evening, a patrol of them came into our camp. We sat around the campfire and talked with them through an interpreter. It was an interesting sight to see. These fighters, sitting in a circle, armed with grenades and AK assault rifles, and wearing machine gun belts across their chests were almost the perfect stereotype of what you would expect a guerrilla fighter to look like. Behind the Peshmerga, stood our guys. It's too bad that I didn't have a camera to take this night photo; it would have made a great recruiting poster! The Peshmerga helped both to keep the camp safe from Iraqis and to maintain peace and order. There was only one incident in which the refugees swarmed and overwhelmed the supplies. In this case, the Peshmerga walked out and surrounded the food. They simply told the refugees to behave themselves or they would confiscate all of the food. The three family clans got together and came up with a plan. Once all of the food was delivered, it was separated into three, even piles. Then the clans came and carried it back to their respective camps, all under the watchful eyes of the Peshmerga. They placed two guards at our clinic to regulate when the Kurds could come in. They established an opening hour of around 8:30 a.m., with an hour break at noon for lunch and the clinic closing at dusk. This kept the Kurds from coming in at all hours of the day and night, and allowed us to establish a schedule. From what I could assess from the campfires we could see, there were at least three major Peshmerga encampments located on the high ground around our camp.

The typical Kurd wore a turban and jumpsuit-type clothing in light colors, normally browns and grays. Some wore regular western-style shirts and pants. For the most part, they wore what they had on their backs when they made the exodus to the safety of the mountains. The vast majority of them were armed with AK-style assault rifles, probably taken from the Iraqis. Those associated with the Peshmerga carried either a knife or a bayonet on the left front of their belts. Most of the women, except the young girls, wore a middle-eastern style dress with a headscarf. A headscarf signified a married girl or woman. During my tour of the camp, I checked up regularly on a 13-year-old mother and her young child. The "mom" would be swinging on a homemade swing with the baby kept in a basket in the shade. I noticed that there were a lot of Kurds with western features, perhaps I believe due to the crusades which long ago passed through the region. It looked as if some of the crusaders had stopped for some recreation. I knew one man who was the spitting image of an Irishman, except that he spoke Kurdish and wore a headdress. I visited him and his family one day as he was putting on his headdress. He had flaming red hair and the ruddy complexion often seen in Ireland. For the most part, the Kurds were a friendly people, who were very happy to have us there and cooperated with us fully. I was amazed how they adapted and made the best out of whatever they had. They cooked their own meals, making their own style of pita bread, which was readily offered to us.

To help out in the clinic, the Peshmerga provided two men who could speak English and work as translators. They were college students, who had been studying computer technology in Mosul before the war and the crackdown on the Kurds. The Teacher's 16-year-old daughter, Media, came down to serve as a translator as well. I also became acquainted with the rest of the Teacher's family, including his son, Kenananch, and his grandsons, War and Aheen. I am not sure of the exact spelling of the names; I just know the sound of their names. With the help of these three people, I quickly learned to speak the Kurdish language. I even made myself a phrasebook in English/Kurdish to help me communicate with my patients. This was real immersion language training in the truest sense, and I was amazed at how fast I picked up their language. To this day, I still carry that little phase book, and I would need it again one day. As part of my routine, I regularly stopped by and visited the Teacher and his family, whose tent happened to be the farthest east of the camp. I soon began to know his family well: his wife, son, and two nephews, as well as his daughter, who was working down in the clinic. Sometimes when I visited, he would be busy talking with some of the other Peshmerga leaders and I would leave him alone unless I was invited to join them. We believe he was the commander of various Peshmerga units from Zahko and had meetings with his officers from time to time. I rarely understood what they were talking about; I believe it usually concerned the security of the city of Zahko. These refugees were from that city, and the Peshmerga would not allow any of them to return home until they felt the city was safe from the Iraqis.

We received another tent that we could use to sleep in, and we had some of our "self-proclaimed stick boys" help us to set it up. It was a medium-size, heavy green canvas military tent. Glen, Lee, and I, with the help of about five kids, were able to get it up. However, we had no sooner got the tent up than a low-flying helicopter with a load of supplies slung below it flew over our camp and blew the tent down. Shrugging it off, we set it back up again. The rest of the fourteen men of my team moved in that evening.

Sometimes we received some added support from the helicopter crews who were flying in the relief bundles. Because we were situated inside Iraq, mostly Marine helicopters brought the supplies up to the camp, but sometimes Army Blackhawk helicopters or British helicopters would sling load supplies in. One day, a member of the Marine flight crew asked our guys who were running the LZ if we were Army Special Forces. They replied that we were, and he reached inside the helicopter and threw a large cardboard box to them. Inside were steaks and pork chops, which we roasted over our campfire that evening for a very enjoyable dinner. Now and then, the Peshmerga also brought us some of the supplies that had been dropped off by the helicopters.

I couldn't help but be amazed by what I saw being brought to the camp in these United Nations supply bundles. When I made my way through the camp, I noticed piles of the military Meals, Ready to Eat (MRE), which had been stripped, with about half of the items used and the other half just dumped on the ground. When I wasn't out checking the camp or working in the clinic, I sometimes helped out on the landing zone. There, I was able to see what was in these food bundles. Mostly it was the standard fare -- bags of flour and rice and vats of cooking oil, but sometimes there were really strange items. Once we found mix for making chocolate chip cookies in the bundles. The Kurds looked at it, shrugged, and piled it off to the side. In one shipment, they received several large sacks of lentil peas. They had no idea how to cook them, but they did use them for a special purpose. The landing zone was located on a flat plateau on top of a rise. It was a steep climb to get to it, and with all of the people using the same trail, it became slippery. The Kurds took all of the sacks of lentil peas and used them to make a sidewalk up to the landing zone, a rather ingenious idea. The peas worked like gravel to help them keep their footing on the trail. I still wonder who came up with the packing list for these bundles, in which a lot of items went to waste.

While helping out on the landing zone, the "worker bees" mostly worked air traffic control and guided the helicopters in. Once the helicopters landed, the Kurds unloaded the aircraft and carried the supplies to the main pile. Our engineers built a makeshift control tower by using four or five sandbags to make the corner support pillars for the corners of a metal pallet. Our radio operator sat on top of it and maintained communication with the helicopters, or sat under it and used it for shade. One day, a helicopter asked over the radio if we had a name for our landing zone. Roger Moore, in one of his more energetic and happy mood, replied, "Why yes, this is Sinat LZ, the Happy LZ!" After the long silent pause on the radio, the pilot called back, "You don't really have a name for the landing zone, do you." Roger replied that we didn't. We were simply known as Landing Zone number five, but Sinat LZ sounded good at the time. We had learned that the area we were in had once been a town known as Sinat. The plateaus were too well made to be natural; we believed they were once terraced farm lands. We later learned that Sinat was one of the towns Saddam had purged. It had been attacked with chemical weapons, and then completely bulldozed under. You could see where the foundations of the homes had been. Nothing grew near the former village, and in some parts, the grass had turned a shade of yellow. To be on the safe side, we avoided the village location to prevent any possible contamination.

Working on the landing zone was sometimes boring, but now and then it proved to be very interesting. The Kurds had developed a well-organized system of collecting the supplies and distributing them into their three piles. One day, we heard a helicopter coming toward us, but we could not see him. As we scanned the surrounding area, mostly as a traffic control safety method, we spotted the helicopter very low in the valley. It must have had a very heavy load slung under the aircraft, for it was only about 100 feet above the valley floor, and flying very slow. It was so low we became concerned that the sling load would crash into our tent, knocking it down again. The pilot was able to give it enough power to fly over our camp without knocking the tents down, and he safely landed his cargo on the landing zone. Sometimes, there were so many helicopters coming into the landing zone that some landed on nearby ridges and waited their turn to enter the pattern and land their cargo.

During another day on the landing zone, I had an interesting moment with one of our Marine helicopter crews. A CH-46 transport helicopter landed, and a member of the flight crew came running over. The first thing I thought was that they had seen something on the way in and needed to warn us. Instead, he ran up to me and asked if I was an Army Special Forces guy and if I could speak with the Peshmerga who were standing with me. I told him that I could speak to them. I was standing next to one of our translators, but the pilot didn't know that. He produced a camera and asked if he could get his picture taken with the Peshmerga. Turning to our translator and asked him in English (I don't think the pilot could hear me through his helmet and the noise of the landing zone) if the pilot could have his picture taken with the Peshmerga. The translator smiled and spoke with a couple of our guards, who smiled and walked up to the crewman. One thing I noticed about both the Kurds and the Peshmerga: they liked to have their pictures taken. They posed together, the crewman with his pistol out and two of our Peshmerga with their AK rifles. I snapped his last two photos and handed the camera back to him, telling him he was out of film. He ran back to his helicopter and returned with a new camera, saying he had more film. After a couple more shots, he climbed aboard his helicopter and took off.

Most of the time, it was serious business around the camp, but from time to time, there were some rather funny moments. Once again I was introduced to the Teacher's wit when I was walking with him one day, and he asked, "My friend, I hear your colleagues call you Aag, what is this Aag?" I explained to him that it was a nickname that I had received when I joined the team. Aag was a caveman character in a comic strip. He nodded his head in understanding and said, "Ah Cro-Magnon man, you look like Cro-Magnon man!" My teammates burst out laughing at his response. However, it stuck and soon circulated around the camp. Most of the Kurds referred to me as "doctor," but after they heard about my nickname, I was greeted by "doctor Aag, doctor Aag!" when I entered their living areas.

One of the best phases I learned from the translators was "I must go see more patients" which sounds like, "Asdichen hesh halkay be-beanum." Every time I stopped to see the different camps, they made me tea and gave me bread. This delayed me. To be polite, I partook of their tea and bread. However, if I ate at every camp, I wouldn't get anything done. After I learned this phrase, the Kurds understood and allowed me to continue my rounds without delay. I still had an escort of two or three stick boys, more as of a status symbol for them than because I needed protection. Every day I stopped and said hello to a little girl I named "Toothless" because she was missing all of her front teeth. We had earned their trust, granted warily, and had developed a good rapport with them.

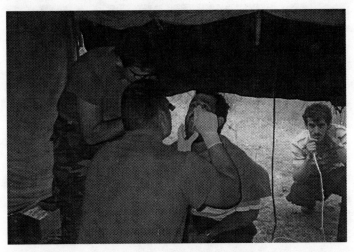

The author and Jerry Zunich perform dentistry on a Kurdish refugee while his friend looks on from outside of the tent.

"Toothless" is the little girl on the far right in orange with three of her friends during one of her daily morning greetings with the author.

A picture of "Corn HLZ" with the UH-60 that was going to carry our equipment to the base camp in the distance. The HLZ is the most southern part of the refugee camp.

MAP 2: Operation Provide Comfort, showing the location of the UN camp in Silopi, The refugee camp at Sinat and the way-station camp near Kesann

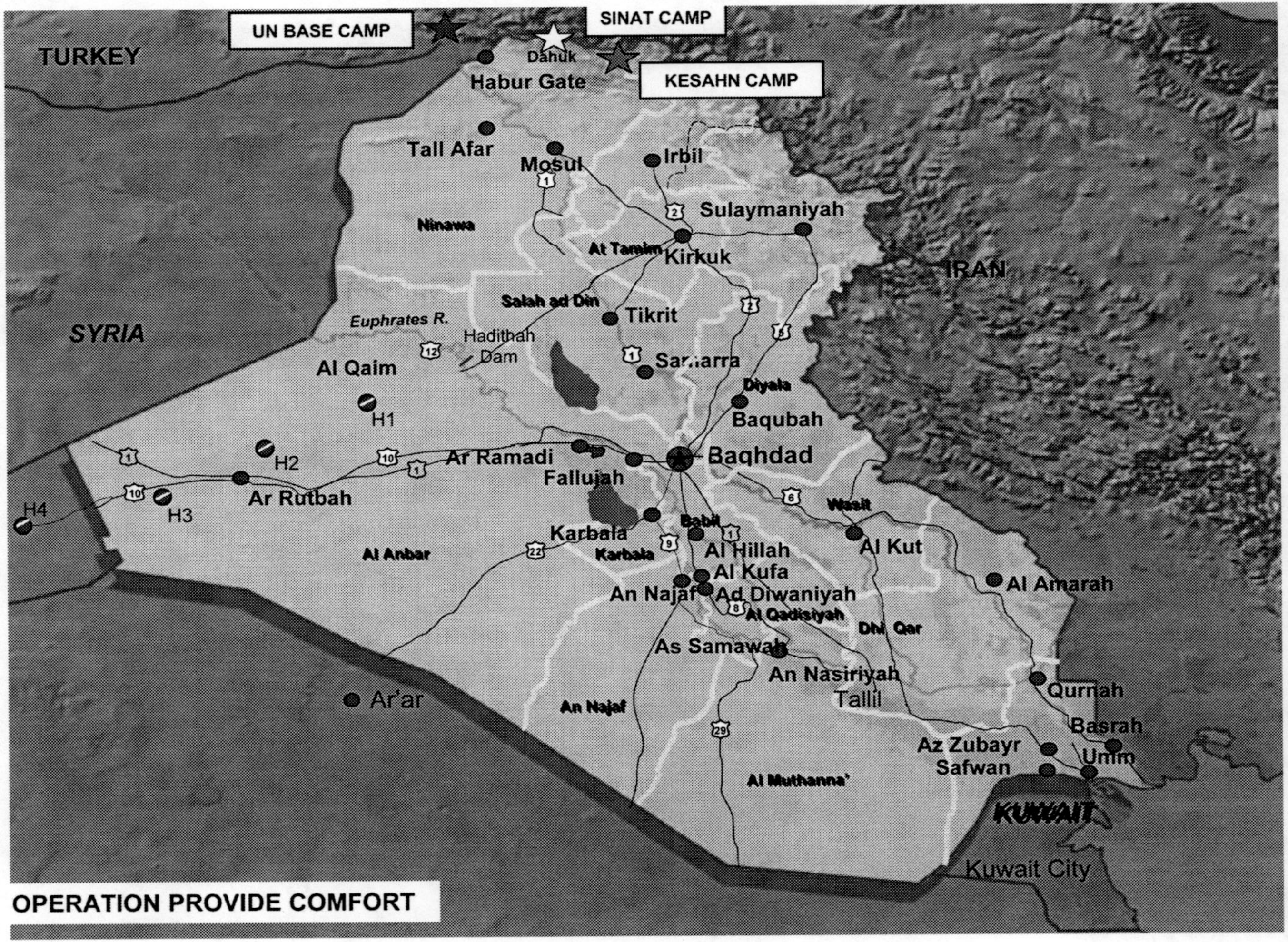

OPERATION PROVIDE COMFORT

CHAPTER 5

MEDICAL CHALLENGES AND THE ZAHKO PEOPLE RETURNING HOME

As the temperature became warmer, we began to see changes in the medical condition of the Kurdish people, who were becoming sicker with an unknown illness. Our engineers developed a program to clean up the camp. Glen McMurry and Lee Tomasic came up with an ingenious idea to help clean up the garbage around the camp. They had bags of candy dropped off by the helicopter crews. They then recruited a small army of kids to take garbage bags and go around the camp and collect the garbage. When the kids returned with full bags, they received candy. In a matter of a couple of days, the camp began to look better, with most of the garbage collected. It was Lee who finally discovered one of the causes for the mysterious illnesses. During one of his surveys, he discovered several rotting carcasses of goats that had been hidden at the top of the stream. The refugees had cleaned and butchered goats for food and dumped the carcasses in the water supply for the camp. They did it at the very top of the stream, and the people all drew water from below the rotting carcasses. Lee requested a case of Thermite grenades, which burned with an intense heat. He then pulled all of the rotten carcasses out of the stream and burned them with the Thermite. If there ever was a man who deserved a medal, it was Lee for that heroic act. Within a couple of days, the illnesses started to go away.

Tony Hernandez took me under his wing and really showed me the ropes to help me become more proficient in medical care. Keith Nease, a medic from the other team, also helped me out. I learned a lot from these two, especially from Tony. I was always amazed at how Tony interacted with the Kurdish children and made them feel relaxed in the clinic or when we were seeing them in the camp. I had learned most of the medical steps by being an Emergency Medical Technician and studying during my off duty hours. Tony taught me about serious injuries, diseases, lab work, and the non-routine work a medic does. I was thinking hard about going back to the qualification course to become a medic, and Tony encouraged me to do so.

As a whole, the health of the camp was remarkably good. There were only a few deaths, and we found out about these by finding the freshly dug graves during our daily walk around the camp. I worked with several interesting cases while helping out in the clinic. With the warm weather, the insects began coming out. This especially meant spiders, and a few young children came in with spider bites. One young boy had a bad bite on his foot, which had ulcerated and filled with puss. In order to drain the puss, I had to open the wound with a scalpel. My friend Kirby McWhithey helped out by distracting the little boy so that he looked away. As he turned his head, I quickly opened the wound with the scalpel and the puss drained out, coming out in large "cheesy" chunks. The boy cried, but at least I didn't have to fight with him when he saw me come toward him with a knife.

Now and then, a Peshmerga soldier would come in to have us take a look at his shrapnel wounds. In one case, a Peshmerga came into the clinic, complaining that his foot hurt. After removing his sock and shoe, we found that the front half of his foot was missing because he had stepped on a landmine. He had what was known as "Phantom Limb Syndrome," in which the patient still feels pain where a missing limb once was. He was given some pain medication, and the medics, with my assistance, checked his scars to be sure there was no infection. Another day an old man came to me with a vial of clear liquid, used for injections. Through the translator, this man told me he needed an injection. After checking our medical references, we could not determine what this injection was for. So I gave him the injection using all three methods: in the shoulder, right under the skin, and in his thigh.

Due to the cultural taboos, working with the Kurdish woman was a delicate procedure. I made sure I asked permission of either the woman's father or husband before I touched or examined a female patient. In one case, my "buddies" set me up when they called me over to look at an older woman's legs. They told me she was complaining that her legs hurt and wanted me to look. Why they would want my opinion had me baffled, but I checked her legs anyway. I found nothing, so I started to check her feet. As I looked between her toes, I found she had no webbing; in fact there was nothing there! This woman had a slight case of leprosy in both feet. The other medics had used her as a training tool to show me what leprosy looked like. It was a slight shock for me, because I had heard of the disease but had not had actually seen it in real life. I bathed her feet in a cleaning solution of Betadine and wrapped both of her legs up in bandages to help keep out any dirt.

Another case I worked on was a young girl who had first-degree burns on both legs. I guess she had gotten too close to the fire. After asking permission from her father, I bathed her legs in a Betadine solution to keep them from getting infected. As I was washing her legs, I looked up to see her giving me "the big eyes," which in a way I could understand. In the Kurdish society, men don't bath women's feet, so she must have felt pretty special, and was giving me the "I-am-not-married-yet big eyes." Sometimes, the lack of knowledge caused more injuries than the original problem. A young girl came in who started out with a spider bite. Her father took a burning stick from the fire and cauterized her injury. So now I had to treat both a spider bite and a second-degree burn!

In between seeing cases, I helped out by cleaning our medical equipment. We were limited on what supplies we received, so we had to wash and sterilize our surgical instruments by hand. The only cutting that I helped with was the removal of an infected toe nail from a young boy. We numbed his toe up, and then Keith Nease removed the toenail with my assistance. The boy watched in amazement and curiosity; the fact that his toe was numbed really helped. Additionally, Jerry Zunich and I received dentistry duty. We had a few patients who came in with rotten teeth. Unfortunately, we did not have the proper needles to numb the tooth in order to extract it.

Jerry and I became very proficient in using a material known as Irm. Basically, it was a paste that hardened into a temporary covering for the tooth. It was rather a simple procedure. We mixed the paste, and then filled the hole. Most of the times, out of the four points of a healthy molar, three of the points were completely gone and there was a large hole into the gum. We simply placed the Irm (a type of dental cement) on a gloved finger, filled the hole, and waited for it to harden. It provided temporary relief for the patient, which was better than nothing.

Perhaps one of the most difficult problems with the Kurds was their misconceptions about Americans. Every one of them thought we were fabulously wealthy indeed. In their eyes, the fact that I was a medic or doctor must have meant that I was very rich. When I stopped at the campsites and opened my medical bag, I was normally surrounded by those who needed help. In the Kurdish culture, a young girl with no headdress was of marrying age. This meant a young girl of 12 or 13 could be married off. Now and then, as I sat and provided care, these young, doe-eyed girls would be pushed toward the front of the circle. I would smile politely but inform them tactfully that I was already married. Another misconception was the belief that we could use "magic' in healing. Some of the cases I worked on were young children with fevers. I used my knife to cut an aspirin in half, crushed the aspirin up, put it in a small cup with water, shook it up, and told the parents that the children should drink it over the day. Normally by the next day, the fever was gone. This belief that I could use "magic" made for a difficult situation when a young father brought his baby son to me. To keep him warm, they had placed the child too close to their fire, and an ember had fallen into one eye and burned a hole through the cornea. The cornea was clouded over, and I could see that the child was blind in that eye. I asked the man what he wanted me to do. He asked me to make his son see again, but I had to tell him that it was beyond my power to do so. To help with dehydration problems, we were provided electrolyte packets to be added to drinking water. These packets may have been filled with necessary elements to keep these people healthy. In any case, they were the foulest concoction we had ever tasted. We overcame that by making sure that as many packets of Kool Aid as we could get were flown up to the camp. Once again, we made these "magic" elixirs that were both colorful and tasted good, and made the children better.

Sometimes the difficulty rested with the parents of the patients, rather than the patients themselves. During one of my morning patrols in the camp, I found a young boy about six months old with a herniated testicle. I informed the father that he needed to take himself and the child to the clinic, so he could be evacuated. He was quite happy to hear this, and I continued my rounds. On the way back, he was still in his camp, getting ready. I stressed to him he had to get down to the clinic "now." After having my lunch, I started with my afternoon patrol and found he was still at his camp. I asked him what he was doing, and he replied that he was washing and getting ready. That was the final straw! When I saw the Teacher I asked for some assistance, and five Peshmerga came with me to the camp. One of them took the child and carried him to the clinic, while two others carried the father! These people had learned that if one of their family members was ill, they would get a free ride down the mountains to Zahko, where the hospital was located.

He was using his sick son as a way of showing off, and spent the whole afternoon before he was escorted to the landing zone to primp and brag to his friends, instead of moving quickly. Again, this may also be partly due to their belief that children were expendable, and he could also have another child. This was one of a few of the peculiarities of the Kurdish culture and within their families. They held their older people in high regard and took the best care of them. This was because the elders were the patriarchs who possessed the family history. But the Kurds did not place a high priority on their children. This was contrary to how most Americans approached this situation, but it was something my teammates and I had to deal with.

Now and then, I took Lauren Sharp with me as a "bag boy" to carry an extra medical bag. Though most of the cases I found were genuine, there were some instances in which the patients were only looking for sympathy. When I could find nothing physically wrong with them, I gave them a placebo. I carried five types of vitamins with me, and used different ones depending on the case I found. Though these patients were faking, they were smart enough to see the different colors of the pills I provided. If one guy had a different injury and I gave him the same pill as the faker, the faker would figure it out. So I gave out multivitamins, children's vitamins, chewables, etc. Lauren carried the extra vitamins in the extra bag. I could see him shake his head when an obvious faker wanted some attention.

For the most part, the illnesses were genuine, and I tried as best as I could to help. Some of the cases I found were self-inflicted. One poor pregnant girl was dehydrated from wearing five sets of clothes because she had no bag to put them in. I gave her some prenatal vitamins and some of the rehydration packets and asked her to take it easy. Another young man was wearing a ski suit and suffering from dehydration.

Other difficulties were caused by my fellow Americans. During one of my days in the clinic, we had to evacuate an older woman who was running a high fever we couldn't break. Once the evacuation helicopter arrived on the LZ, I led three other teammates in carrying the stretcher from the clinic up to the landing zone. It was difficult to climb the steep grade in the slippery grass through the strong rotor wash from the helicopter. To make matters worse, a reporter had come with the helicopter and was in front of us filming as we struggled up the hill. He ignored my warnings to get out of the way, so I "encouraged" him to move by grabbing him and moving him off to the side. A few months later at home, some friends informed me that they had seen me on the news. It was the film from that reporter who had been blocking my path. They said they could see my face getting redder and redder as I got closer. The next thing they saw was blue, green, blue, green as the reporter tumbled down the hill. I guess when I moved him, I threw him by mistake. From then on, my wife always reminded me to be nice to reporters every time I deployed!

One morning we woke to the sound of gunfire, which wasn't unusual because the Peshmerga frequently test-fired their weapons. However, this morning it was more intense. As we observed the mountain tops, we found out that non-Kurdish Iraqis were bringing mule trains of weapons to sell at the Turkish border. The Peshmerga were trying to keep the peace with the Turks and did not want the

Iraqis to sell guns to the refugees on the border. To "encourage" the traders to go away, the Peshmerga fired at them with the heavy machine guns. The only problem was it didn't scare them. I guess the lure of easy money was more important. As we sipped our morning coffee, Vic Allen said, "If we get on the radio now with the sound of gunfire, CIBs (Combat Infantrymen Badges) for everyone!" Though he was joking, we knew that if we got on the radio, every fighter jock out there with bombs would be on this valley in a heartbeat. We decided to keep quiet and enjoy the show.

Now and then, we had to deal with visitors to our camp, mostly Red Cross workers or Doctors without Borders, another humanitarian aid group. Most of the time, it was no problem. They observed and provided some help and advice, but for the most part allowed us to perform our duties without interference. Sometimes though, their personal feelings about the military or our government caused some friction. We kept our opinions to ourselves and went about our business. One day we had three Austrian Red Cross workers show up, two men and one woman, who were very vocal about their opinions and the fact that they didn't like us (Americans). We took it in stride and basically ignored them. They made a lot of comments in their own language, believing we could not understand them. Finally, I and a couple others who spoke German told them we didn't care for their opinions and asked them to go away. As they wandered around the camp, a large Marine CH-53 Sea Stallion flew over low and knocked the three Austrians off their feet. In the process, the girl's shirt was flipped over her head as she tumbled down the hill. I will admit it was a cheap thrill, but we laughed our heads off, thinking it was only fitting after all of the grief they had been giving us earlier.

During one of my daily patrols through the camp, I observed some men in American uniforms who were approaching the camp. We had visitors! I confronted them and found out they were from the Psychological Operations unit and were assessing the camp. I escorted them towards our base camp. I asked them about the "pointee-talkee" cards which we had been given prior to arriving in the camp. The idea was that if we wanted to communicate with the Kurds, we would point to a phrase in English, with the Kurdish translation next to it, and that would help us get our ideas across. These men were in fact from the unit which printed them and were very proud of their accomplishment. Unfortunately, I pointed out to them that first of all, most of the Kurds couldn't read. The second point was that they had used a Southern Kurdish dialect, from the tribes that live in the southern portion of Iraq. These were northern Kurds, who had difficulty understanding the cards. I had discovered that when I had shown the cards to Media and the other translators and they observed that the dialect was wrong.

Perhaps the most troublesome visitors we had were men from the British 2 Commandoes. About a platoon of them had marched up to our camp from the valley below along the winding mountain trail. We didn't think too much about it, welcomed them, and went back to our work. But when a British helicopter arrived with a TV crew, we became suspicious. After the film crew arrived, a bunch of British military helicopters showed up, and they began to shuttle some of the Kurds down to Zahko. First they took the medical cases and then anyone who wanted a ride, with the film crew taping the British soldiers helping the Kurds onto the helicopters. Needless to say, the camp came apart. Many Kurds rushed the landing zone, believing it was finally safe to return to Zahko. The Peshmerga interceded, and we regained control of the landing zone. We found out that the Commandos were actually support personnel from the unit, who had climbed up to get on the news. They were politely, but firmly, asked to leave our camp, and it took a couple of days to restore order. There was still a question about Iraqi security personnel in the city of Zahko, and the Peshmerga did not feel it was safe for the town's people to return home.

Once again, a strange illness developed in the camp, and we could not figure out what it was. It seemed to affect the younger children, causing a severe fever. Unfortunately, the lab sets that would normally come in the medical bundles had been removed before the bundles were delivered to the camp. There was no means of identifying what was afflicting the camp, other than sending samples to the main hospital outside of Zahko and waiting for a result (which rarely got back to us).We provided medication and IVs, but nothing seemed to work, including building a bathtub and immersing the sick children in cold water. It was decided that as soon as a child arrived with the fever and the symptoms, we would evacuate both the child and an accompanying parent down to the hospital.

Unfortunately, this illness attacked some of our guys as well. About a quarter of our folks succumbed to one type of illness or another. Some cases were not bad; others were terrible. One of our guys got something that forced him to curl up next to the latrine because whenever he wasn't vomiting, he was having bad diarrhea. To save time, he slept next to the latrine. He was evacuated down to the hospital. Roger Moore caught something bad as well. We had him inside the clinic with IVs in him, but he recovered and didn't have to be shipped off.

It was a real challenge to remain neutral when dealing with the Kurds. It was normally our job to train guerrilla fighters, but in this case, we had to obey the instructions we had received prior to coming to the camp. I cam e close to crossing this line one day when, I saw two boys playing with an expended American-made Turkish Light Anti-Tank Weapon (LAW). They were playing with the now-empty fiberglass tube. I showed them how to press the release button on top of the tube to collapse it and how to extend and lock it. They caught on quickly and were soon opening and collapsing the tube. Some of the older Kurdish gentlemen saw this and nodded. I smiled and returned to my rounds.

Now and then, another minority sect would show up in the camp, the Assyrians. These were the Christian minority who also lived in the North. They came into our camp from another camp either up in Turkey or further down the border to try to get supplies. Normally the Peshmerga chased them off. We had only enough supplies for our refugees, and the Peshmerga aggressively defended them. The Assyrians tried the "fellow Christian" route with us, but we had to abide by the Peshmerga's wishes and ask them to return to their own camp near the border.

On a couple of occasions, some men, who were about 25-28 years old, came into our camp and told us they were friends of the Peshmerga. Not knowing who these fellows were, we held them until the Peshmerga came and identified them. There were two incidents in which men, who had claimed to be friends, simply disappeared after being led of up to the mountains by the Peshmerga. We weren't sure what exactly happened, but normally there was a far of rifle shot echoing through the mountains after these men were led off. I never really found out who they were, but rumors of Iraqi Special Police circulated around the camp.

Eventually, word reached camp that there were no Iraqi security personnel in the city of Zahko, and it was safe to return. The joyful news raced through the camp, and the families began to prepare to make the trek home. The following morning, some of the families headed down the trail toward Zahko. I saw these huge bundles of blankets with two tiny feet below them, as the children were loaded up as well as the parents. Again with the assistance of the Peshmerga, as helicopters arrived, we organized the families into an orderly procession for loading. One of the first groups to go was the Teacher and his family. It was a happy day for them when they were loaded aboard a Marine CH-53 for the flight back down to the city. We all said our farewells and wished them the best, and then we returned to our duties.

A couple of days later, we received our orders to return to Silopi. All of the refugees were returning home, and the Army had a new mission for us. We were going to return to base, refit, and move out to a new location to set up a "rest area" to provide medical and support services to the refugees as they made their way home. After we packed up all of our stuff, the team was loaded on to a Marine CH-53 and flown back to Silopi. It was a shock when we returned; the camp had grown even larger while we were away. We made our way back to our old tents and started to reload our equipment to get ready to leave. The first half of our mission was now complete, and the adventures at "the Happy LZ" had come to a close.

I would return home after this deployment and about a month or so later, I received a letter from Media who had it smuggled out of Iraq and mailed to me (I had given her my address) by a CNN reporter whom she had met later. The letter basically thanked me along with my team for our efforts with the refugees. It was a big surprise to receive the letter, and it felt really good to be appreciated by the Kurds for our hard work.

The family, L to R, unknown Kurd with red hair, Aheen, Kenananch, Media's younger sister (in red), Media (waving), Media's older brother, whose name I didn't learn, and War.

The Teacher's family, along with other Kurds, is being loaded on to a Maine CH-53 with the author, Lauren Sharp and Ricky Williams helping.

CHAPTER 6

MOVING DEEPER INTO IRAQ

Once the team arrived back at the main compound at Silopi, we had approximately twenty-four hours to repack our stuff and be ready to move out. The first thing we wanted to do was to get our uniforms washed. We had been up in the mountains for approximately a month and a half, and our uniforms could have used a real wash. However, this turned out to be easier said then done. As it had happened in Desert Storm, the Air Force built a large laundry facility in the camp. When we arrived to have our uniforms washed, we were informed that the Army's days for laundry were Tuesdays and Thursdays, and today happened to be Wednesday. We tried to explain to the young Air Force soldier running the place that we had just arrived from the mountains, we were heading out again in the morning, and we had no time to wait until the Army's days. To highlight the problem, we pointed out that the stains on some of our uniforms were from blood, not mud, and they needed to be washed. Unfortunately, this Airman stood to the rules and would not budge. No clean uniforms for us, other than what we had done for ourselves up in the mountains.

With the laundry out, we next went to see the unit supply sergeant to see if we could exchange our old uniforms. Once again, we ran into a roadblock. The supply orderly said they had no more uniforms to issue, all of their extra uniforms had already been issued, and we were out of luck. He did provide us with some Israeli boots; which were green canvas and rubber-soled, like Converse sneakers. As we made our way back to our tents, we observed some of the rear support personnel sporting their new uniforms. They not only had new uniforms, but new boots, new Bonnie caps, the works. Some things in the military never change.

Feeling dejected, we returned to our tents to wait for further word from our commander as to when we would leave and where we would be going. As I was hanging out, our Company Operations Sergeant came up and asked if we could spare a couple of guys to ride into Zahko with him. Lauren Sharp, "Bunky" Burton, and I volunteered. Why not? We were doing nothing, and this would give us a chance to get out of the camp and see some of the countryside. After grabbing our equipment and weapons, we loaded up in a Jeep and headed off toward Zahko. We followed the main road southeast toward the Iraqi border. The area the road passed through was very flat, with mountains off in the distance toward the north. Along the way, we passed a Turkish compound/prison that was being used to house some of the refugees. With the land being so flat and open, we could see we were approaching the border area known as Harbor Gates. This was the main and only route into and out of Iraq, and there was a large customs/border checkpoint.

We easily passed through the Turkish checkpoint and headed out onto a large, four-lane bridge that crossed the Tigris River, which marked the border. The bridge itself was relatively intact, except for one bomb crater in the center of the far right lane. After we crossed safely, we entered the customs/border checkpoint on the Iraqi side. There were still a good number of large trucks moving wares across the border. The fighting may have come to an end, but commerce continued at full speed. On the other side of the checkpoint, each of us became more security conscious. Granted, there was a cease-fire in effect, but we were not going to take any chances and go in with our guard down. We all took up sectors of responsibility and scanned for anything that looked unusual. This was more out of instinct and training, than a spur-of-the-moment decision. There was an abandoned village on the Iraqi side of the border, with a small checkpoint next to the road. It was flying the Iraqi flag, and we all thought that the flag would make a good souvenir. However, we left it alone and continued on our way to Zahko.

The road began to climb into some high country, and then it quickly fell away into a large valley. The terrain was similar to what we had seen around Silopi. It was all open grass and farmlands, with scattered vegetation. Way off in the distance we could see the mountains where we had just spent the last month and a half. As we approached a four-mile stretch of road leading into Zahko, we began to see more houses and businesses. We also began to see a large number of children lining the sides of the road. They had come out to beg for food, but we had nothing to give them. What scared us the most was that these children had munitions with them that they wanted to trade for MREs. They had everything from ammunition to pieces of uniforms and equipment. I watched these two kids, who had to be around seven years old, drag a large belt of ammunition for a 30-mm anti-aircraft gun! The belt must have weighed more then both kids put together, and yet, here they were dragging it across the road with big smiles on their faces.

Once we were able to make our way through the gauntlet of kids, we arrived in the city of Zahko. It was a medium-size city that seemed to be filled to bursting with people. Mostly Kurds lived there. We recognized the clothing as well as some of the people who had been in our camp, and we kept our eyes open to see if we could spot some of our friends. We made our way over to the military compound that was arranging all of the humanitarian aid being distributed around the north. After dropping off the Company Operations Sergeant, Lauren, Bunky, and I parked over in a corner of the parking lot to wait for him as he attended a meeting that was going to take some time. After waiting there for about an hour, watching all of the logistical and military traffic coming into and flying out of the city, we observed an Iraqi Military delegation arrive at the meeting place. There were a lot of press personnel, both military and civilian there, and out of habit, we avoided them. It wasn't the press who came over to us, however, but some more Iraqi children. Three boys, who had been begging from everyone in the parking area, walked over. As before, we had nothing to give them, so we asked them to go away. For some reason, we piqued their curiosity, and they wouldn't leave. We tried every language we knew, from my Kurdish to the little Farsi and Arabic we knew, to get these kids off our jeep. They kept climbing up, and we kept lightly pushing them away.

This caught the attention of a reporter who started to walk over toward us. Seeing his approach, we started up the jeep and drove over to where we had dropped off the Operations Sergeant to check on his progress. He was not finished with the meeting, so we returned to our parking spot, waiting there were both the kids and the reporter. Accepting our fate, we allowed the reporter to come over and speak with us. He was interested in us because of our sterile uniforms. The original idea of the steriles was that they would not draw attention, but I have noticed that the steriles have the tendency to attract more attention than we want. For some reason, not wearing unit patches always attracts attention, especially from conventional officers. The reporter was actually from the Air Force, so we gave him more answers then we would normally have given to civilian reporters. We politely answered his questions, within what we could tell him under operational security (OPSEC). He was amazed to find out that we were Special Forces; he didn't know any of us were here. We told him of the refugee camps up in the mountains and the care we had provided to them. To show his appreciation, he offered us cigarettes and the use of his cell phone to call our families. I didn't use his cell phone, but I did grab some cigarettes for my teammates back in the camp.

The fact that he didn't know that Special Forces were there was normal for us. Whenever we deployed, we never told anyone who we were. We had a good laugh over this a few months after we got back home, when one of our guys appeared on the cover of *Time* magazine, being kissed on the cheek by a Kurd. The caption read something like, "Kurds welcome American Marines," but we all knew it was our unit and not the Marines.

The time had come to go pick up the Operations Sergeant, and we bid our reporter farewell. After picking up the sergeant, we had to stop at one of the large refugee camps outside of the city. This camp made the one we had worked in look tiny in comparison. As we waited for the Operations Sergeant, we were assailed once more, but this time it was mostly Kurds looking for medical assistance. I answered their questions as best as I could in my broken Kurdish, but there was nothing I could do. The Operations Sergeant finished his business, and we got back on the road, driving back across the border to our camp in Silopi.

As we entered one of the gates, we discovered a new addition to the camp. Air Force Security Police were manning the gate, and they stopped our jeep. They wanted to make sure all of our weapons were unloaded. This was new to us; we had been carrying loaded weapons for so long it was second nature. There had been a rash of accidental discharges, mostly from inexperienced soldiers who did not know how to handle their weapons. We followed their instructions, cleared our weapons, and returned to our tent area. There we found out that we were in fact flying out the next morning. Our destination was an area known as Kesann, which sounded just like Khe Sahn. We were going to build a "rest area" and provide medical and nutritional support to the refugees, who were walking from the large camps in Turkey back to their homes. After we received our instructions, we finalized our equipment preparations and went to sleep.

The following morning, we went over and had a big breakfast, then grabbed our gear and headed out to the helipad. Instead of our normal Air Force MH-53, we were going to be flown in by an Army CH-47 Chinook. There was a pile of supplies waiting next to the helicopter, which we were going to need at our new camp. Four of the guys were going to drive to the site in a jeep, and they would link up with the rest of us there. The jeep would give us some flexibility to scout the countryside and if need be, drive back to Silopi if helicopters were available. At least we wouldn't be stranded out in the middle of nowhere without a means to travel. Some Army support personnel from the 8th Infantry Division were loading the supplies into the helicopter as we climbed aboard and stacked our rucksacks on the floor. After the supplies and our equipment were loaded, the support personnel climbed aboard as well. They were coming along for the ride and to "earn" their shoulder-sleeve insignia (combat patch). I shook my head and made myself comfortable in the webbed canvas seat. During the flight, we watched one of the door gunners trying to look as cool as humanly possible. A girl with the support personnel was flying with us, and I guess he was trying to impress her. Once these kids found out we were Special Forces, they lost any interest in the "styling and profiling" door gunner.

71

Our new camp was even further into the Iraqi interior and further east of our old camp at Sinat. We had flown for about an hour or so when we began our approach to the site. The pilot maneuvered the helicopter into an opening and landed. We quickly began carrying our equipment and supplies off the helicopter. Once everything was unloaded, we waved goodbye and got down to business setting up our camp. Tony and I erected a small, general-purpose military canvas tent that would serve as our clinic. Once the tent was up, we organized the medical supplies and set up a stretcher to be used as an examination table. The rest of the team set up their tents and completed setting up our new home. After making a fire, we cooked dinner, made ourselves comfortable, and waited to see what would happen next. The camp was located in a mountain valley in more rugged terrain than our former camp. There was a good stream running through the middle of it, which allowed for thicker vegetation, but the area still looked like the American Southwest with its mountains and trees.

The next couple of days were quiet. We saw perhaps ten refugees walk by. The high point was a Kurdish soldier, who stopped by so we could check his wounds. Tony and I checked his old injuries, which were healing nicely. He thanked us and went on his way.

With nothing really going on, we decided to fall back upon our old training and begin an area assessment of the region in which we found ourselves. Lauren Sharp, Bob Spears, and I went out one morning to check an area west of our camp. There, we found a couple of old Iraqi bunkers and cleared them. We became concerned when we found a chemical protective mask filter in one of the bunkers. The search also turned up pieces of old uniforms and equipment. I secured myself an Iraqi beret that I found in one bunker. The bunkers were more like blockhouses, constructed out of sandbags and logs and as tall as a single story building. They were roughly ten feet by ten feet, some surrounded with barbed or concertina wire.

Some of the guys took the jeep out and checked the areas down the road. There they discovered the old cars that the refugees had used to get up into the mountains and then abandoned. The industrious non-Kurdish Iraqis had come along and stripped the vehicles, leaving the hulks along the road and taking the parts back down to the cities to sell.

A few days later I went out again, this time with Lauren, Lee Tomasic, Glen McMurry, and Dave Talarczyk. We explored the area to the southeast of the camp. Most of the same type of stuff we had found earlier was found here as well. Old pieces of Iraqi military uniforms, field gear, and equipment were scattered along a stream running through our valley. We also found what appeared to be an explosive crater on the side of a hill. We could not determine if it was a bomb or a land mine, and we decided not to approach it. Next we found what appeared to be five graves. They had concrete slabs across the top, with the letters "PKK" written on top. The PKK were Kurdish, Socialist guerrillas who fought against the Turkish Government. Now, we wondered whether the blockhouses/bunkers we had found before belonged to the Iraqi military or the PKK insurgents. After recording their locations with a Global Positioning System (GPS), we decided to head back to camp since the sun was beginning to set.

On the way back, we decided to cut across an open field that would take us back to our camp more quickly. While crossing, one of the guys got his pant legs caught on some barbed wire. I was up front and had everyone freeze. We were crossing a large, open and rectangular field that had high grass growing in it. The barbed wire was found on the outer edge of the field. The first thing that popped into our heads was that we had just entered a minefield! Prior to hostilities, we had been instructed on what Iraqi mine fields looked like, and this closely resembled the description. Deciding to play it safe, we backed out the same way we had come in and took the long way back to our camp. Once there, we reported everything we had found and decided to avoid that open field. All of the information was sent back to the main camp so our intelligence people could update their data.

The team developed a routine, and we settled into it. It was very quiet up there, with little activity to observe. The team continued to assess the region while Tony and I treated an occasional patient. During one of these quiet times, I decided to go take a bath. On my scouting expeditions around camp, I had found a nice water hole in a flowing stream. Granted, it was going to be cold, but it would be better than how I had been bathing. I wore a cleaner uniform and brought my dirtiest one with me. Stripping down to my "birthday suit," I immersed myself in the cold water. It was refreshing, if a bit cold, and I washed my uniform and myself. Alerted by a cracking twig, I was able to cover myself before my teammates, who had snuck up, could take a photo of "nature boy" in the wild. After cleaning the rest of my uniform, I got dressed and returned to camp. We had found a serviceable large pot with a lid, and we combined our MREs and made a potluck stew with rice.

It wasn't very long after this that we received word that our mission out here was over and we were to prepare to come back to Silopi. The team celebrated by firing off all of our flares and throwing all of our smoke grenades, filling the valley with colored smoke. The camp was torn down and most of the supplies were moved out to the trail so the refugees could find them. I was lucky enough to be allowed to ride back on the jeep instead of having to fly back. We had left a monument to ourselves by writing our team number, "031," in white stones on a hill overlooking the camp. One of the guys took a picture of it as they took off in the helicopter. We photographed them from the jeep as they flew back to Silopi.

After the team had departed, Ricky Williams, Dan McLean, Bunky, Glen McMurry, Dave Talarczyk, and I headed down the valley. The dirt road snaked alongside the stream, with numerous abandoned and stripped cars along the way. One of the more interesting vehicles we found was a stripped fire truck. The road broke out of the mountains and into an open plain. I was amazed to see a nice paved road out in the middle of absolutely nowhere. There were no villages, just the high mountains.

We followed the road westward until it joined with a major road, heading west. After driving for a while, we began to see signs of civilization as farms and small villages started to appear. As we were driving, we came across an old man walking along the road. We stopped and were able to determine through our broken Arabic and Kurdish that he was walking to Zahko. Taking pity on him, we gave him a seat in our jeep and drove him the rest of the way. Ricky gave him a pair of goggles to keep the dust out of his eyes. This old man looked very happy and must have felt like royalty as we entered the city. He thanked us as we dropped him off on the outskirts. We then decided to see if we could find the Teacher and his family. We had a rough idea where his house was located, and we had some time to go look. As luck would have it, we spotted his young nephew, "War," on a sidewalk. He was happy to see us, and he climbed into the jeep and led us to the Teacher's house. War ran inside and soon the Teacher was greeting us warmly at the gate to his house. He invited us inside and told us not to worry about our jeep; it would be watched. We accepted his hospitality, but still left Dave and Dan back to keep an eye on the jeep.

The house had been untouched, and it appeared to be in good shape. The Teacher started offering us everything, from food and tea to the use of his bathtub. We accepted tea and sat down with him for a while. He even offered us "Raki," a very strong drink that smelled of black licorice. We accepted only a small drink, but it still knocked us for a wallop. We hadn't had any type of alcohol for the last couple of months, so this little bit was enough to cause some coughing. Media, the Teacher's daughter, arrived from school as we were talking. She was dressed in a school uniform, which was different to us. We had only seen her dressed in her bathrobe, since it was the only clothes she had when the family evacuated the city and ran for the hills. It was good to see that life went on and everyone was returning to there normal routines. We stayed for only a short visit and then got back on the road again. The trip back to the camp was uneventful, even though we faced the gauntlet of kids along the stretch of road outside of the city.

We drove over to our old tent and unloaded our gear. For the next couple of days, we cleaned and repaired our equipment, washed our clothes, and waited for our next mission. After a few days, the whole company received orders. We were to escort a convoy of refugees across the border and drop them off outside of Zahko. A couple of us would ride in each truck that was carrying refugees to insure their safety. We were to link up with the trucks on the Iraqi side of the border, at the abandoned village we had passed when we had driven into Zahko with the Company Operations sergeant. At the designated meeting place, the company dismounted and wandered around the place. The flag at the small checkpoint that I had seen earlier had been taken down. As time dragged on, we all started to walk through the abandoned town and look at the damage. We assumed that this had once been a Kurdish village. What struck us as odd was that there was no bomb damage. The Iraqi military must have come into this town and looted it. As we explored, we could tell where the Iraqi's had emplaced anti-aircraft guns by the large piles of spent 30mm shell casings strewn about the town. We also found abandoned pieces of Iraqi equipment.

All of the houses had been looted and trashed, including a Mosque. Respecting their laws, we looked inside but did not enter. The whole place had been ransacked, with windows broken and every room completely torn up. In one of the abandoned houses, we found large military crates. Stenciled on the front was Jordanian military identification, even though Jordan was with the coalition and was not a supporter of Iraq. We wanted the box because it would have made an excellent and rather unique team equipment box, but we left it behind. The Iraqi guards at the checkpoint began to shadow us through the abandoned village. We ignored them and returned to the link-up site. Eventually, the convoy of trucks arrived, and we climbed aboard. These refugees were from the Turkish compound/ prison that was located just south of our camp in Silopi. The convoy pulled out onto the road and headed for the city of Zahko. Just outside of the town, the convoy pulled over and the refugees began to get off. Some of them wanted us to drive them to their villages, but our instructions stipulated that we were to drop them off there and return to base. Once they were all off-loaded, we returned to Silopi.

The next couple of days were spent packing our gear and getting ready to head back to Incirlik and, eventually, to Germany. Before we could load our equipment boxes, the customs officers made sure we had no contraband in our gear. Mostly they were looking for Iraqi weapons, since a few senior officers from the regular service had attempted to smuggle them back. We did not have any weapons, but we had spare parts and magazines for the AK assault rifles we had all been issued as part of our normal team equipment. This practice was left over from the Cold War days. We deployed with AKs instead of our American weapons in case the Russians had invaded Germany. Using the AKs would have made it easier for us to recover necessary supplies from the battlefield. During peacetime, we had limited supplies, and so we gathered up as many magazines and spare parts as we could find. The customs officers didn't see it our way; to them, a no-weapons order included weapon parts as well. Even after we explained about our equipment and lack of spare parts, they would not budge.

The customs officials parked a Hummer near our row of tents, and we quickly filled it up with spare parts, magazines, and broken pieces of salvaged equipment. I had kept an expended Turkish LAW, thinking it would make a cool plaque for our team room's wall. Like our normal LAWs, it had instructions on how to put it into operation, except the instructions were in Turkish. Basically, it was an empty fiberglass tube, but the customs officials wouldn't allow it. They went strictly by the book, refusing to use common sense. We obeyed their instructions, and soon that Hummer was completely filled with spare parts. After only a couple more days, we were on our way back to Incirlik, our part in operation Provide Comfort coming to a close. This time, we were housed in a tent city on Incirlik instead of a hangar out in the middle of the airfield. It would be a couple of days until our transportation back to Germany arrived, so we were allowed to relax. We visited the "Wagon Wheel," a western-themed club located on post, as well as the Base Exchange and the gym. The team was also allowed to go off-post to visit the Turkish city of Adana.

I was not interested in seeing the city and decided to stay on post and keep an eye on our stuff. Later that day, I sat and listened to my teammates' tales of adventure, which were rather comical since they were a little drunk at the time. Most of them had gone into the city to purchase Turkish rugs. The Turkish tradition during the sale was to serve beer to the customer. Dan McLean's motive was simple; he just wanted free beer. The Turkish rug merchant kept bringing him rugs, but none was what he wanted. Getting frustrated, the merchant finally asked Dan what type of carpet he was looking for. With a straight face, he replied, "A flying carpet!" After leaving that store, he continued down the street and did the same thing in the next merchant's store, looking for the fabled Flying Carpet while enjoying the free beer. Ricky went into the city and purchased a leather duster at a fairly inexpensive price. When I returned to my tent, I found Bunky passed out on his cot wearing a "Mister-T Starter Kit." Every finger had a gold ring, and he had at least ten necklaces around his neck. Gold and silver were easy to get here and also fairly inexpensive. It didn't bother me that I hadn't gone into the city; I enjoyed listening to the tales of their exploits. I hadn't bought any gold or silver jewelry there, but I later purchased a silver ring that a member of the company had designed. It was known as the "Batman Ring." It had our Special Forces crest on it, with the Batman symbol on the side. Eventually, I donated my ring to our battalion's museum before I went back to the states on a new assignment.

We enjoyed our time in Turkey, but soon our aircraft arrived and we were on our way back to Germany. This trip was less eventful than our return from Operation Desert Storm. We arrived once again at night, and family members were there to meet us. After being home for about a week, we found out that our base was going to be closed, and we were going to have to move to Stuttgart.

CHAPTER 7

INTERLUDE, THE GLOBAL WAR ON TERROR AND ON THE ROAD TO WAR AGAIN

Following Operations Desert Storm and Provide Comfort, I continued with my career in Special Forces. Within Special Forces, we have what is known as the "Iron Triangle" when it comes to assignments. For the most part, a Special Forces soldier will serve in a stateside unit, a forward deployed unit, and as an instructor at the John F. Kennedy Special Warfare Center and School (JFKSWC). After the 1st battalion was moved to Stuttgart, I participated in Operation Silver Anvil, the evacuation of American citizens from the African country of Sierra Leon.

Next, I, along with about a hundred others in the unit, received orders to report to Fort Bragg to become an instructor at the school. Eventually, I was assigned to Camp Mckall, a small area on the far western part of the extensive Fort Bragg military reservation. This is where Special Forces soldiers begin their training as part of the Special Forces Qualification Course (Q-Course). My first year and half, I was an assessor and evaluator for the Selection and Assessment program. This wasn't a bad job. I was out ruck marching with the students, and I didn't have to validate being a graduate of the first selection course. Normally, a new instructor would have to go through the selection and evaluation course if he had not gone through prior to 1988.

Since I had attended the very first one, I would not have to be validated and could start right into evaluating. However, I was not allowed to make suggestions or instruct, and I had to remain stoic

79

and aloof. This ended when the Q-Course was changed back to the three-phase program that I had gone through as a student. In between the time when I had gone through as a student and the current curriculum, the phases of the Q-Course had been changed. Students went through their respective Military Occupational Specialties (MOS) specific training, then would be sent out to Camp Mckall to learn land navigation and small unit tactics. What was being discovered was that some of the candidates were excellent academic students, but when they arrived at Camp Mckall, they couldn't land navigate or conduct small-unit tactics. This required a student to stay longer and be continually recycled through the program, a waste of money. The Special Warfare Center and School decided to return to the older three-phase program

I volunteered to join the Phase I Committee, responsible for training the students in small-unit tactics. At least now I could do what I was trained to do and instruct. However, this was a lean time for the cadre of the Q-Course, with a reduction in the number of instructors and an increase in the number of students. We were told to do more with less and to "make it happen." I was soon helping out the Selection and Assessment Committee as well as supporting the Phase III, the Unconventional Warfare/Robin Sage Committee. I would no sooner finish up a Phase I class and write my reports and evaluations, than I was on my way out to the training area to prepare the backside support for the Robin Sage exercise. I used my experience with the Peshmerga guerrillas to help make the training as realistic as possible. I was away from my family for a month and a half at times, covering one phase or the other. I had served my three years as an instructor when the call went out for volunteers for Germany. I volunteered to return to my old unit, and soon I was back in Company C, 1st Battalion in Boeblingen. During this time in Germany, I became once more a player on the world stage.

Within my first year back in my old unit, we were alerted and sent to Sarajevo, Bosnia, where President Clinton was going to meet with the other confederation leaders. The Secret Service decided they did not have enough security personnel, so we were alerted and sent to augment their forces. I was responsible for the ground security of the old Natural History Museum of Sarajevo, where the President would meet with the leaders. Our security element consisted of two of C Company sniper teams, a secret service sniper team, and two, four-man ground security elements composed of a team from ODA 033, and my four-man team from ODA 036. The President arrived, along with the Leaders of Serbia, Bosnia, and Croatia. The meeting went without any incidents, and the President and his large caravan of vehicles left for another part of the city. I would spend more time in that city, returning the following year to provide security once again for the President along with other members of NATO for a large meeting. I would also spend a four-month rotation as a member of the Combined Joint Special Operations Task Force-Sarajevo, providing security and force protection to general officers, dignitaries, as well as conducting special operations. This tour occurred during the millennium, from the end of October through February 2001. Most people want to remember where they were for the millennium; I was in Sarajevo.

I continued to respond to one crisis after another around the European area. It seemed every year we were alerted and planned for contingency operations in Africa, which included deploying to Gabon in case we were needed in the Congo. Then the situation in Albania and Kosovo exploded, and we were sent to an old Naval Air Station called San Vito in southern Italy. Not all of my missions were contingency operations; I was able to take part in a parachute jump onto a drop zone along Normandy Beach in France during the anniversary in 2002. There I was able to meet and speak with the Ranger veterans who had climbed Point Du Hoc as part of the invasion. When these old veterans who had faced the cliff called calling us "crazy" for jumping out of airplanes, it came as a big shock to us. However, we were kindred spirits and brothers-in-arms.

While I was an instructor at Fort Bragg, the 10th Special Forces were still busy supporting Operation Northern Watch. To insure that Saddam Hussein would not attack the Kurds in the North and the Shi'ites in the South, a "No Fly" zone was put in place to protect these areas. This effort was known as Operation Northern Watch for the northern half and Operation Southern Watch for the southern half of the country. Teams from 10th Special Forces Group were rotating into Turkey, providing Combat Search and Rescue (CSAR) support in case any aircraft went down. The teams rotated out of Incirlik for the next couple of years, in addition to continued support operations in Bosnia. While we were busy supporting other operations around the world, the United Nations attempted to maintain a trade and military embargo on the country of Iraq. The United Nations sent survey teams into Iraq to make sure Saddam was obeying the U.N. resolutions that were enacted following the war, including arms inspections. However, there were signs that he was not complying with theses resolutions.

To encourage Saddam to adhere to the United Nations resolutions and allow the inspectors better access, a series of air strikes and Tomahawk cruise missile strikes were launched at key military targets within Iraq, known as Operation Desert Thunder. Following these strikes, Saddam seemed to become more aggressive and non-compliant than he had been before. Iraqi Surface to Air Missiles (SAM), frequently were tracking the aircraft that were supporting Operation Northern Watch from Incirlik Air Base, with their radars. Being threatened, the aircraft attacked these missile sites and radar installations in self- defense. Back in our team room in Germany, we watched these events and commented on how Iraq was becoming a live-fire bombing range for the Air Force.

While all of this was going on, I received my orders to report to the Group Headquarters, 10th Special Forces Group at Fort Carson, Colorado, for my new assignment. Now a senior Sergeant First Class (E-7), I was assigned to the Group Headquarters, where I worked as the Group Exercise coordinator and planner. We took current world events and incorporated them into our training scenarios, to keep the detachments ready in case something went very wrong in the world.

In fact, the world fell apart for us on Sept. 11, 2001, when Muslim extremists hijacked four passenger aircraft and slammed them into the World Trade Center and the Pentagon, with one that had been destined for a target in Washington, D.C. forced to crash into a field in Pennsylvania. My family and I, living out in Colorado Springs, had no idea what had occurred. With the two-hour difference between Eastern Standard and Mountain Standard Time zones, we hadn't seen the news yet that morning. After putting on my uniform for work, I walked my daughter Samantha to school, as I had every day since we'd moved there. But this morning would be very different from normal. When we arrived at her school, some of her classmates came up and said that we had been bombed. I did not believe them at first, thinking the kids were just telling stories or repeating rumors. However, as my wife Karin and I walked back home, one of our neighbors came out and said the same thing. The first thing we did once we reached our house was to turn on the news, and sure enough, there it was. We began seeing the news from the Twin Towers, and I decided I had better get to work immediately.

The shock of what I just witnessed on the news haunted me on the way into work. I had heard of the Taliban, the Russians began to fear them more than the United States. Now I could see why, they were radical fundamentalists who had no fear of dying for their cause. Earlier I had seen news reports how they had destroyed ancient statutes because they believed it violated Islamic law. All I felt was a deep anger that I still feel to this day. As a soldier, I understand waging war and killing an enemy soldier. But to attack civilians because of a different belief was against everything I had been taught and brought up on. Now I was waiting for my turn to pay them back in full for what they had done to my country.

We continued to work as if nothing had happened, except we watched more news to keep up with what was happening. There were signs that things were in the planning phase. As we began putting together the next Group exercise, we were told to find areas to train in that were close to Colorado. Originally, we had been looking at areas in other states, but now we concentrated on Colorado. My family and I spent a Saturday up in Cripple Creek. There was a bikers' festival going on, and one of the announcers informed the crowd that we had begun bombing Taliban targets in Afghanistan. It was determined that Osama Bin Laden, once an ally during the fight against the Soviets in Afghanistan, was now our enemy. It was his terrorist network that had sent the hijackers to attack the Twin Towers and the Pentagon. What would become known as the War on Terror had began. A shiver of electricity ran through me, I knew it was time to get even.

As the United States sent troops and aircraft to Afghanistan, we continued to plan exercises and to get through our day-to-day routines. During all of this, Saddam Hussein continued to be a problem for the United Nations. The United Nation's weapons inspectors were either brought to sterile or already inspected sites, or not allowed into others. Once the Taliban were for the most part defeated in Afghanistan and stabilization operations had begun, the United States turned its attention back to Saddam and the country of Iraq. Plans were begun or reworked in case Iraq continued to be uncooperative and military action was needed. This changed our situation in Colorado, when our exercises were canceled and the detachments were trained locally.

With no exercises to plan, I was basically out of a job. With my background in Personnel Recovery (PR), I was teamed up with CW/4 William McPherson (Chief), and we became the PR experts for the Group. Chief McPherson, the Group's Operations Warrant Officer, had been in Special Forces for a long time. We were both sent to Fredericksburg, Virginia to attend classes at the Joint Personnel Recovery Agency's (JPRA) Personnel Recovery Training Center-East (PRTC-E) school. After attending their Introduction to Personnel Recovery Course, we returned a few months later for the Personnel Recovery Operations Management Course. These courses prepared us as we continued the path that would lead us down the road to war with Iraq.

As we prepared for our second war in Iraq, my position had changed. I was no longer a member of a team preparing to go out on missions. Instead, I had moved up to the Combined/Joint Special Operations Task Force (CJSOTF). A CJSOTF is a special headquarters where elements from either two or all four military branches, such as Army and Air Force personnel, along with coalition allies, become a single headquarters element. The CJSOTF would usually be responsible for a specific area of operations. This Task Force oversaw the planning and would be responsible for the command and control of operations in northern Iraq.

For the vast majority of the Group Staff, the only experience we had in running a Combined/Joint Special Operations Task Force (CJSOTF) staff was through training and schools. Some of us on the staff had some experience with CJSOTFs, but very few had actually served on a combined, let alone a CJSOTF staff. So staff training began in earnest to prepare us for what we might encounter when we deployed. To assist us in our training, the Joint Forces Command's Special Operations Component (SOCJFCOM), came out to train our staff in CJSOTF operations. We spent a week listening to seminars, and we received instruction from their experts on our duties and responsibilities. The staff began to receive augmentation from the Special Forces National Guard (19th Group) as well as from other branches of the military, including active duty, Reserves, and National Guard. These newcomers included officers who were not in Special Forces and had to be shown how we did business. As I was the Assistant Director for personnel recovery, I sat in on the seminars and briefings, while CW/4 McPherson coordinated with other Governmental agencies. During these seminars, I ran into Mike Dozier once again, who had retired and had gone to work with JPRA.

The training and seminars served two purposes. The primary reason was to prepare us to run a CJSOTF staff when we deployed; the secondary reason was that we were preparing for a major staff exercise. This exercise, hosted by the 5th Special Forces Group, was known as "Internal Look." It was a staff exercise, in which the staffs would be linked across Colorado, Fort Campbell in Kentucky, and the Joint Forces Command (JFCOM) in Norfolk, Va. via satellite and secure Internet. This served as a means to rehearse scenarios and work out battle drills in our Joint Operations Center (JOC), as well as to work with our counterparts with the other CJSOTF staff. The exercise was intended to conduct our staff operations in the same manner as they would be conducted for real. The JOC sat us in our classroom/isolation facility within our compound. We all worked twelve-hour shifts; half of the staff worked during the day, and the other half during the night. The only difference from a real deployment was that we could go home to sleep. I was amazed at how far we had advanced in technology since Desert Storm. Back then, it was pencils, maps, and notebooks. Now we had Internet chat, video conferencing, and real-time exchange of information.

While the exercise was being conducted, I handled most of the staff portion, doing personnel recovery planning and monitoring, and Chief (McPherson) continued the coordination process. The most beneficial portion of the exercise, other than working out the kinks, was that I was able to interact with the very people I would be working with once we deployed. This allowed me to get to know their procedures for operating and to build a rapport with them prior to the conduct of operations. Instead of going in cold and not knowing anybody, we had already worked together. For personnel recovery, there was an established pyramid of responsibility. At the very top was the Joint Search and Rescue Center (JSRC) located in Qatar in the Joint Air Operations Center run by the Air Force, which was responsible for the planning, coordination, and execution of all recovery missions within Iraq. Underneath the JSRC was the Rescue Coordination Centers (RCC) of the participating component commands within the Joint Force that were conducting the military operations. This included the Army, Air Force, Marines, Navy, and Special Operations. To assist in the coordination within the extensive Special Operations forces, each JSOTF had its own Personnel Recovery Coordination Cell (PRCC). Within our PRCC, Chief and I, who were responsible for the coordination and planning of Combat Recovery of our forces and Chief McPherson, would additionally be responsible for coordinating Unconventional Recovery operations. In these operations, an outside organization from within our government would recover the isolated person, and return them to friendly military control. We helped each other out as needed. Luckily, before we deployed, we had practiced this flow of control and information during the Internal Look exercise, making it easier for us now. Chief and I had already met some of our counterparts with 5th Group's JSOTF while attending the training in Fredericksburg, which helped us to quickly develop a rapport.

One of the more interesting aspects of the exercise was the Capitulation Matrix. In normal military operations, the goal is to reduce your enemy's fighting capability through combat attrition. In this operation, we expected the majority of the Iraqi military to surrender, except for the Republican Guard, who were considered some of Saddam's best and most loyal troops. We rehearsed combat operations, contingencies, and numerous "what if" scenarios. The idea was to develop plans and battle drills, step- by-step procedures for staff actions, depending on the situation. During these events, a slide would be shown on one of the screens so the staff could follow the steps. Just like our SOPs and Battle Drills for a detachment, these staff battle drills were practiced over and over again, so the right procedures would become second nature and would not require a lot of thinking.

Following the exercise, we continued to refine the plan and wait for the order to deploy. The detachments continued to train, and I worked with the JPRA to arrange a High Risk of Capture (HRC) training seminar for the Group's personnel. Because we were working with Central Command (CENTCOM), I began to read up and study their procedures and regulations. For the most part, however, their procedures were identical to what we normally followed, with only minor differences. While waiting for the order to deploy, I also reviewed the Group's Isolated Personnel Reports (ISOPREP) cards. These cards would be used to identify our personnel in case they were captured or recovered if they had became separated or isolated from their units/detachments. In a digital world, all of the ISOPREP cards had to be transformed into a digital medium so the information could be sent via computer over a secure Internet. All of the 10th Group, from the team members to the support personnel who were going into harm's way, filled them out and put them into digital form. I then checked them and passed them on to the Special Operations Rescue Coordination Center (SOCRCC). There was a lot of grumbling, especially when I sent cards back because they had mistakes. I understood that the teams were busy, but this was one of the requirements I had received from CENTCOM that was to be completed prior to our arriving in country. They wanted as many of our digital ISOPREPs sent to them as possible so they could be placed into their database before our deployment.

The waiting game continued, which worked out well for me because I was able to spend the holidays with my family. As 2002 arrived, we continued to wait for the deployment order and to refine the plan. It was not a matter of "if" we deploy; it was a matter of "when." By late January, we began to get clues that the deployment order would be coming soon. First, there was no change to the political situation with Iraq. There was a tremendous amount of diplomacy going on between the United States and her allies in Europe. President George W. Bush worked to build a coalition, similar to what his father had achieved during Operation Desert Shield/Desert Storm. This time, there were fewer Muslim and Arab nations willing to support us, due to the War on Terror. These fanatics had a lot of influence with various Arab national governments. Great Britain, our strongest ally stood with us, however France, Germany and Russia were not as supportive as they were back during Operation Desert Storm. The diplomats at the United Nations must have been working in overdrive to get enough support for a resolution in favor of military action.

Not only was it a difficult situation internationally and with the United Nations, but the situation with the average American was becoming intense. There were two sides, a strong anti-war movement and a strong pro-war movement within the United States. Sometimes I wondered if this was really due to personal views, or if the college generation was trying to do what the college students back during Vietnam had done. Unfortunately, I felt there was more attention given to the anti-war movement than to the pro-war movement by the press. This was the situation with my own family, especially with my stepmother. She was a strong supporter of the anti-war movement and active in that cause. All of my family was concerned, because they knew if a war with Iraq began, I would more than likely deploy. I had not informed them of our pending deployment. I never talked to them about when and where I was going in the world due to the sensitive nature of my job. I understood their concern and respected their views, though they differed from mine. Having seen first-hand what Saddam had done to the Kurds, I knew what he and his regime was capable of doing. The problem was, I and the other soldiers who had served over there before were in the minority, and the press was not presenting all of the facts.

I will admit that I felt, along with other military historians, that Desert Storm ended far too soon. If we had driven on to Baghdad then, Saddam would have been overthrown and removed from power. The United States would have taken more causalities and would have had more men killed, but the United States wouldn't have spent the last ten years and billions of dollars supporting Operations

Northern and Southern Watch. However, it was politics. We had achieved the military objective of removing the Iraqis from Kuwait. Had the Americans and the Coalition pushed on to Baghdad, more than likely, we would have lost a lot of support from the Arabian nations. That was then and this was now, and we had to deal with it. In any case, our wait was over. When March arrived, we received our orders to deploy. Fate always seems to deploy me on or about my daughter's and my birthdays. In my military career, I have missed her birthday (which is two days after my own) about half of the time. This time, it wouldn't be any different.

We began our pre-deployment activities, received our desert uniforms, and began the Anthrax vaccination cycle. The bags and boxes were packed; we received our deployment and threat briefings. Part of the pre-deployment activity is to go through the Fort Carson Readiness Center to complete the Soldier's Readiness Packet (SRP). It is a centralized facility where our paperwork was updated, we received a medical screening, and we received our necessary vaccinations to make sure everything was in order before we deployed. Most of our equipment was loaded into large, square metal containers, which made securing and transporting our gear a lot easier. Some of our equipment, however, was loaded on the old-fashioned flat metal pallets. The equipment was inventoried, locked, and secured, and then moved over to Peterson Air Force Base. The hardest time was waiting for our turn to go to the airfield and load the aircraft. The word for my section came in the first week in March, when we departed to what would become known as Operation Iraqi Freedom.

CHAPTER 8

OPERATION IRAQI FREEDOM AND THE "UGLY BABY"

It started out as any other typical military operation. We arrived to depart, but found out the aircraft had broken down and we would leave the following morning. Though being able to spend another day with the family was a nice surprise, it prolonged the difficulty that is going off to war and, in a way, made it that much harder. The next day, March 4, 2003, I arrived at our Company Headquarters around 5 a.m. and continued the tradition of hurry up and wait. I was traveling light, a small rucksack with a meal and enough snacks, water, books, and toiletries for two days in case the aircraft broke down. Additionally, I had an aviator's kit bag in which I was carrying my mission-essential paperwork and bloodchits so I would be ready to go to work as soon as I hit the ground. A bloodchit is a piece of waterproof paper which has an American flag on it as well as a statement in numerous languages of the area, "If you help me to return to my unit, the United States will give you a reward." We normally all carried one and hoped it wouldn't be used.

After putting our bags on a flatbed trailer, we loaded the bus for the ride to the airfield. It was a quiet ride, with most of the guys keeping their thoughts to themselves. When we arrived, we were pleasantly surprised to see a contracted L-1011 instead of a military transport. Most of the Air Force's heavy lift assets were busy moving men and material to Kuwait and Saudi Arabia. I helped to load our bags and equipment inside the aircraft, which was better than sitting around and doing nothing. As we finished loading, it began to lightly snow at the airport. I once again would miss a good snowfall while being away. Coming from upstate New York, I love snow, and we hadn't seen much of it while we lived in Colorado. Now it was snowing when we had to leave.

We began to file aboard, with Fort Carson's Deputy Commander standing at the bottom of the stairs and seeing us off. The 200 or so of us filled that airplane, but we still had more room and a more comfortable seat than we would have had on a C-5 Galaxy. Those on the plane included most of the men from the second battalion, along with some of us from the group staff. It was around noon when we taxied out to the runway and took off for the first leg of our deployment.

The first leg of our journey was only an hour and a half to Indiana, where we landed to top off the aircraft's fuel tanks. The airplane could not be fully fueled in Colorado Springs, because the altitude made it necessary to restrict the weight it could carry for takeoff. As the aircraft was being fueled, we hung out in one of the terminals, receiving some funny looks from the other passengers, who were waiting for their flights. After about an hour, we filed back onto the plane for the second leg of our journey, which brought us to Gander, Newfoundland. It was dark, and the temperature was six degrees with a strong, cold wind tugging on us as we made our way to the terminal. We waited another hour as the aircraft was topped off with the fuel needed to carry us across the Atlantic. Since it was so late at night, the only people in the airport besides us were some folks running the small restaurant and gift store. To kill time, I looked through the gift shop to see if I could find anything for my daughter but didn't buy anything. The hour was soon up, and we re-boarded the aircraft for the third leg of our journey. The flight across the Atlantic wasn't bad; we watched two movies, "The Transporter" and "I Spy," and had something to eat. I tried to get some sleep, but the attendant kept running into my shoulder and waking me up when he walked down the aisle. As the sun was coming up, we landed at Sandy, Ireland, where the aircraft would be refueled and the flight crew replaced with a fresh one.

This time the wait would be two hours, so we made ourselves comfortable in the empty terminal. There was a small bar open, but we were under Rule #1, no alcohol, so we purchased coffee. However, another aircraft full of soldiers arrived, and apparently ignoring Rule #1, they drank beers. More than likely, these soldiers were reservists, and a few of our guys envied them and the good Irish beer they were enjoying. I found myself a quiet corner to stretch out on the floor and take a nap. On the airplane, I had shared the row of three seats with one other guy, so we had enough room to snooze on the plane, except for the problem of my shoulder sticking out into the aisle. It felt nice just to stretch out on the floor for a little bit. Once the aircraft was ready for us, we loaded and began the final leg to our destination. Our original plan had us going to Batman, Turkey, but this had to be changed when the Turkish Government refused to assist us in this operation. It would have been nice to see what the place looked like now, but it wasn't to be. Once more politics had raised its ugly head, and a key piece of our plan fell through. Instead, we were heading to an unlikely destination, one I wouldn't have thought of, Constanta, Romania. We flew for about three and a half hours and then landed on a Romanian Air Force base outside of Constanta.

Being based on a Romanian military installation was very strange for me. For the first half of my career, I had been training to fight the Soviets and their Allies, including Romania. With the situation in the world changed and the Cold War over, those who were once our enemies were now our allies. In a way it seemed fitting that when, Turkey, who normally is one of our allies, wouldn't help us, we ended up here. Romania was really pushing hard to be allowed into the North Atlantic Treaty Organization (NATO), and I guess this was a way for them to bolster their case. As we taxied past their aircraft sitting along the side of the taxiway, I saw Mig-29s and SU-27s, some looking as if they had bird nests in their air intakes. I guess they don't get much flight time with their aircraft. As our plane taxied over towards the terminal, I noticed the MC-130s and MH-53s from the 352nd SOG sitting on the tarmac as well. After our plane came to a stop, we were brought into a terminal where we once more followed the military tradition of hurry up and wait. Here we passed through an in-processing center, filled out paperwork, and received our area orientation briefing. Once completed, we all loaded up on buses to be brought to our new barracks while the second battalion went to their new area.

New, only in the sense that they were in Romania. These were old military barracks that had been freshly painted and smelled of chemicals. I guess they had used chemicals to kill all of the bugs and lice. Finding myself an empty bunk near a window, I noticed I would be sharing the bay with about sixty other people. After stowing my bags, and settled into my new surroundings, I began to look around my new home. Billeted on the floor above us were some old friends of mine, who had left 10th Group and joined the 96th Civil Affairs from Fort Bragg. After getting caught up on what they had been doing, I went to my bed to get some sleep. The heaters definitely worked; it was very warm in the room. The heat mixed with the chemical smell made for a very restless night and some very strange dreams. With my bunk being next to a window, I opened it to try and get some fresh air and was finally able to get some sleep. In the morning, I went over to the dining facility, where we had catered Romanian food. The food itself wasn't too bad, and it was certainly better than an MRE. I hung out in the barracks for a little bit, taking in my surroundings. We had two Romanian guards, armed with AK-74s, and a BRDM armored personnel carrier nearby. It was still strange to me to be with these folks after all of my years of training to fight them.

It was now March 6, and I headed over to where the Joint Operations Center (JOC) was set up. The barracks that I was living in was located on one base, and the JOC was located on a smaller base next to the airfield down the road. After taking the bus over, I linked up with Chief, who had came over a week or so earlier. He briefed me on where we were in the scheme of things, and told me that I would start that evening on night shift. Returning to the barracks, I did a quick workout of push-ups and sit-ups, stretched to get the kinks out, and took a nap. I kept having a feeling that there were bugs on me while I was asleep, either from the smell of the chemicals or my imagination. As night fell, I made my way back to the JOC and got down to business. I mostly spent the night going over more ISOPREP cards and sending them on to the Special Operations Rescue Coordination Center, as well as reviewing our detachment's Emergency Plans of Action (EPA). These plans detailed what a team would do if their aircraft crash-landed while they were infiltrating. The political situation with Turkey was not resolving itself, and we knew it could become a major problem for us. The shortest route to Iraq was over Turkey, and the Turkish Government was still not cooperating. I believe this was because they were Muslim, and since we were about to fight another Muslim country, they didn't want to become involved. Or perhaps they were holding out for more financial support.

Once my shift was over, I was told we were being moved to a hotel in Constanta. There were more people coming in, and they needed our barracks space. So I want back over to the barracks, grabbed my gear and returned to the JOC area. We didn't actually move over to the hotel until 12:30 p.m., so I sat around and waited in our support center, which was a large tent erected in a parking lot across from the JOC. I couldn't get any sleep while I was waiting due to all of the activity, so I just sat there and watched the world go by, waiting for the bus to take me to my new home. We finally boarded a bus and headed toward the city of Constanta, about a twenty-minute drive. Along the route, we passed an air defense missile site. I recognized the radar arrays from earlier reconnaissance classes. The city of Constanta itself was a tourist/resort city, situated on the western coast of the Black Sea. Because it was early March, most of the hotels were empty, so it was easy for our government to contract rooms, a job that was handled by our embassy personnel. The city itself, from what I saw during the ride, was drab and gray. Tall apartment buildings lined the road. It seemed to be a cross between a second-world and a third-world country. Most of the buildings had a dingy color to them with a lot of garbage around them. With no tourists around, the strip of hotels along the beach looked like a ghost town.

I imagine that during the summer months, this strip was a hive of activity, considering the number of hotels and clubs that we passed. The hotel where I would be staying was situated on the beach, and I caught a glimpse of the Black Sea. We were told we could not go out on the beach, only to our rooms and to work, nowhere else. This was a force protection issue for our safety, as well as a way of keeping our signature low so the whole world wouldn't know we were there. After being assigned my room and receiving a briefing from the embassy personnel on procedures, I went to my room and stored my bags.

The room wasn't very big. It had two single beds and a bathroom. The ceramic green tile floor was very cold, and very slippery. The hotel had only been recently opened to provide rooms for us. The room had a heater, but it would take some time for me to figure out how it worked. My roommate was supposed to be an old teammate of mine, Mike Fite, who was now a medic with the second battalion. I believe he came to the room at night while I was on night shift. This worked out rather nicely; I had the room all to myself. The room did have a TV with cable that showed mostly Romanian channels, but CNN International and the Discovery Channel were in English. The bathroom wasn't very big, but it had a toilet, a sink, and a shower. After putting away what little stuff I had, I grabbed my poncho liners and tried to catch some sleep before going back on duty. The cold temperature helped me to fall asleep. This would be the hardest challenge for me, adjusting my body to sleeping during the day and working during the night. The other challenge was not breaking my neck walking on the smooth, slippery tiled floor. I took a shower and as I walked across the tile, nearly slipped. I had to literally be on my toes so I wouldn't fall down and hurt myself. What an embarrassment that would be!

The next week was spent doing a twelve-hour shift on, and then twelve hours off. The first week is always the most difficult, because you need to attune your body to the routine. Chief, Wolfgang Kaiser, who was attached to us from JPRA (and an old 10th Grouper as well), and I worked at getting our workstation, maps, and information boards set up as we had been taught in Fredericksburg. I spent most of the time reviewing ISOPREP cards and EPAs. Because we were working with CENTCOM, they wanted the EPAs in their format. The teams grumbled when I sent the EPAs back, but we had to play by CENTCOM's rules. We had the time. The political situation was still not working in our favor, and none of the teams was being launched.

Another drawback to working nights was that the majority of the other soldiers who lived in my hotel, were on a different time schedule than mine. When I arrived at my room to go to sleep, most people were getting up. When I was on my way to work, they were hanging out in the hotel lobby. I also had to deal with the cleaning ladies. They came into my room to clean, even when I was asleep. I am a very light sleeper, and I awoke as soon as the door opened. I became frustrated trying to speak to them to get them to understand my situation. I put the "Do Not Disturb" sign on my door, but, unfortunately, they ignored it, dedicated to their job of cleaning the room during the day. The fact that I slept during the day baffled them. None of the cleaning ladies spoke English, so I tried German, which for some reason didn't go over very well. I tried what little Russian I could remember, which seemed to work. Eventually we came to an understanding, and I was no longer disturbed while trying to get some valuable sleep.

While we were getting the staff organized here in Romania, more Army and Air Force units were positioning themselves in Saudia Arabia and Kuwait. Two aircraft carrier battle groups along with the Marines were moving into the Persian Gulf. Along with the American forces, coalition partners were moving their forces into the region and moving to staging bases along the Iraqi border. As we were responsible for the north, the 5th Special Forces would be coming in from the west and were establishing their personnel recovery architecture there. Additionally, the majority of the Air Force and other Special Operation recovery forces were being staged along the Iraqi/Saudia Arabia borders.

The JOC was set up just as we had rehearsed back in Fort Carson. At first, I was located in the front row, in the very center of the JOC, which allowed me to interface with the key planners. Next to me were the coordinators and planners from the 352nd Special Operations Group (SOG) and the 21st Special Operations Squadron (SOS-which flew the MH-53), as well as the Ground Fire coordinators. This allowed me direct access to them in case I had to plan a recovery mission. Immediately behind me was the shift Operations Officer, and behind him, the JOC Chief of Staff. In the row behind me were the key intelligence coordinators, both Army (ground) and Air Force (air). Our JOC was set up so the key players were located on the left side of the room, and the other coordinators were on the right. These included Liaison Officers from the various battalions from our group, as well as Space Command, Medical, Judge Advocate (JAG), and our support center. The JOC was set up as a "One Stop Shop" for coordination.

The room itself was about seventy-five feet long by about twenty feet wide. Crammed into this space were eight rows of tables, four rows on the left and four rows on the right with a central walkway between them. The rows were composed of about eight workstations each. That's roughly sixty-four personnel, with sixty-four computers on. Needless to say, we never worried about it being cold in there; sometimes it was quite warm and muggy. In the very front were three large screens used to project the Blue Force Tracker (BFTs-a way to tell where friendly units are located on the battlefield), battle drill slides, and any other pertinent information. Also located along the front rows were radio boxes, where we could monitor radio traffic and different frequencies. I wore a headset so I could listen to the missions and block out the noise of the JOC. The only time the JOC's activity came to halt was during the changeover brief. This meant that there were twice as many people in the room, plus some extras to listen to the morning and evening situation updates. This was designed so that the personnel coming on duty were kept up-to-date on what was going on and what missions were occurring. In this way, everyone maintained Situational Awareness (SA) of the fight.

The JOC itself was in what I believe was an administration building for the Romanian base on which we were located. The JOC was on one side, and the 352nd SOG had the other side for their planning area. Our Headquarters First Sergeant had a small administration area in an office located in the central hall. Located along a hallway inside the building were several offices used by our future planners and our intelligence section. When Chief, Wolfgang, and I were moved out of the JOC because space was becoming critical, we were given an office located along this hallway for our recovery planning cell. Within our tiny corner of this base was a large festival tent, or in simplest terms, a circus tent just behind our building, which was dedicated to the communication and computer personnel, who were supporting both us and the Air Force. Located within the tent were our planners, who coordinated with other government agencies. Off to the side was a large dining facility, and the catered food was served there. The bus stop where we were picked up and dropped off from the hotels was located on the airfield, about a fifteen-minute walk from the JOC. In an open field, a medical clinic was set up in a couple of tents. The little base was becoming crowded real fast, and the Romanians who worked there also continued to do their jobs. We tried to stay out of their way as much as possible.

I still had not located my bags, which had come on the pallets and the containers. I was using what I brought in my ruck, which was designed for two days and not a week. Still wearing the same uniform that I had deployed in, and there were no facilities yet for washing clothes, my uniform was starting to become a little ripe. The JOC itself was in an old briefing room, and space was at a premium. We did have a place for the coffee maker, and soon I was having caffeine shakes from all of the coffee I was drinking. Some amenities had been established on the compound. We now had a single computer and a single phone for morale purposes.

As we waited to see how the political situation with Turkey ended, we continued to work on improving our area in the JOC. At the moment, Personnel Recovery was a low priority, so we were moved around four times. Most of the staff felt that the chances of a PR/CSAR mission coming up were slim to none so the job was given a low priority. Top priority went to supporting combat operations, which for the time being meant getting our forces into Iraq. Chief, Wolfgang, and I, continued to prepare ourselves, as well as help the other sections get established and running.

Constanta always seemed to be gray, both because of the color of the buildings and the cold, overcast weather we had most of the time. Working night shifts limited my exposure to the sun in any case, but instead of sunsets or sunrises, all I saw were lead-gray clouds. The wet and damp air had given me a cough that didn't want to go away.

The days were numbered now as "Groundhog Day" number 2, 3, etc., a reference to the Bill Murray movie in which he was stuck in the same day over and over again. This is how it felt for us on duty; we did the same thing day after day. I reviewed ISOPREP cards and EPAs, so much so I was seeing them in my sleep. It must have really been bad for the teams who were waiting to go.

As we rode the contracted shuttle bus to the base from the hotel, we could see our Special Operations MC-130s from the 352nd SOG parked on the tarmac, the teams and their vehicles waiting. Every night they headed out to the aircraft to load, waited for a few hours, and then were told that it was not going to happen and so they should return to their barracks. The level of stress within the JOC was growing due to the waiting; I was becoming frustrated with the lack of support in getting the necessary materials to do my job. Understanding I was a low priority, I felt I needed to make sure our portion of the operation went smoothly and was a textbook example on how to run a PRCC. After waking up, I watched CNN International for an update on world events before heading over for my shift. As I got ready for work, I relieved some of the stress by doing push-ups, sit-ups, crunches, and stretching in my room while I listened to the Romanian version of MTV, which played mostly music videos in their language.

There was a small victory for me on March 14, when I finally received my equipment. As I came in for my shift, I was told where to find my rucksack and duffel bag. When I reached the spot where the pallet had been stored, I found them, sitting out in the snow! Someone had opened the pallet to get their gear, and in the process moved mine off. Instead of putting it back under the plastic cover that protected the pallet and the equipment from the weather, they had left it out, and had been snowed on for about a day. Of my three bags, one was completely soaked, the other duffel was half soaked, and only my rucksack was OK. I had placed waterproof bags inside them, which helped a little. I took my gear back to my room after my shift was completed and laid the half-wet clothing out to dry. The hotel now provided a laundry service for us, so I took most of the wet clothes to the laundry to be washed.

My cough developed into an infection, so I had to take antibiotics. I had already caught the tuberculosis virus during one of my trips to Bosnia. Romania is also bad with the virus, so I was taking every precaution that I could. By now I had sent over 800 digital ISOPREPs to the Special Operations Rescue Coordination Center (SOCRCC). They had the overall responsibility of coordinating all the Special Operation Forces CSAR missions, and we as a Personnel Recovery Coordination Cell (PRCC) assisted them. The waiting game continued. We worked on our plans and waited to see what would develop with Turkey.

On March 16, I once more celebrated my birthday away from home, and I called my daughter on her birthday, March 18, by a cell phone leant to me from Wolfgang. As we waited for a decision to be made concerning how we would infiltrate our detachments, I ran a computer drill with the SOC RCC so we could rehearse our procedures. During the drill, we had a complete power failure in the JOC, so I was able to rehearse that contingency.

I went over to try and get some body armor. The only thing they had which would fit was a carrier, which is the outer vest. They didn't have any armor plates, so I would have to do without. At least the carrier would protect me from shrapnel, but not from direct fire.

One of the new items we were using this time was The Blue Force Tracker (BFT). Each Coalition unit had a transponder so they could be tracked on a large map. Everything from aircraft, to tanks, to teams on the ground could be tracked in real time. This definitely beat the old grease pencil on a map overlay, even though I brought all of the stuff to do that in case the computers failed. Working with technology has taught me that when you need it the most, it will break on you.

On March 20, Operation Iraqi Freedom began. I found out the same way I did back in Desert Storm. We had an idea when it was suppose to start. The Blue Force Trackers confirmed this as the signals began to fill our screens. We also had a television in the JOC tuned into CNN, and that's how we learned that the war had started.

Operation Iraqi Freedom started south of Iraq coming from Kuwait and Saudi Arabia, while we were still on hold due to the political problems with Turkey. The next couple of days, I monitored the situation in southern Iraq. One of the first aircraft lost was one of our MH-53s, which had landed hard while infiltrating a team into Iraq. The second helicopter recovered the helicopter's crew, and the Air Force bombed the plane so it wouldn't fall into Iraqi control. Our teams actually got airborne and were halfway there, until they were forced to turn back at the boundary of Turkish airspace. There was nothing we could do, except monitor the situation. To make matters worse, we continued to have power outages. The building was not designed to handle the entire draw on electricity that we had placed on it. Our commander and the chief planners had had enough with the waiting game, and a decision was made. Our teams would fly into Iraq from Jordan instead of flying over Turkey.

By March 21, the portion of Operation Iraqi Freedom known as "Shock and Awe" had began. This was a massive air campaign designed to weaken the Iraqi military's will to fight. As we watched this unfold on the news, we could hear our MC-130s running their engines and beginning the trip to Jordan. I continued to watch the development of the operation in southern Iraq. The night of March 21 and the early morning of March 22 were not a real good few hours for the Coalition. A Long Range Surveillance Unit, call sign WARPIG 12, was discovered by civilians and was on the run. Two British helicopters collided in the Persian Gulf, and our Marine helicopters went in to assist in their recovery.

We continued to monitor what was going on in the south while we were still trying to get into the war. Some of the JOC staff felt that the war would be over by the time we got involved. The idea was that we would link up with the Kurdish fighters in the North, and elements of the 4th Infantry Division (some of their units were from Fort Carson as well) were supposed to attack from the North. Combined with the offensive from the South, we would catch the Iraqis in the classic pincer envelopment. However, thanks to our Turkish allies, neither the 4th ID nor we were doing anything in the North. In fact, members of the 4th ID were still on their ships waiting for an area in which they could offload. As a result, the Iraqis were fighting on a single front, which was to their advantage.

The night of March 22 would be remembered as the "Ugly Baby," the name we gave to the infiltration of our detachments into Northern Iraq. The detachments had arrived in Jordan and waited for night to conduct the infiltration. It was not going to be easy, even for the specially equipped MC-130 aircraft, which were designed for this type of mission. Instead of flying over Turkey and into the north, where there would have been little to no threat, the aircraft would approach from the west. The aircraft would fly from the westernmost part of Iraq, follow the western border to the North, and then cross over into their designated landing areas. My biggest concern was the worst-case scenario, one of our aircraft being shot down. The Turkish Government not only refused permission to fly over their territory for the infiltration, but they also made it clear than none of our helicopters could fly over Iraq for a rescue. This included the recovery aircraft that were stationed in Turkey to support Operation Northern Watch. They could leave, but they could not enter Turkish airspace. This was a difficult situation, but we had to deal with it and continue with our mission. It was very frustrating, watching the diplomacy and the politics. The United States continued to offer them financial support, and yet they would not help us now. I felt we should have voided any financial deal with them, but that was just my opinion, and I may not have seen the bigger picture that our diplomats saw.

As we watched the situation and kept track of the progress of the infiltration, the JOC received a morale booster of Big Macs. Each of us received one. Though they were a little cold, it was a nice gesture from our support center and a big boost to morale.

We received a report that the British had lost one of their Tornadoes down south. This was an unfortunate friendly-fire incident in which one of our Patriot missile systems detected and fired upon them.

Our situation began to turn bad when we received reports that our aircraft were under fire along the route. The third aircraft was taking anti-aircraft fire. From what I could assess, the lead aircraft startled the Iraqis as it flew low and fast near them. The second aircraft a few minutes later must have brought them to their senses, and by the third aircraft, they were ready. The next report made my blood run a little cold; the third aircraft had taken a hit in one of the engines and had to feather the propeller (which was turning the engine off and stopping the propeller from spinning). They could not finish the mission and were diverting to Incirlik Air Base. I kept my fingers crossed that the aircraft would make it across the border in one piece; we didn't really have any CSAR capabilities if it crashed-landed. At least the Turkish Government allowed them to land at Incirlik.

I contacted Richard Ferguson who was working as a Liaison Officer at Incirlik and told him they were on their way. I found out the next day that the aircraft had taken some serious hits. One of the cannon shells went through the wing and punctured the fuel tank. There was just enough fuel left in the fuel tank to taxi off the runway onto the taxiway before the engines gave out. Another shell had gone through and broken one of the windows on the left side of the cockpit. A couple of other shells through the aircraft came very near to the wing roots, which held the two wings to the fuselage of the aircraft. Not a single member of the aircrew or our detachment were hit or injured, but they endured one very interesting ride. The Turks may have allowed them to land, but they would not allow them to cross over into Iraq. Eventually, a few days later, the two detachments returned to our base in Romania via Germany, and they would be re-inserted into Iraq later. The other three aircraft made it to their airfields and landed safely. Two of them flew to Bashur and unloaded the detachments there; the fourth flew to an airfield designated AS-West and unloaded their detachments. Our teams had finally infiltrated and begun operations against Iraq. This difficult infiltration under fire, with one aircraft diverted, was how the operation earned the name, "The Ugly Baby."

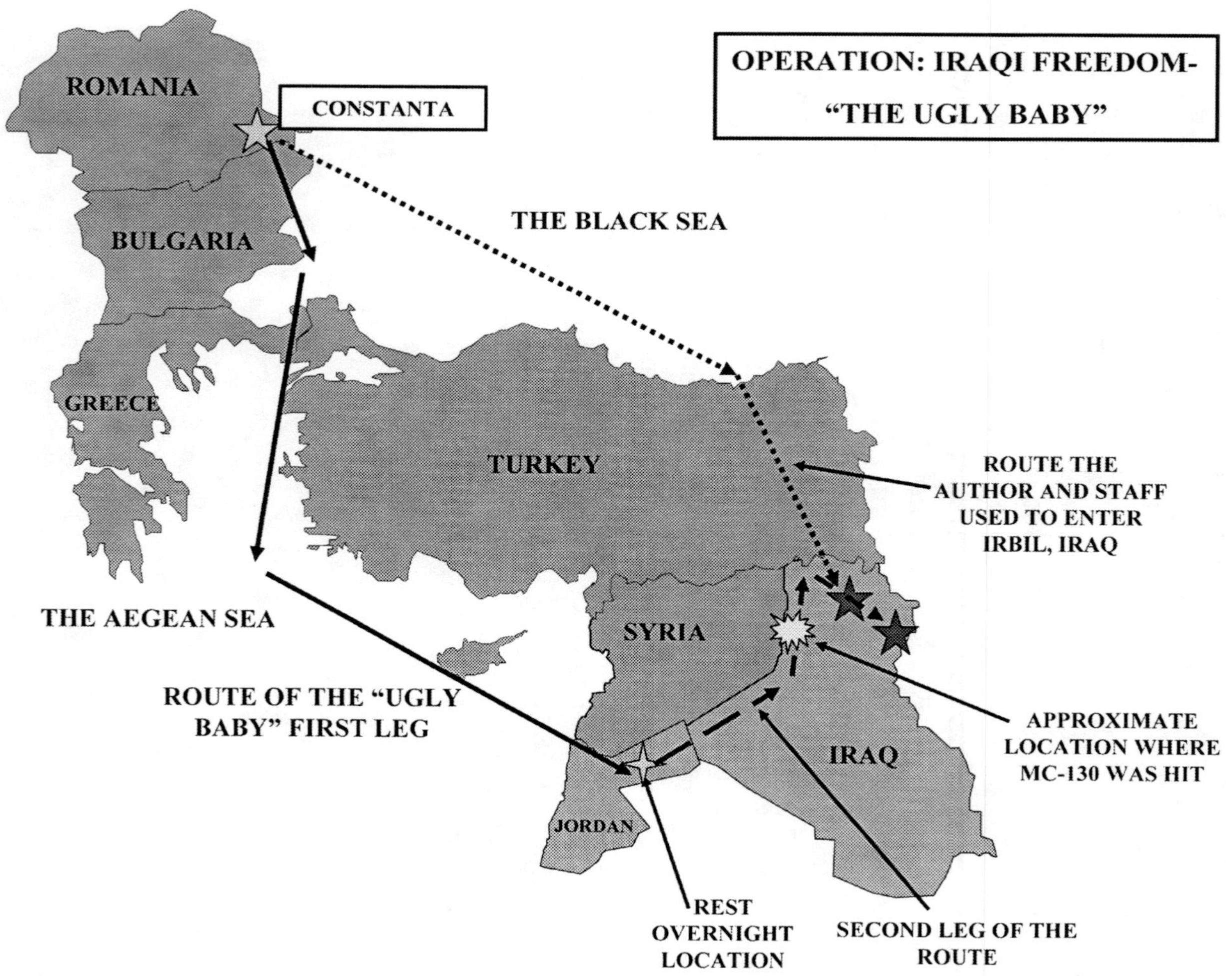

OPERATION: IRAQI FREEDOM-
"THE UGLY BABY"

ROUTE THE AUTHOR AND STAFF USED TO ENTER IRBIL, IRAQ

APPROXIMATE LOCATION WHERE MC-130 WAS HIT

SECOND LEG OF THE ROUTE

THE BLACK SEA

CONSTANTA

ROMANIA

BULGARIA

GREECE

TURKEY

SYRIA

IRAQ

JORDAN

REST OVERNIGHT LOCATION

THE AEGEAN SEA

ROUTE OF THE "UGLY BABY" FIRST LEG

MAP 3: Operation Iraqi Freedom showing the initial deployment to Constanta, Romania, the "Ugly Baby" route used to infiltrate our teams into Iraq, as well as our staff's route to Irbil.

CHAPTER 9

MOVING FORWARD TO IRBIL

Meanwhile in Romania, watching the news brought us information about events occurring back in the United States, as well as other news concerning the war. The current situation was stressful enough, when on the night of March 22nd we saw the news concerning an attack on a command post at Camp Penn, Kuwait. At first it was thought to be a terrorist attack, but soon we found out that it was a disgruntled American Muslim soldier, who was accused of throwing hand grenades into the 101st's command Tactical Operation Center (TOC). He was believed to have killed two officers and wounded fourteen others. This was a sign of things to come. This soldier adamantly believed the United States was going into Iraq to conquer, rape, and pillage. He decided to take matters into his own hands and throw two hand grenades into the TOC. He was later tried by military courts-martial at Fort Bragg, North Carolina (2005) and was found guilty and sentenced to death.

Following the "Ugly Baby," our situation continued to be stressful as we fought with Turkey for the right to send aircraft over its territory while our detachments on the ground were now coming under fire. During the shift one night, we all filed into the main hallway to receive our smallpox vaccinations. The next couple of days would be itchy as the injection site scabbed over and healed. We had to make sure it stayed covered, and we washed our uniforms so no one could become infected.

It is a belief in the military that if there is a chance for something to go wrong, it will. For our staff, one such occurrence took place on the night of March 23, when we lost contact with one of our teams. Their last radio contact had informed us that they were under mortar and small arms fire and they needed close air support. Then they went off the air. Repeated attempts to contact them failed. To compound the situation even more, their Blue Force Tracker blip also disappeared from our screens. As the situation still remained unknown, the operations officer leaned over to me and asked what capabilities we had if we had to go find them. Due to our helicopters still being stuck in Romania, the only option we had was to send some of our teams with the Peshmerga guerrillas to the team's last known point. In fact, this was what we did when we had had no communication with the team for twenty-four hours. A large element of Peshmergas and team members made their way over to the location. The team was found safe and sound. The batteries in the radio had died, along with the Blue Force Tracker transponder and their replacement batteries were no good. That was why they lost contact and could not communicate with their command post.

Another situation went bad for the United States on the night of March 22nd. A convoy became lost and was ambushed by Iraqi forces. This was the famous Jessica Lynch convoy, and she and several members of her 507th Maintenance Company were captured. All of the personnel recovery coordination elements were alerted, even those of us who were operating up north. We had no idea where the prisoners were being held, so we all used what resources we could. I made contact with our Special Activities people, who in turn contacted their intelligence sources. One of the hardest but most important tasks in personnel recovery is to locate anyone who is reported missing or taken prisoner. Without a location, there is no way to launch a successful rescue/recovery operation. The report concerning the prisoners of war was sent to all of our detachments, so we could keep our eyes and ears open for anything that could help us locate them. Mostly, we were working with the local Peshmerga and their contacts to see if they spotted anything that looked like the prisoners. Normally the Iraqis would have separated the prisoners, which would have made it very difficult for us to find them. But we had to try. I waited and hoped for the best for them. I knew what the Iraqis did to prisoners, and I doubted any of our captured soldiers had received formal training in resistance to interrogation.

While all of this was going on, we were preparing for the next major operation in our area. Other than the detachments from 10th Group who went in the night of the Ugly Baby, the only conventional Army unit that would enter up north would be the 173rd Airborne Brigade, formerly known as the Southern European Taskforce (SE-TAF) stationed in Vencenzia, Italy. They were going to fly in and drop by parachute onto Bashur Airfield in northern Iraq. We had a Liaison Officer from the 173rd with us to help with coordination. I did not feel comfortable with this drop, especially seeing it was completely unnecessary. Anytime a major airborne operation is conducted, even during training in peacetime, the potential for injury of the jumpers is great. Personally, it seemed to me this jump was being done because the brigade hasn't conducted a combat jump since Vietnam, and they wanted to make their mark on history. My other concern was over fratricide, because the potential for a friendly-fire incident was also great. The jump would be conducted at night onto an airfield we already controlled. We would have our detachments there along with the Peshmerga. My concern was that an excited eighteen-year-old kid would be so jacked up that he might fire on one of our own personnel or our allies.

It was starting to become very confusing as to who was or would be in charge of the northern sector. Right now, our Group Commander, Colonel Charles Cleveland, who was the CJSOTF-N's Commander, was in command of the northern area of operations in Iraq. A general commanded the 173rd, and once they jumped in, there was going to be a conflict over who was in charge seeing he outranked Colonel Cleveland. I was also concerned because our helicopters had finally made it into Iraq and were stationed at the Bashur Airfield. The 173rd was going to airdrop both personnel and heavy equipment, such as artillery and vehicles. Our helicopters had to be moved to a different airfield in order to protect them from the heavy equipment drops, in case they missed the drop zone. I worked with their Liaison Officer, asking for number of aircraft and manifests in case something happened and an aircraft was damaged. I never did receive the information. On the night of March 26, we tracked the line of C-17s by their Blue Force Trackers as they entered our area and conducted the night jump.

We watched on CNN as the troopers exited the aircraft. I sort of felt bad for the 173rd's Liaison Officer, a conventional officer in a JOC full of Special Operation soldiers, because we gave him a hard time out of fun. During the CNN broadcast, a jumper froze in the door and missed the drop zone. The Liaison Officer took the ribbing in stride and just shook his head. After the successful jump, he got back at us by saying "You can all go home now. The 173rd will take it from here."

We did not receive confirmation that 100 percent of their personnel had been accounted for until 24 hours later. There were only three injuries on the jump, which was amazing considering the number of personnel who had been dropped. None of our personnel or equipment was damaged, and the detachments that had been operating out of Bashur began to help out the newly arrived 173rd. Unfortunately, 173rd soldiers had jumped expecting warm, desert conditions and were not ready to face the several days of cold rain that had been falling in Bashur. They jumped wearing desert camouflage uniforms, which really stood out against the greens and browns of the surrounding terrain.

A break in some of the monotony of the day-to-day grind came when I was asked to help a scout platoon from the attached 10th Mountain Division. They were issued brand new M82A1 Barrett .50-caliber sniper rifles. They had asked Enos Ward, who had been a teammate of mine, if we had a Barrett shooter, and he directed them to me. Luckily, I deployed with my "dope" book on ballistics and sniping, even though I wasn't serving in that capacity. I always brought it along in case I needed it, including the data my friend John had given to me back at the start of Operation Desert Storm. I gave the scouts a class on both the weapon system itself and on what I knew about sniping in Iraq from my Desert Storm experience. I passed on everything I knew about the environmental conditions of northern Iraq and what to expect from the Peshmerga and the Iraqis. The class was well received, but giving it made me miss my old profession of being a sniper.

Most members of the staff who worked the night shift were for the most part down-to-earth kind of people. However, from time to time we tried to do things to change the monotony of the nightly grind. The Air Force planners from the 352nd SOG decided to wear their flight gear while on duty one night. They came in, wearing their full flight gear, including their flight vests and helmets, and sat down at their workstations. They plugged their helmets into the radio receivers we use to monitor the situation and went to work. It was an interesting sight, and a neat way to break up the monotony, and add a little color to the JOC floor for an evening.

I immersed myself in the next major operation, which was Operation Viking Hammer. After finally infiltrating all of our teams, we were launching an offensive with the Peshmerga against the Ansar al-Islam, an al-Qaeda linked terrorist group that had camps in Northern Iraq. The camps were hit by extensive close air support operations, directed by our teams on the ground. To make our jobs more difficult, an AH-64 Apache attack helicopters was shot down during a deep penetration raid near Baghdad. The two-man crew was captured and shown on television. Now we were working to locate both the convoy survivors and these two crewmen.

A morale package of McDonald's hamburgers from our Support Center folks arrived that evening while we observed and monitored our operations. Even though our operation against the Ansar al-Islam (AI) was proceeding well, we heard that CENTCOM was going to order a pause in the operations so the newly arrived 4th Infantry Division could catch up and we could consolidate our forces. The only major problem we had was that the terrorists were escaping into Iran, and we could do nothing to stop them. Even the AC-130 gunship crews were getting frustrated with watching the terrorists run across the border and being able to do nothing about it. A delay would have made things worse. The pause in operations did not happen, however, and we continued our operations at full speed. On March 29, I was given a warning order to pack my bags and be ready to move forward. We are going to establish a forward base of operations closer to the fight than Romania.

Our forces were pounding the Iraqis hard with a lot of air support. Our detachments, the Peshmerga, and the 173rd were facing three Iraqi Corps of almost twenty divisions, two of which were elite Republican Guard. They may have outnumbered us, but we compensated by using our overwhelming air superiority. Both Air

Force and Navy aircraft were hitting targets all across the operational area. Our controllers, who coordinated all of the close air support in the JOC, were very busy. This was the first time that B-1 bombers with their GPS guided bombs were being used for close air support missions. If a team needed help, aircraft were on the way, normally within five minutes.

Our night JOC Director had a single goal on his mind: he wanted to drop a MOAB (Mother of All Bombs). This was a 25,000-pound bomb that was dropped out of the back of an MC-130 aircraft. He thought he had his chance one night when one of our teams spotted an Iraqi Armored Battalion in an open field. He was all excited and the air controllers tried to make it happen, but it didn't work out.

On March 30, I was informed there had been a change of plans. I was going into Iraq the next morning. I had twelve hours to get my kit together and be ready. After working my shift, I packed what I needed, and stashed the rest in my extra bags. The next morning, I checked out of my room and brought all of my bags to the Support Center. The bags that were not going forward were to be shipped back to Colorado. Once my bags were dropped off, I headed over to draw my weapons, grenades, and ammunition. Along with my M-4 carbine, I was issued an old faithful M1911 .45-caliber pistol, which was fine with me. I haven't been a strong fan of the Army's M-9, 9mm pistol, having grown up carrying a .45 back in my ranger battalion days. Only the old timers who had carried a .45 before were issued one. We went over to our ammunition holding area, and loaded our magazines sitting on the ground. Along with ammunition for my pistol and rifle, I was given some hand grenades and a Thermite grenade, for "just in case."

After everything was issued, we went over to the airfield and began the tradition of once more hurrying up and waiting. There were about thirteen of us going on this flight, including Major Higgins, some of the group staff and some of the support center personnel. To help with the wait, we were brought a morale booster of Big Macs for lunch. This was a pretty good deal, getting burgers while we wait.

As the sun began to set, we moved out to the tarmac and a waiting MC-130 aircraft. During combat operations, there are no seats in an MC-130, so we sat on the floor with the equipment, using a tie-down strap as a seat belt. While the aircraft was being loaded, our Operations Officer, Major Higgins, got with me and another former C Company assaulter, Shawn Murphy, and informed us we would be in charge of security when we hit the ground. As we briefed all of the staff officers, I informed them of Shawn's and my responsibilities. I told them to look for a large figure on the airfield -- that would be me. At least I am easy to see in the dark, and our guys can key off of me. We loaded the aircraft, and everyone spread out to find what nook and crannies they could sit in or on. I took up a position at the rear ramp of the aircraft, so I could be the first one off when we landed. The Turkish government was allowing us to fly over Turkey and into Northern Iraq. I guess our diplomats had finally worked something out. The flight was uneventful, but I kept looking out of the single window in the jump door on my side for any sign of tracer fire. Our last twenty minutes were conducted at low-level, and the ride wasn't too bumpy. The aircraft was completely darkened so there were no lights to give us away. It felt good to feel the adrenaline rush before a mission once more as we made the approach to the airfield. I was at last in Iraq.

The aircraft landed on a dark strip, and as the ramp opened and the aircraft halted, Shawn and I rushed off and took up a position about 75 feet behind the aircraft. The shock of the hot, strong engine exhaust and propeller wash hit us as we ran off the ramp. I looked over at Shawn and saw a memorable image. As he took up his position, he held his M-4 in one hand and his laptop computer case in the other. What a great recruiting photo that would be for modern Special Forces, a soldier armed with his weapon and his computer! I guess this is what you could call the modern age of battle. The rest of the staff came off the aircraft, and I directed them to an assembly point. We unloaded our gear and piled it up near the assembly point. I did a final check of the airplane to make sure nothing was left behind, gave the loadmaster thumbs up, and headed back into the night. The MC-130 took off, and we linked up with the transportation provided by our advance team and headed to the new base. It was a very dark night, with the lights of Irbil far off in the distance. It was also very quiet once the MC-130 took off. The only sounds we heard were insects, the jet aircraft high overhead, and us. After we made sure everyone and all the equipment were accounted for, we all broke off to go to our respective areas. The support center personnel moved off to a spot on the airfield where they were going to set up a tent, which would become the new forward operating base. The rest of the staff was going to be moved over to the temporary forward command post. I loaded my gear into the back of a Landrover truck, wedged myself inside and we were on our way. We followed a dirt road, and passed several Peshmerga checkpoints before we arrived at our new destination.

Our new command post was the Rozhgar Primary School, which had been abandoned and would now temporarily serve as our forward operating base. We were led upstairs to an empty classroom and shown a pile of mattresses. After setting up a foam mattress on the floor, I went downstairs where they had some chicken left over from dinner. This was going to be my new home for a little bit, and I looked around the building before going to bed.

The following morning, April 1(April fool's Day) dawned bright and sunny. After changing into my desert uniform, I walked around the building so I could check it out in the sunlight. I went up on the roof to look around and to take some photos. The school was located at the northwest corner of the city of Irbil. It definitely smelled better than Romania, even though the houses surrounding us were a bit rundown. I could see that this area was a sniper's paradise, both for and against us. From the roof, I had clear fields of fire, but there were numerous places where an enemy sniper could hide to shoot at us. Luckily, the area was for the most part friendly, and we had Peshmerga guarding the school. The rest of the day was spent observing,

Staying at the school were members of our staff along with support personnel from the 528th Special Operations Support Battalion. A small JOC had been set up in a room that once had served as a small auditorium. They had a single computer set up for morale purposes, so I sent an e-mail to my family. In a corner under some stairs, there was a TV set up with some couches where we could watch the news and other stations, since we had a satellite feed. The food was catered by the locals and was quite good. That evening, I climbed up on the roof and saw the lights of Mosul way off in the distance.

The following morning I went on my first mission. I went along with our supply sergeant into the city to purchase supplies. Our first stop was out at the airfield where construction was beginning on our future camp. Only a single tent was up in the middle of a large open field. The airfield was only a runway, with no buildings or control tower to speak of. I believe it was once a military airfield used to forward stage Iraqi aircraft for military operations, based on old Soviet doctrine. After talking with the personnel there, we drove into the city of Irbil, which appeared to be doing quite well, contrary to what was being shown on the news. Granted, most of their revenue came from black marketeering and selling oil to the Turks. The Kurds had benefited from Operation Northern Watch and had been able to get their infrastructure well established.

Accompanying us were two contracted translators and a Peshmerga guard. It was a full truck, and I rode in the very back where I could barely fit with all of my gear. I had to admit, it felt good to be wearing armor and kit once again, like I had done in the old days before I became a staff NCO. The city appeared to be in very good shape, and the people seemed very happy to see us.

One of our first stops was at a cell phone company, which was very modern and fully operational. CNN and other news agencies had reported that there were no private cell phones in Iraq. They must not have gone up north. This was also true of the many stories about how badly the sanctions were hurting the Iraqi people. The Kurds in the North were doing very well; the news only showed those in the south. Our supply sergeant worked with the cell phone company to contract phones for the JOC. While this transaction was going on, a man and his son entered the store with us. He came up and shook our hands, and his son was very pleased to be seen with Americans. As we waited for the business to be finished, we were served free sodas and tea. After we finished with the cell phone company, we headed to several market places and stores in the city to purchase supplies. We stopped at a small store, but could not find what the supply sergeant needed. Our small group was still given free sodas though, even if we didn't purchase anything. That Kurdish hospitality that I had experienced during Provide Comfort was still there and going strong.

Next, our small party drove to the main market district, located near the center of town. As we drove around the city, we passed several statues and, located on top of a hill, a large stone fortress that was very old. It now served as an apartment complex, but it still looked very impressive. The city roads seemed to be well maintained, and there was a good amount of traffic, but most of the people we saw were armed Peshmerga and Kurdish men. The market was a very large, very crowded area, with shops on both sides of the street. I walked in the rear of our group, keeping an eye on things and staying out of the way. Many curious faces watched us as we went by, and a few followed us to see what we were doing. While our supply sergeant was inside a shop purchasing supplies, I stayed out front to watch the street.

There, I watched a young kid, showing off to his friends. He slowly made his way toward me, trying to sneak up. He kept looking over at his friends as I watched him approach. I kept looking away so he thought he was successfully sneaking up, but I kept him in the corner of my eye. When he turned to look at his friends to show them how he was doing, I quickly moved toward him. He was still looking at his friends when I crouched down to his level. As he turned back towards me, he came literally face to face with me, and he nearly jumped out of his skin and ran off. The crowd who had been watching broke out in laughter, and I went over and shook the kid's hand, making him look good in front of his friends.

Remembering some of my Kurdish, I spoke with a couple of people, some of whom could also speak English. They wanted to know if we (the United States) were really coming to stop Saddam. I said we were, and they were overjoyed. The supply sergeant finished up with his purchases, and we headed to our next stop.

We stopped along the road at the airfield to see about getting fuel and oil for our generators and vehicles. Even though there were major oil fields operating in northern Iraq near Kirkuk, there were no gas stations operating yet in the city of Irbil. Gas was sold on the side of the street from plastic jugs and fuel cans. After speaking with a garage owner, we headed to the airfield, our truck needing to be fueled up. Unfortunately, when we refueled our truck, we fueled it from the wrong storage drum. Instead of the diesel we needed, we filled it with regular gasoline, which would not work in our truck. We pushed the truck out into the field, and six Kurdish truck drivers worked with us to repair it. They drained the fuel tank right there in the field, which was a surprise to us. In all of my years in Europe, we were conditioned to be very conscious of hazardous materials. It was a major problem if we leaked fuel on pavement, let alone on grass. Here, they were dumping a full gas tank into the ground, which was against everything we had been taught. It was their country, so we did as they did. The truck was dead and had to be left out on the airfield. Another truck came and brought us back to the school.

For the time being, that would be the only mission I participated in. There really was no place for me to work personnel recovery in the small command post established there, and, until the new forward operating base was built, Chief and Wolfgang had it covered from Romania. Then I would assume the duty and cover them as they come forward to Irbil. I, therefore, became a guard for the school. We were busy fixing up the school, even though we knew we are going to move out to the new camp on the airfield, once the construction was completed. The school would be turned over to the Kurdish people in better condition than we found it. I spent the next couple of days on 12-hour guard shifts, watching the workers as they moved in and around the school.

At night, I sat outside with our Peshmerga guards, and we talked about events. Some of them spoke English, and I worked on my Kurdish. One of the guards had been a little boy in our camp in Sinat. As I spoke, his eyes widened and he exclaimed, "Doctor Aag!" Talk about a small world! What would be the chances that a Kurdish child I had known in 1991 would now be here as a soldier during Iraqi Freedom?

Some of the guards had borrowed some of the school's textbooks that taught English so they could try and speak with me. During one of our talks, one of our guards, with a big smile, said "I love you" to me. I politely explained it should be, "I like you," and he nodded his understanding, happy to have spoken with me. At least I hope that was what he intended to say. The nights were enjoyable as we sat around outside of the old school, talking with each other and I listened to their stories and plans for the future.

Some of my guard duty was broken up with perimeter defense. I went around our building, and developed a base defense plan incorporating the school's construction. I don't know if it was built specifically for this purpose, but it had great defensive positions around the roof. Sketching the perimeter, I used my compass to make sure each position had interlocking fields of fire and that all of the positions mutually supported each other. I doubted the Iraqis would attack our position, but it was better to be safe then sorry. At least I was doing something remotely in my professional field as a weapons sergeant.

To help with our perimeter defense, 1SG Brad Boyer, myself, and a bunch of the other support soldiers manhandled about 40 large concrete culverts into place to be used as barriers. We constructed a wall that would limit any vehicle approaching to a single lane so it could be checked. It was a great workout, and the locals enjoyed the show. Some of the boys came over to watch us roll these culverts into place from the near by houses. On April 4, the news reported that our forces had reached the Baghdad International Airport. My Kurdish friends said, "Let's go to Baghdad. You lead, and we'll follow!" As much as I would have liked to, I explained that we had to follow our orders, and, for us, that meant staying here. They smiled and accepted it, but it was a good idea.

Driving between the school and the airfield, I noticed we were located in the Christian section of the city. Along with the small churches we saw, we also observed stores selling bottles of Jack Daniels and other spirits. Christians were allowed to drink alcohol, as well as sell it in their stores. Still under the CENTCOM Commander's rule about no drinking, we watched the bottles go by as we drove to and from the airfield.

We began watching the news with the hope of seeing the Iraqi Minister of Information, who became known as "Baghdad Bob." He reminded me of Joseph Goebels, the German Propaganda Minister during the closing days of World War II in Germany, who talked about how everything was going their way as their cities burned around them. In the same way, "Baghdad Bob" reported that the

Iraqi military was pushing our forces back. I guess he was getting wrong intelligence reports.

Mornings, I went up on the roof with my cup of coffee to watch the aircraft overhead. During one of these mornings, I watched a B-52 Bomber fly over and head toward a ridge line about 20 miles away. We knew there were Republican Guard units dug in along that ridge, and I thought the B-52 must have been heading for them. I could see the bomber turn away and head away from the ridge. Seconds later, the concussion rumbles of the bombs' impacts reached us and shook the school. Whoever was on the ridge got a rude wakening.

At night, sometimes the lights of Mosul were dark, but with our night vision goggles, we could see anti-aircraft fire and flashes from the vicinity of the city. During the days, I returned to my roving guard duty to watch the workers. The medical personnel had established a small clinic in the school, and I lent them the Kurdish dictionary I had made during Provide Comfort. A day later, they actually used some of the words and phrases when they had to work on some Peshmerga causalities. I was glad that my little dictionary helped a little during the crisis.

One day, Major Higgins asked me if I would like a mission, and I said I would be glad to take one on. Anything was better then standing around and watching the workers. This mission would not be as simple as going into town with our supply folks. I was going up to the Iraqi/Turkish border to escort a fuel convoy to our camp. It would prove to be a challenging journey.

The staff and support personnel preparing to load the MC-130 Talon II from the 352nd SOG in Romania for the flight into Irbil during Operation Iraqi freedom. Shawn Murphy is the soldier standing in the front with his back to the camera (and hands in his pockets).

The elementary school occupied by JSOTF-N as a forward command post while Camp Loki was being built. A rebuilt and modernized school building was returned to the people of Irbil.

The Author and the commander of the Kurdish
fighters providing security at the school.

CHAPTER 10

THE MISSIONS AND CAMP LOKI

The mission sounded simple enough. We were to drive up to the Harbor Gates, meet some tanker trucks carrying diesel fuel, and escort them back to our camp in Irbil. On the morning of April 5, I rode over to the camp on the airfield to pick up the rest of the escorts. We would drive up to the border in two Landrovers. Our group consisted of SFC Dave Eckenroth (a communications specialist), SFC John Gates (from the support center) and one of his Support Center personnel, and a guide from the Peshmerga/KDP and me. The day was bright and sunny and everything pointed to an easy mission.

After we received our brief, were issued a satellite cell phone, and went over the map once more, our small convoy of two trucks started on our way. With Mosul still under Iraqi control, we had to take the long way around through the mountains to the border. I sat in the back of the Landrover, while our guide sat up front. I never understood why we placed so much stock in these trucks. First of all, they were painted a bright white; anyone who saw them knew we were Americans. Every time we drove along a road, everyone we passed waved at us. I could barely fit in the back, and that was when I was wearing only my vest. My helmet and kit (my load-bearing vest with my ammunition) sat next to me on the seat. There was no way I could fit in the back with all of my stuff on. Even without it, my head hit the roof of the truck (which did every time we hit a bump), and it was very cramped. My theory was that the enemy would be laughing so hard watching me roll out of the back that I would have ample time to grab my gear.

We departed from the airfield and drove into the city of Irbil. We then took the highway out of the city and headed northeast up into the mountains. Irbil sat in a large valley that was surrounded by farmers' fields and grasslands. Along the road were fruit stands and more gasoline stands. The road snaked its way up into the first major town along the route, named *Salah ad Din*. The town sat on top of a large, pointed hill named *Pirmum Dagh*, the road cutting back upon itself and zigzagging upwards. When we passed through the town, I noticed a large concentration of Peshmergas. This must have been one of their bases. We went back down into another valley, with the snow-capped peaks of the mountains way off in the distance. When we drove first northeast then northwest along the foothills of these peaks, we passed Bashur airfield and looked at all of the activity there. It was a great sight to see the MH-53s sitting on the airfield, as well as all of the desert-uniformed 173rd soldiers who stood out against the green vegetation. The Bashur Valley was very wet and green with thick grass. The soft terrain must have been one of the key reasons that only a few 173rd soldiers were injured on the jump.

Once past Bashur, we headed up into the rugged mountain passes. *The Chiyane Barat* mountains were steep and very rocky, a light brown color like the mountains near Colorado Springs. The road followed a rolling river, called the *Great Zab*, which was full of run off from the rain from the past week. There were few vehicles on the road, mostly large transport trucks hauling goods toward Turkey or into the Iraqi interior. For the most part, the road and the mountain passes were devoid of any houses or buildings. I commented that this area would be an outdoorsman's paradise if someone wanted to invest in it. Mountain climbing, white water rafting, and fishing could all entice outdoors-types.

After climbing out of that valley, the road skirted around the foot-hills, then once more climbed into the mountains, called the *Chiya e Marla Kirza* and the *Chiya e Khere*. It may not have been a direct route, but the territory was all under both our and Peshmerga con-trol, with the Iraqi military forces some 12 to 20 miles to our south near Mosul. As we entered this next group of mountains, we stopped for a break at a roadside rest area. It was a single building on the side of the road, with no other structures nearby. Some of the guys went in to partake of the local fare. I volunteered to watch the trucks and eat the bag lunch I had brought. As I looked around and scanned the countryside, I continued to be amazed by the landscape and its rugged beauty. There was a rolling stream with a waterfall just behind the rest area. The mountains shot straight up from the road into the crisp blue sky. The Kurds had goat and what appeared to be chicken cooking on an outdoor rotisserie, but I still kept to my own food. Some of the Kurds who were there had their pictures taken with us, and then it was back on the road. Our route snaked higher and higher into the mountains. We saw very little evidence of other humans as we continued on our journey. We also noticed that there were no guardrails along the side of the road, just the road and the steep embankments down into ravines. As we began our descent, small villages began to appear and dot the countryside. I believe they were Assyrian settlements, for there were small churches in the villages. The Assyrians were the only Christians in this region.

We finally came out of the mountains and turned onto the main east-west paved road that led to Dahuk, the next city along our route. Dahuk, which was situated in a mountain valley, seemed to be very prosperous, judging by the large number of cars and people in the area. There were Peshmerga guards in the center median along the main route we were following. The Peshmerga were dressed in green uniforms and for the most part wore helmets. It was am impressive sight as we drove by.

As we left the city, we passed a Peshmerga checkpoint that blocked the road to Mosul, mostly to keep people from entering the combat zone where they would not be safe. Like back during Operation Provide Comfort, the Peshmerga went out of their way to insure the safety of the civilians, so they wouldn't get caught in the fighting. The road was now heading northwest and toward my old stomping grounds of Zahko. Our route took us across a large open plain, with the mountains in the distance. After climbing another series of mountains, we entered the valley and saw Zahko off in the distance. I also noticed what appeared to be mine fields along the side of the road and along the side of the hill and made a mental note to pass this on to our intelligence folks once we got back to Irbil. The city seemed to be in better shape than it had been back in 1991-92. We had no time to stop, and I didn't think I could remember how to get to the Teacher's house anyway.

The rest of the journey went by quickly. Near the end, we stopped at a Peshmerga camp just before Harbor Gates. Our instructions were a little vague about where we were to meet the tankers, so our guide spoke with the local Peshmerga commander. Our vehicles were surrounded by a large group of curious Peshmerga soldiers. I saw a reporter behind them, trying to maneuver himself to take our photographs. Pointing him out to the other members of the mission, we made it very difficult for him to snap a picture of any one of us. He moved one way, and I moved another to keep either the truck or a pole in his view so he couldn't get a clear photo of me. After our guide received what information he could, we made our way into the Harbor Gate complex.

It looked about the same as I remembered it from Provide Comfort, except it was a lot busier and in better shape. The other thing that was different was that there were now Turkish soldiers stationed on the Iraqi side of the border. Following Desert Storm and Provide Comfort, Turkey had launched a series of military operations into Northern Iraq and the mountains to eliminate PKK strongholds. There was still a Turkish presence in the northern mountains, roughly about the size of a brigade spread across the region. The only thing missing was our tanker trucks. Unfortunately I had not been provided with a time or a description of the trucks during our pre-mission briefing, so we made ourselves comfortable and waited. How hard is it to spot fuel trucks coming across from Turkey? I soon realized it would be very difficult with all of the truck traffic coming into Iraq. We had our work cut out for us.

We pulled out the SATCOM (Satellite Communication radio) and attempted to make contact with our base. Unfortunately, the satellite off which we had to bounce our signal off of was very low to the horizon, and we were trying to send a beam through the mountains. The cell phone (which used a different satellite) was not working either. We were able to pick up one of our detachments near Bashur on the SATCOM. They were reporting that they had received mortar or rocket fire. Checking the location they sent on our map, we saw that it was very near a spot we had just traveled through. We thought it may have been a mistake and went back to waiting for the trucks. The day turned to dusk, then soon to night, and I was seriously thinking about heading back. We had been waiting for a couple of hours, and there was still no sign of our tankers. But I knew how important these tankers were; they were carrying diesel that we badly needed for our trucks.

I was getting very close to calling it off when the first tanker truck rolled through the checkpoint. In all, there were a total of four tanker trucks, all with Turkish drivers. None of us spoke Turkish, and none of the drivers spoke English or Kurdish well. Using hand and arm signals to get our point across, we convinced the drivers to climb back into their trucks and follow us out of the Harbor Gate.

My truck took the lead, and our other truck bringing up the rear with the tankers between us. I thought that it had been interesting driving this route during the day, but it was going to prove to be an even bigger challenge at night. My other big concern wasn't about any Iraqi military forces that may have been in our area, but about the possibility of local brigands. Four tankers of diesel fuel would fetch a big profit, so we stayed vigilant as we drove through the night. We stopped the convoy just outside of Dahuk to allow the tankers to refuel.

The drivers wanted to find a restaurant and a hotel to spend the night at Dahuk, but we convinced them we must continue. Understanding that there is some animosity between the Turks and the Kurds, we decided to press on and not risk a confrontation. We handed the drivers an MRE and some bottled water. They may not have liked it, but we couldn't afford to spend the night there.

What had first been estimated to be only a five- to six-hour mission was now in its tenth hour, and looking to be even longer. As the convoy entered the first mountain range and began to navigate the winding roads, our speed dropped to a crawl. Understandably, the drivers were uncomfortable navigating roads that had no lights and no guardrails. There was not even a moon that night.

It was now around one o'clock in the morning. I was leaning out the window for some fresh air and to check on our trucks, when I heard a sound that made my blood freeze. During one of our breaks as we waited for the tankers to catch up, we had seen some flashes off in the distance and made the comment that Mosul was getting blasted again. We could hear the sound of the jets overhead and didn't think much about it. About a half hour later, a jet fighter (I assumed an F/A-18) screamed over the top of us! With the mortar/rocket attack near Bashur, our fighters were probably out hunting targets of opportunity. They may have mistaken our convoy for an Iraqi column, but luckily for us, they buzzed us to confirm our identity. I guess having bright white trucks can be a good thing, but that was a close call.

By three in the morning, we had finally arrived outside of Bashur with all of our trucks. Then the next challenge began, for we were supposed to have one of the tankers top off the fuel tanks for our detachments stationed on the Bashur airfield. I went up to the front gate to talk to the guards there. This was a U.S. base and we were fellow American soldiers, but I could see at least three machine guns aiming and tracking me as I approached their position. I moved slowly with my hands in plain view, and with a very loud, bellowing and cursing (I would admit it would have made a sailor blush) voice, I identified myself. My big shape in the dark and the rather colorful way I expressed my displeasure of having weapons pointing at me alerted the guards that I was an American and not a threat. Being allowed to approach, I spoke with the sergeant at the gate. He apologized, but he had thought we were going to attack his position. I pointed out that we were driving on a road with our headlights on, and asked if the would enemy do that if they were attacking. He saw my logic and apologized once again.

Somehow either our camp did not alert them that we were coming or the information was not disseminated to the guards. In any case, we were not allowed in! An American convoy was not allowed to enter an American installation. The guards from the 173rd stubbornly followed their orders, even if it didn't pass the common sense test. I pointed out where our vehicles were, informed them they were full of diesel, and said we were going to park right there and wait until morning.

I was very disgusted by the time I reached the trucks and told them we were not allowed on the base. Their base policy was that all trucks had to be cleared ahead of time, and somehow our convoy description had not reached them. To add to my growing frustration and anger, their sergeant of the guard was nice enough to wake up for a second and ask, "What part of NO didn't they understand!" Although I was senior to him in rank, he was just doing his duty, and there really wasn't much I could do. Using my hands, I explained to the drivers that they were to sleep in their trucks. Since it was so late, it was safer to catch some sleep before facing the last set of mountains in the dark. We stayed up and ran a rotation guard for the trucks while the drivers slept.

About an hour later, one of the guards came out and said they did in fact have our description and that we could come onto the base. I didn't want to wake the drivers, so I thanked them though it was a little late now. Somehow, the message had been misplaced in their Tactical Operation Center. We took turns watching the trucks and caught a quick nap when we could. I stayed up most of the night and watched the sunrise the following morning.

After enjoying a wonderful breakfast of MREs and coffee, my truck escorted one of the tankers onto the base to refuel the detachment's storage tank of diesel, while the second Landrover went over to check with the support center on Bashur. I watched the beehive of activity on the airfield as the various units woke up and started their day. We drove along the flight line to talk with the aircrews, and I observed all of the improvised shelters made from the parachutes that had been used in the 173rd's jump. Almost every tent had a patio covered with a parachute canopy. What a waste of material! I guess they did a "Hop and Pop," which meant the parachutes were left in the drop zone instead of being collected.

Once the tanker finished, we lined up our convoy with my truck taking the lead once more, and we got back on the road for Irbil. Due to the slow pace of the tanker drivers, it took us another five hours to reach our camp. Along the way, I kept my eyes open so I could pass on what I saw to our intelligence folks. Mostly out of old habits, I always observed what I saw and reported it. Our truck had gotten ahead of the tankers while they navigated down the steep, zigzagging road near *Salah ad Din*. While we were waiting for them to catch up, I was caught in an awkward position. I was standing outside of our truck stretching and yawning when I observed an SUV pass us, with a man videotaping the convoy. I didn't like this, believing we were being cased for a hijacking. We were able to contact one of our detachments operating in the area and give them a description of the SUV and the people inside. I found out later they were a German news crew and were just filming us for a story.

Finally, our convoy rolled into the camp, and my mission was complete. I talked with our intelligence folks about the Peshmerga activity I saw, as well as about possible minefields and the German news crew. They wrote down the information and thanked me for it. When I returned to the school, a package containing birthday wishes from my family was waiting. I sat on my mattress, opened it, and it brought a big smile to my face. After a mission like that, I could use some cheering up. After putting everything back inside the box, I settled onto my mattress and after pulling my poncho liner up, fell into a welcomed deep sleep.

After catching up on some necessary rest, it was back to guard duty, though the support staff did make me the Sergeant of the Guard for the day. Basically this meant I was responsible for keeping track of all of the local Kurdish workers and caterers moving around the building, keeping an eye on them and escorting them around for breaks and lunch. I found out from Chief McPherson that the Air Force rescue squadron that had been supporting Operation Northern Watch might be moving into Bashur to help us. I had made contact with them earlier. They were the Air National Guard's 129th Rescue Squadron out of California. I had been coordinating and helping one of their intelligence folks get enough information to justify their being sent forward. It would be a big help, having dedicated rescue aircraft so our MH-53s could concentrate on supporting our teams.

We continued to watch the news as more of the Marines and the 3rd Armored Division pushed their way into and around Baghdad. It looked like the war wouldn't last too much longer if their capital fell. Also on the news was a report of another air strike going after Saddam, although we didn't get him. The Kurdish fighters with us still seemed very pleased with the progress of the war. They were extremely happy to learn that we might have killed "Chemical Ali," the man responsible for the gas and nerve attacks against the rebels. They had a personal grudge against him.

However, my time at the school was over, and I moved over to the new camp on April 9. It seems that some reporters found out we were living in old schools and raised a cry about violating the rules of war. What they forgot to talk about was all of the improvements that were made while we were there, so that an almost new facility was turned over to the town.

Camp Loki, as it was called, had grown immensely since the night I arrived in Irbil. It now held about two thousand troops, including our JSOTF Staff, Support Center, 528th Support Battalion, and 2-14th Infantry from the 10th Mountain Division, as well as all of the Air Force support personnel. A large domed maintenance tent served as our new JOC, surrounded by the other tents for the Support Center and Intelligence people. As I went over to the new compound, I was able to pick up my laundry. Due to the lack of washers and dryers, our support element contracted with a local laundry facility in the city. The problem was, you never knew if you would receive your own clothes back or not. In one laundry return, I got a pair of desert trousers, only they were a "small" size and not my "extra large." We moved into a temporary tent as our permanent tent had not yet been built. Basically, we had a large tent with cots in it with roughly twenty of us sleeping in it. However, more of our personnel were beginning to come forward from Romania, and the tent quickly filled up to about thirty-five. I had brought my foam mattress with me from the school. There was no electricity wired to the tent, and there was no air conditioning, so we baked during the day.

With the JOC up and running, I assumed my personnel recovery duties on the night shift once again. Sleeping during the day proved nearly impossible. The temperatures were now 90 degrees on the average, and we baked inside our tent. With no means to cool the tent, the temperature hovered between 95 and 100 degrees inside. The tent was also located in the very middle of the camp, so there was no peace and quiet. Along with the warmer temperatures, the flies were now out in force, which made sleeping during the day even more difficult because we had to keep the windows open for fresh air. I had brought a bug net, which I set up on my cot to provide some protection.

Needless to say, I started my shift with little or no rest. There were only a few of us on night duty, because the rest of the night shift had not yet arrived from Romania and were slowly filtering in.

The 1-63rd Armored arrived at Irbil to support the 173rd. Their tanks and armored personnel carriers (M-2 Bradley) had been delivered by C-5 Galaxies, and they were a welcome sight. I stood outside of the JOC tent to watch them as they drove past our camp on their way to the forward positions. It was nice to see M1 Abrams and Bradley fighting vehicles roll by, even though one of the tanks had to be towed by another.

Our operation against the Ansar-al-Islam was going well. Along with our detachments and the Peshmerga, AC-130 gunships were flying at night and attacking the terrorists. However, terrorists were still escaping across the border into Iran where we couldn't follow due to the rules of engagement. Having the armor in our area was a great asset, because they were the only friendly armored unit in the area. Our detachments and the Peshmerga had been facing the three Iraqi Corps with modified Landrovers and Hummers, loaded with Javelin missiles and supported by a robust air package. Everyone watched the great progress of the armored units in and around Baghdad on the news, but our elements were facing Iraqi armor with just missiles and air support. We did not have reporters with any of our units, so no one knew of the fantastic job our detachments were doing against the Iraqis. On April 10, we learned that the city of Kirkuk had fallen under our control. The Iraqi V Corps quickly capitulated. We were beginning to see a domino effect as more and more Iraqi units decided to surrender.

I also learned that I would lead another mission to the Harbor Gate. This mission, however, would not be as simple as the tanker escort. This was a politically sensitive undertaking, for I was to escort Turkish Special Forces Observers to our camp in Irbil. The Turkish Government was concerned about the oil fields around Kirkuk falling under Kurdish control, and so the Turks decided to send their own observers to keep an eye on things in the region. On the morning of April 11th, my team of two Landrovers was preparing for the mission when we learned that Mosul had fallen the night before. The roads were going to be full of Kurdish fighters, which would make this trip very interesting. Knowing the strong dislike between the Kurdish fighters and the Turkish Military, I tried to get an update on our rules of engagement. My biggest concern was what to do if the Kurds fired on the Turks or the Turks fired upon the Kurds. Do we engage? Who do we engage? Or do we stay out of it unless we ourselves are attacked. I couldn't let my personal feelings cloud my judgment. If it were left to me, I would fire on the Turks before firing on our Kurdish allies. Unfortunately, I didn't receive any clarification of the rules of engagement and was told to use my best judgment and obey the standard rules of engagement and right to self-defense.

This time, six of us were going on the mission. This included SFC Gates, and Eckenroth again, but we brought two other support company personnel and a translator. We took the same route we had driven the last time, and the trip went smoothly. There was a lot of celebrating along the road and in the towns as we drove through. It reminded me of a European soccer match, with banners everywhere and people lining the roads waving their hands and the banners. We also observed a lot of captured Iraqi equipment being driven into the hills. Dump trucks and tractors were towing artillery pieces and anti-aircraft guns. Now and then, a captured Iraqi tank would drive by with a bunch of smiling and waving Kurds on top. As we passed through Dahuk, a very happy and quite drunk pair of Kurds pulled up alongside of us in their car. They were celebrating, drinking as they drove, and swerving now and then toward us. They were happy drunks, and we soon left them behind and continued on our way.

Also on the road were large convoys of Kurdish fighters stuffed into the backs of large, open-bed trucks. Escorting them were "Technicals," regular trucks converted to carry heavy weapons, mostly 23-mm anti-aircraft cannons. All of this increased my concerns about escorting Turkish soldiers into Kurdish territory while the roads were filled with Kurdish fighters. Hoping everything would turn out for the best, we arrived at Harbor Gate in good time and began to wait for the Turkish soldiers. As we waited, a member of the Kurdish Security police pulled me off to the side and asked me about the expected Turkish soldiers. He almost pleaded with me not to allow them into Iraq. I told him I had no choice. I was following my orders to escort them to our camp. I explained that it was a small observation element and not a major force. He seemed to understand and went back to his office. We didn't have to wait long before the Turks arrived. There were driving five civilian trucks, but they were in uniform. I introduced myself to their commander, a Turkish Special Forces Colonel, and we began our return trip.

As we had done with the tankers, my truck was in the front and the other Landrover driven by the support company personnel followed in the rear. Once we were up in the mountain passes away from any signs of the Kurds, we stopped for a quick rest break. The Turkish soldiers stretched their legs, smoked, and talked with some of the support folks who were accompanying me on this mission. I think one of the reasons we were left alone was perhaps the fact that the Turkish uniforms looked just like our United States woodland pattern camouflage uniforms. There were no problems along the route. The Kurds still waved at us as we drove by. Another Turkish truck was at Bashur, having driven down from one of the Turkish elements in the mountains, and we were to meet them there. We parked alongside the road, and I drove up to the gate, not wanting an incident between the Turkish soldiers and the Kurdish guards. There was no problem with my getting on the base this time, but no one seemed to know where the Turkish soldiers were. I was bounced through five different TOCs before I found out where the soldiers were staying. They had been sent to a tent in a remote corner of the base, having been almost fired upon by the Kurdish guards that morning. We found them in their tent and then rejoined the convoy. The rest of the journey went by quickly, and we arrived back at Camp Loki. The trip took only 14 hours instead of the two days it had taken us the last time.

I later found out that the Turkish Colonel had spoken with my commander on how professional the convoy had been run and how his men were well treated. He said some other kind words about me, which must have impressed my boss. Along with the potential international risk and sensitivity of the mission, the successful escort of the Turkish observers into the region was one of the contributing reasons for being awarded the Bronze Star later.

Of course returning to camp did not mean getting back to luxury living. We were still living in our temporary tents while waiting for the construction of our permanent tents. Sleep was the greatest challenge of all, dealing with a stifling temperature of 90 to 94 degrees. Adding to our comfort was the wonderful smell of burning waste from our latrines. Just as during Desert Storm, we had wooden latrines with half barrels to catch the waste. A detail was assigned every day to change the barrels and burn the waste. I tried my best to sleep normally, but I made up my mind that if sleep continued to elude me, I would seek sleeping pills from our doctors. Finally, I gave up and obtained some pills from our medics. I hate to use sleeping aids, but with them, I had a real good sleep for a change and woke up refreshed and ready for duty.

On April 13, one of our soldiers was slightly wounded, and I worked the causality evacuation (CASEVAC) by one of our helicopters. Insurgents fired upon a mounted patrol in vicinity of Mosul, and a soldier was wounded, with the bullet passing through the fleshy part of his hip and exiting. Another soldier took a round in his Kevlar helmet, but suffered no injuries. Helicopters picked the injured soldier up, and we had him on his way to Landstuhl Hospital in Germany within hours.

During the night, we received reports that our POWs had been found near Tikrit. The survivors from the convoy (except for Jessica Lynch who had been recovered earlier by a combined Marine/Special Operations raid) and the two captured AH-64 pilots were all located. It appeared that whoever was holding the prisoners decided to cut and run because our armored advances were moving quickly. All of our prisoners had been centrally located in a house in Tikrit and left alone. The guards decided to make a break for it, before getting caught up in the fighting. Our folks did the right thing by staying put and keeping their eyes open for a patrol. They were rewarded when they saw a Marine squad making its way along the alley toward their house. They waved at the squad and shouted in English, and the Marines secured them. They were all checked out by medics while being moved outside of the city, where a MC-130 landed to pick them up and move them to safety. It was a big relief to find them all, remembering that we had one pilot still missing from Desert Storm, Major Scott Spiecher.

At night, I often went outside and did some pushups and crunches to keep my body toned as well as to relieve stress and get the kinks out after sitting in front of my computer for hours. During the day when I couldn't sleep, I walked around the camp to watch the activity and to see all the improvements being made. Surrounding our camp was an open and thickly grassy field that stretched toward the city, about a mile away and off toward the mountains in the west. Rumor had it that the field was so green because of the hundreds of Iraqi soldiers whom Kurds had killed and buried in the field. I wasn't sure if it was true, but I did suspect there might be some unexploded ordinance out in the grass, and I didn't go exploring. It looked like we had rented every Land Rover or sports utility vehicle in Irbil, as well as contracting for all of the heavy earth moving and construction vehicles available to work on the camp.

The Peshmergas still provided a ring of security around the camp. Normally around seven to ten men would man these checkpoints. The Peshmergas laid out their blankets in a communal area, and then set up a machine gun and watched the road. As construction continued around the camp, our perimeter defense remained strong. Our engineers helped the Peshmergas build up defensive positions with sandbags, with positions watching down every road coming into the camp area. We manned an immediate checkpoint just in front of the camp with our own soldiers in a sandbagged bunker. We had no perimeter fence, however, except for right next to the front entrance.

Our camp received several pallets of mail each night. Most of us had nothing to do, so we helped the mailroom clerks unload and carry all of the mailbags to their sorting tent. These large orange bags were filled to capacity. I thought some of the guys might have been trying to smuggle their wives in to them from the size of the bags. While unloading the mail, we heard that there was a major backlog of mail stuck at Ramstein Air Base in Germany. Mail wasn't a high priority; the Army tried to fit what they could on supply runs into Bashur, and then to ship it down to us. We helped the clerks sort the mail into separate piles for each unit. I had not received much mail since my move into Iraq, but that was OK. We had some phone lines set up, so I called my family whenever I had a spare chance late at night. Actually having a phone connection with my family so we could stay in touch nearly real time was a big improvement from when I was in Desert Storm.

I learned that the rest of the 129th Rescue HH-60 helicopters had arrived in Bashur, although their tanker aircraft was still in Romania. Any extra support we could get was great, but the signs showed that the war was beginning to wind down and might not last much longer. Still, I was glad they had arrived. I had worked with them in preparing the justification for their entering the country. Why has a dedicated and trained rescue outfit nearby, but unable to do anything? Their arrival took some of the burden off our Air Force comrades and allowed them to focus on mission support.

The author prior to departing from Irbil to pick up the fuel convoy at harbor Gate.

Camp Loki, JSOTF-N's location outside of Irbil, Iraq.

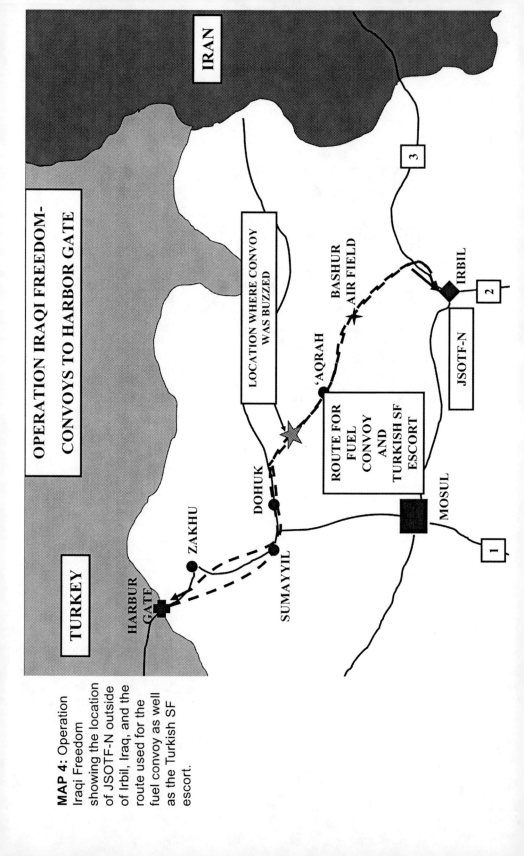

OPERATION IRAQI FREEDOM-CONVOYS TO HARBOR GATE

TURKEY

IRAN

HARBUR GATE

ZAKHU

DOHUK

SUMAYYIL

LOCATION WHERE CONVOY WAS BUZZED

'AQRAH

BASHUR AIR FIELD

ROUTE FOR FUEL CONVOY AND TURKISH SF ESCORT

IRBIL

JSOTF-N

MOSUL

1

2

3

MAP 4: Operation Iraqi Freedom showing the location of JSOTF-N outside of Irbil, Iraq, and the route used for the fuel convoy as well as the Turkish SF escort.

Sand storm striking the camp in northern Iraq

CHAPTER 11

THE WAR WINDING DOWN TO MISSION ACCOMPLISHED

One of the greatest advantages to working the nightshift is that the cover of darkness can sometimes hide some very embarrassing moments. Normally I can see very well in the dark and do not need to use flashlights to see where I am going. A lot of this is probably from my earlier years as a Ranger, where noise and light discipline were stressed. Because this was literally beaten into me by my Ranger NCOs when I was a private, I can't stand to see people using flashlights. To make it worse, a lot of the Air Force personnel wore headlamps with very bright lights. They always turned them on, even if it was a full moon out and you could see clearly. I guess they didn't realize if they shined their bright white light into someone's eyes in the dark, that person would loose his night vision. There were several instances where I growled at them for temporarily blinding me. They would feel offended if I growled at them for light discipline, but that was the difference between Army and Air Force rational I guess.

During one of my shifts, I was making my way to the latrine on the perimeter of the camp, and I failed to follow one of my own cardinal rules, not allowing time for my eyes to adjust to the outside darkness. I had walked this path numerous times, and I felt I knew it like the back of my hands, but suddenly I dropped into a deep trench and crashed after falling about six feet. I had stumbled into a new trench that had been dug for our protection in case of an artillery or mortar attack. Quickly, I looked around to make sure no one had seen me fall in and then pulled myself out of the trench. Luckily for me, no one witnessed my embarrassing moment.

Though the shift work was becoming routine, it was still a challenge. One of the greatest problems we faced was caused by our own technology. We had come a long way since my early days when we relied on radios and did a lot of paper and map work. Now, everyone used computers, and we sent data nearly instantaneously to one another. I had always preached that you must be able to do the "old school" style of manual work and shouldn't rely on technology because when you need technology the most, it will fail on you every time. It's always hard to rely on equipment that has to use electricity or batteries. Our first problem was keeping our electricity, which came from generators, working. The camp was trying to wire into Irbil's power grid, but it was taking a long time to build the needed power lines. From time to time, the generators ran out of fuel, broke down, or needed to be serviced. I kept a flashlight at my workstation for these emergencies, but I had nothing to power our computers except their internal batteries. If the power went out, so did our server and any connectivity with our higher units. Sometimes the problem originated in CENTCOM's area with high winds messing up the satellite feed.

Happiness arrived on April 15, even though nearly everyone else dreads "Tax Day." We finally moved from our temporary living quarters into our permanent tent with power and air conditioning. Our tent was located a good distance from where we worked, and the area was still under construction. There were about twenty of us, all from the night shift, composed of senior officers and sergeants. Even though we hung signs out that we were nightshift and slept during the day to limit interruptions, we still had to deal with the noise of construction and the activities of the majority of the camp. There was a tent of young soldiers across from ours, and they liked to hoot and holler during the day. They figured out to leave our area alone and move their antics somewhere else when a few of our senior officers and me growled at them one day and gave them a quick class on how to read signs.

A Morale Welfare and Recreation (MWR) tent for the camp had been built next to the parade field in the center of the compound. In the MWR, we could watch movies, play games, and such. Inside our eating tent, there was a large-screen TV on which we could watch the news. Since it was mid-April, another popular activity was storm watching. With the camp located in the middle of an open valley, we had clear views of our surroundings. This made thunderstorms and lightning shows very spectacular. One evening, our weather guys and a few of us from the JOC watched a storm approach, and we "oohed and aahed" like it was a July 4th fireworks show. Though it was a spectacular show, a little common sense voice reminded me how muddy it got during Desert Storm. I had brought my Army rubber boots with me. Before the storm hit, I went back to my tent to fetch them and was glad that I had. The thunderstorm lasted most of the night and finally broke by morning. All of the rain turned the camp into a sea of mud. I pulled out my rubber boots, slipped them over my desert boots, and walked through the standing water with ease. At first, everyone thought the rubber boots were funny, but soon they were envious as the camp became thick with mud and water. Sometimes a little experience can really pay off.

The weather continued to be wet for the next couple of days, and except for some large ponds, the camp was nothing but mud. I soon became a "fashion assassin" as I walked around camp in my physical training T-shirt, my shorts, and my big black rubber boots. I watched this poor kid try to jump from one mound of dirt to another to keep out of the water. I asked him why he didn't just face it and walk in the water. He replied that he had only brought two pairs of socks with him. I was amazed. I always deployed with at least 20 pairs or so. I guess they don't train them like they used to. It rained so much in fact that a foundation for a shower, which was ten feet wide, fifteen feet long, and ten feet deep, completely filled with water. Someone commented that it looked like a swimming pool, and some of the younger kids took him seriously. I walked out of my tent one day to watch two of them jump into this makeshift pool and swim around. I wondered if they realized how high the potential was for parasites and who knows what else that lurked in the water they were swimming in. I warned them, but my words seemed to fall on deaf ears and they continued to swim around. I never found out if they got sick or not, but why take the chance? Sometimes inexperience can be dangerous.

Another challenge was dignitaries. The whole camp got into an uproar whenever some general was coming to see us. Everyone rushed around, making sure everything looked pretty. I might understand the need for dignitaries and having the camp all cleaned up for them, but my first responsibility is doing my job by being ready in case our teams in the field need help. One of our visitors was an Air Force Survival Expert named SSG Jim "Jimbo" Wilson, who came up to see how we did things. Chief McPherson and I incorporated him into our rotation schedule so he could see how we ran our PRCC. Jimbo was a character to say the least, but he really knew his stuff. While he was with us, he trained me up on High Risk of Capture briefings and training, so I could instruct our Group's personnel the next time we deployed. I was soon allowed to become the "Token Snake Eater (nickname for SF) in the Bug Eater (nickname for Air Force survival specialists) World."

One of the collaborative tools we used on the staff was a Microsoft chat program known as mIRC. Each major office of the different services branches had their own chat room so they could conduct real-time coordination. This was a great tool to keep situational awareness of what was happening on the battlefield. It was an excellent tool we in the personnel recovery world used to quickly coordinate rescue missions if needed. Additional to the operational chat rooms, there were some "private" chat rooms for pilots or survival specialists. Because I had worked with Jimbo, he allowed me access to their room so we could "sit around the camp fire" and talk about the day's activity.

Jimbo was a character, but I found out that he was also a very thoughtful person. I had been collecting my care package goodies and had them stored in a box next to my workstation. I began to notice that my supply of hard candy seem to be getting smaller and smaller, but thought I had just over-looked it. I found out later that Jimbo, who was on the shift before me, found my goodie stash. He than offered it to everyone in the JOC who partook of my hard candy! They had thought it was Jimbo's and didn't realize it had been mine. Oh well, it was used by our staff folks, so I guess it was OK.

With more and more visitors coming to the camp, was a sure sign that things were beginning to wind down. I commented one night that I used to see the glow of battle in the distance at night, but now all I was seeing was the glow of burning latrine waste. I had heard from friends with the 129th Rescue Squadron that they were on their way home. Things were definitely coming to a close.

Focus was shifting away from supporting combat operations and turning toward future operations. I was asked to start looking into our next Silent Warrior exercise in Europe and to begin working with the exercise coordinator of the Special Operations Command-Europe (SOCEUR). Our command believed that our role was winding down, and they had put our PRCC "on call" in case we were needed. I started to look into the exercise, but it was difficult to coordinate when we were in northern Iraq and the main exercise coordinator was back in Germany. I saw another sign that things were winding down one evening when I went into our future operations tent, and everyone was asleep at their desks. Our helicopters were being used to ferry dignitaries around and could not stand personnel recovery alert. The detachments being used as CSAR teams were sent back to their battalions, their services no longer required.

Napoleon said that an army marches on its stomach, and food is near and dear to a soldier's heart. For the most part, the camp had food catered by a local Kurdish restaurant. I had grown to love pita bread during Operation Provide Comfort, and I enjoyed having it for breakfast. But for those of us on night shift, there was no food, other than the beloved MREs. Normally we would keep several cases of MREs and water in the JOC for our meals. However, the supply system came under a new regime that wanted to control everything. They wanted us to request MREs and water instead of just getting them like we did before. This was a shock for us in the JOC, and I was given the mission of "procuring" food. When I went to request our MREs, I was informed about the request paperwork procedure and came away with nothing. So being a good Special Forces soldier, I adapted and overcame the obstacle. I drove a truck over to the supply yard where stacks of MREs were stored and "liberated" enough meals to cover everyone for a couple of days. This would supply the JOC during the requisition paperwork period. I wondered what had happened to the goal of taking care of the soldier, but times had changed and I was an old timer.

Violating my own rules once again, I tried something different for dinner (which for night shift was our breakfast) one day. Calling their creation "Kurdish Pizza," the caterers took pita bread and put some tomato sauce and meat on it. Whatever it was, a bunch of us came down with a bad case of diarrhea. Having diarrhea in a hot environment was dangerous, and I drank as much water as I could. Unfortunately, I couldn't shake whatever it was that had grown to like my insides and had to take medication.

On April 24, we received word that victory has been declared. Beginning my "on call" status and switching over so I could sleep at night instead of during the day, I was able to watch President George Bush's "Mission Accomplish" speech from the aircraft carrier. Sleep had been one of my many difficulties during this deployment, when I was receiving only four hours of sleep on average. Now I would be able to sleep when it was dark and in cooler temperatures than during the day. I started to eat my meals at the normal dining time for the camp. The meal normally consisted of rice, chicken or beef kebobs, and some vegetables, along with pita bread and a can of soda. I usually took my plate of rice and chicken and went to find a quiet place away from the dining tent. Luckily, I like chicken and rice with some soy sauce on it, because I had it every day for lunch and dinner. I didn't feel too bad though learning from reading some of the reports from the rescued prisoners, that all they ate was chicken and rice. I made up my mind that one of the first things I would eat when I got back to the United States would be a nice, thick, rare steak and that I would avoid chicken for awhile.

As April turned to May, the temperatures began to climb. The days were becoming hot and dusty to the point that the sky was a shade of orange. Wind was more frequent, and the metal beams and poles of our tent creaked in response. With high winds, the chances for a sandstorm increased, and our camp was hit by a large storm. In the distance, you could see the storm approaching, a wall of orange-shaded dust. Before the storm hit, it was breezy, and then the winds began to increase as the storm closed in around us. When it hit, visibility dropped off to only a few feet, with the camp swallowed in an orange haze. The flag stood straight out before it disappeared into the gloom. The storm passed quickly, and we could again see the

143

sky over the camp. The wall of clouds and dust continued down the valley as the storm made its way toward Irbil.

As the temperatures increased, so did the number of flies buzzing around the camp. Most of the tents had bug screens to keep them out, but you had to deal with them in the latrines. There is nothing worse then sitting down to go to the bathroom and feeling the flies crawling on your bare buttocks. Reminded me of the movie, "The Amityville Horror."

I went out to visit a bazaar that had been allowed to set up in one of our tents. Local shop owners brought gold, silver, carpets, and souvenirs. My wife really likes Persian rugs, and I was able to purchase one for her. I had hoped for a flying carpet, but they seemed to be out of stock. The day was cold and rainy, and we all waited out in the drizzle for our chance to see their wares. Most of the troops were checking out the gold and silver while I talked to a rug merchant. I picked up a nice hallway rug for about a $100, and they were kind enough to wrap it in plastic to protect it from the rain. I also picked up some old Iraqi money as a souvenir.

That evening, our military dining facility finally opened, and the occasion was celebrated with steak and shrimp for dinner. However, we had to wait in line for over an hour and a half to get a leather-hard steak and a couple of shrimp. It tasted wonderful anyway, and it was different from what we had been eating, but I still promised myself a good steak when I returned to the states. Our new dining facility offered breakfast and dinner, but the Kurds still provided lunch. The only problem was that our rations had been donated to us from our good friends, the 173rd. The rations were known as "T-Rats," which were large aluminum trays of food that were cooked in boiling water and then served to us. The rations came in meal packs, with a specific main dish, vegetables, and deserts. They had donated all of the rations they did not like and kept the good ones for themselves. So now not only did we have the same Kurdish food everyday, but we also had the same army rations every night. Eating the same thing day after day helped to continue the feeling of "Groundhogs Day" syndrome that had started back in Romania.

Now that I was pretty much free to do as I wished, I spent most of the day in the MWR tent, which had been built up nicely by our support personnel. They had installed a large screen TV with a DVD player, and they had built a bar, which served snacks, sodas, and ice cream for free. I had brought some DVDs with me, and I shared them with the rest of the troops who were relaxing in the tent. I also volunteered to help run the place, seeing that I was available.

It was during one of these days in the tent that I realized how old-fashioned I was when compared to today's Army. I made an on-the-spot correction of a young soldier from the 10th Mountain. He in turn gave me a glare and became "slightly disrespectful" as he left the tent. Another time I corrected a soldier for leaving his weapon unsecured when he walked away and left it on the floor for about 15 minutes. I picked it up and gave it to an NCO from his unit, who said he would take care of it for me. I couldn't believe what these new soldiers were getting away with. When I was a young soldier, I never left my weapon out of my sight or reach, and I would never have thought of being disrespectful to a senior NCO. It was then that I realized I was from the "be-all-that-you-can-be" generation, and not the "Army-of-one" generation. It was time for me to move on, and I began to seriously think about retiring.

They had finally built a shower facility, but you had to go there either when it had just opened or when it was close to finishing to avoid the long lines. Some of the guys had built an improvised shower with a gravity-feed bag next to our tent. At sun up, we took several old plastic water bottles and filled them with water. Then placing them on top of the tent, we let the sun heat the water so that we could have a hot shower that evening. There were some shaving stations along the perimeter of the camp with mirrors where you could shave and brush your teeth.

As the end of April arrived, I celebrated my wedding anniversary again away from my wife and family. We were playing the waiting game once more, except this time I was waiting for the word to go home. Most of the combat operations were small-scale, "mopping up" type operations. The days were becoming hotter, and the flies were becoming more of a problem. It was not uncommon to share the latrine with almost 100 of them during the day. I was trying to convince my body to wait to use the latrine until dark when the flies were gone, or at least when you couldn't see them anymore.

Of course with the hotter days, meant more people crowding into the MWR tent.

As a result, I generally chose to stay near my tent. The laundry service had lost some of my uniforms, and I decided to hand wash my own. I spent the days reading and working out, doing push-ups and crunches near my tent. During one of the slow days, we decided to take a photo of all of us in the JOC, dressed up in our gear, in front of our helicopters. Some of the guys had shaved their heads bald, and they had a group photo made holding a "Mini-me" doll from "Austin Powers." They were known as the "Mini-Me Fan Club."

The senior command staff tried to schedule a bazaar once a week or so, and another was set up on one of the side roads near the camp. I headed out to look for some more souvenirs to bring home. As I was looking at the items for sale, I overheard a soldier comment on how he didn't want to purchase anything because he would never be coming back here anyway. I told him that I had said the very same thing and was now on my third trip over. I warned him to be careful not to jinx himself. Little did I realize that I had probably just jinxed myself and would be back.

My first major step toward going home occurred on May 5 when I turned in my weapons and ammunition. During the day, I received a wonderful care package from Sherry's Kitchen in Albany, N.Y. They knew my mother and sent us a care package with snacks and home-cooked brownies and cookies. I took my share, gave the rest to the JOC, and wrote a thank-you note back. It was nice to receive a care package from strangers, getting support from home.

The disagreements about the war had become a very difficult thing for me during this deployment. This war had galvanized our country, and a heated debate between those who were against and those who supported the war ensued. We had watched the protesters on the news, and they seemed to have received a majority of the coverage. I took it very personally when I saw the protesters and the Hollywood stars marching against the war. I understood that they were exercising their freedom of speech, but most of us over in Iraq felt offended by it. The fact that some of these protesters came over to be used as human shields for Saddam at the beginning of the war was hard to stomach.

As of May 7, we no longer had responsibility for covering Personnel Recovery operations. Our helicopters were standing down, and a medical evacuation unit was moving into the Mosul area. A possible evacuation mission came up suddenly one night, and the 129th wanted to play. They told me they had two aircraft, armed with everything from mini-guns to staple guns and were ready to go. The Marines were able to respond, but I thanked the 129th for the offer.

We had begun rotating some of our personnel home. Out of the original 15 men that I had shared the tent with, only six remained. The days continued to be spent killing time and waiting for the word to rotate home. We had come into this place with a roar, but now it seemed we were leaving in a whisper. A new camp sign was erected, showing a Viking warrior with "Camp Loki" written over him. I mused to myself about the name, the Norse God of mischief and deceit, which did not seem a real good name for a camp. Unfortunately, another type of "bug" had made itself at home in my intestines. It seemed almost every other week I had a bad case of diarrhea. I let it go for a couple of days, and when it didn't improve, I saw our medics and received medication to kill it. We were getting closer to our time to go home, and I did not want to bring this type of "souvenir" with me. Our last night in the JOC was May 12, when we handed the responsibility over to the second battalion. Colonel Cleveland got up during the last official nightly briefing and thanked everyone for a job well done. We were told to begin palletizing our gear the following morning. It was with joyful energy that we dragged our gear out and begin building the pallet that would transport it home. The day was a balmy 97 as we built the pallet and waited for the customs inspector.

Another change to the camp at about this time was that our dining was once again catered, but by a better caterer. Happiness was a good meal and a completed pallet, even if the temperature maxed out at 102 degrees that afternoon. It was a good time to go, before the average daily temperature reached 100 degrees or more.

The fact that everything was loaded and ready to go made the "hurry up and wait" pass by pleasantly. The military couldn't operate without paperwork, and we had to go around the camp with clearing papers, documents that showed you owed nothing to the camp. This was the final out-processing we needed to do, except for getting on the bus. However, we would have to suffer through an extended "hurry up and wait" this time. The aircraft we were supposed to catch on May 14 did not arrive, so we had to hang out in the camp for another day. May 15 arrived, and so did the buses in the early evening. Colonel Cleveland came out to see us off, and gave each of us a specially minted JSOTF-N coin for the occasion. We were to ride the bus from our camp down to the city of Kirkuk, because our large transport aircraft could not land at our camp due to the runway construction. Oddly enough, we watched contracted Soviet IL-76s land on our "limited" airstrip.

The ride was uneventful, with a convoy of buses of returning personnel rolling down the highway. Chief and I made ourselves as comfortable as we could in our helmets and vests at the rear of the bus. We drove down the main road to Kirkuk, passing through the area where the Republican Guard, Saddam's elite troops, had dug in. We could see their old fighting positions along the roads and ridgelines, now sitting vacant and collapsing inward. Along the road, we saw an old military barracks that looked like a huge, walled fort with casements and towers on the corners. Our Air Force had renovated it with a couple of well-placed 2,000-pound bombs.

As we got closer to Kirkuk, we saw the extensive oil fields and the fires from the burn-off towers. Scattered along the route closer to Kirkuk were destroyed tanks and armored personnel carriers. Their burnt-out hulks showed how the Iraqis had tried to defend the road into the city.

Night had fallen, and in the distance we saw the lights of Kirkuk, our first destination for planes, trains, and automobiles. We pulled into the Kirkuk airbase, which was located west of the city, and soon we were herded into a hangar that served as a waiting area. Luckily for us, we had become accustomed to the hurry up and wait game, for we were stuck there for at least eight hours. We all filed by, picked up a cot, and found a space to occupy as we waited. The Air Force informed us that our plane was delayed for four hours and we wouldn't be loading until two in the morning.

There was a big temperature change between Irbil and Kirkuk. We had been enjoying cool and pleasant temperatures at night, but here in Kirkuk, it was in the 80s and muggy. To help pass the time, I wandered around the area and watched some of the C-17s load up and take off. I tried to read, but a pigeon roosting in the overhead rafters decided to bombard my cot with his droppings! He must have been one of those diehard Fadayeen fighters getting in a parting shot. Luckily, he was a bad shot and missed me. He tried again, and missed again, and I prudently moved my cot away and tried to get some sleep.

Around midnight, we were herded up once again and moved to the customs station across the road from the hangar, where we filled out our customs forms and amnesty turn-in. Our waiting area was an area surrounded by concertina wire, which made us feel as if we were prisoners of war. I made myself comfortable on the ground and snoozed for a bit until they called for us to move to the aircraft. It was May 16 (technically since it was after midnight) as we walked out to the waiting C-17 transport. This would be my first time flying on this type of aircraft. We all took seats along the side, because the center was full of cargo pallets and vehicles. I found out that this airplane was one of the transports that had dropped the 173rd on Bashur. Even the crew chief couldn't fathom why they had jumped, when the airfield was under our control and it would have been easier to land. It was such a wonderful feeling when we took off and were on our way home (or so we thought).

Once we were in the air, we all scrambled for a place on the floor to sleep. I wedged my big frame under a forklift and between other sleepers. The cold floor felt good, and I was able to fall asleep, helping to make time go by faster. The sun was up when we awakened, heading for our stop at Rhine Main after which we thought we would proceed on to the United States. Boy, were we wrong! After the aircraft taxied up and began shutting down, we were told to grab our stuff and head into the terminal. No one thought much about it; we normally off-load during refueling. It was while we were waiting that we were told that the air conditioning in the aircraft was broken. We could have cared less, coming from a daily temperature of 95 to 100 degrees. We later learned that Rhine Main was the only destination that had been worked out; from there, we were to somehow get another flight. The buses arrived and took us over to a large festival tent with cots. We didn't know how long our stay would be, but I was in Germany, and that was fine with me. The tent was large, and the showers were located right across from it. Chief McPherson and I found our selves a corner, set up our cots, and prepared our selves for the stay.

The first thing I did was to change into the civilian clothes that I had brought with me. We walked over to a small festival and swap meet going on near our tent. After checking it out, Chief McPherson and I headed over to the base store so I could purchase a warmer shirt. Germany was typically cold and rainy when we arrived, which a drastic change for someone was coming from Iraq. Normally I love the cold, but this time I needed something warmer to put on. I purchased a cheap, tourist sweatshirt that had "Where is Ausfahrt, Germany" printed on it. (Ausfahrt is written on a blue sign seen frequently on German highways. The sign means "exit." Locals joke that newcomers think it's one of the biggest cities in Germany.) Wearing it was an inside joke. Most of the guys in my unit knew that I had lived in Germany for a while, spoke German, and had a German wife. It was warm and cheap, and it served its purpose.

The next thing we did was to patronize the German food stand outside the store. There was something about that Sweinhaxe (roasted pig knuckle) and fries that was near to Nirvana for me. Eventually, most of the other guys found their way over to sample the food and get items from the store. Now that we were fat and happy, we headed back to the tent and settled in for our first night in Germany.

The next day was gray and rainy, another typical day in Germany. Chief McPherson and I went over to a coffee shop and, while having coffee, met some stewardesses who worked on contract aircraft that flew soldiers to and from Iraq. We talked for a while, and these ladies offered us free phone cards so we could call home. I had already done that, so I decided to give them to some of the guys waiting in the tent. We passed the afternoon talking to the stewardesses, and they invited us over to the sports bar to treat us to a beer. Once there, we ran into a bunch more of our guys, and the stewardesses even bought them beers. What a bunch of great ladies they were! That's really showing support to the troops. It was our first beer in several months, and it tasted great. Chief McPherson and I took it easy, seeing we hadn't had any beer for a while. These stewardesses were ready to kick the people (Marines, I believe) off their flight in the morning and take us all home. It was a nice thought. We wished them the best and went to our tent.

The morning of May 17 dawned cold and rainy, but we were told that we would be on our way home the next day. The day passed slowly, but we were happy to be closer to going home, and we killed time the best we could. The following morning, the chaplain talked to us about readjustment and getting reacquainted with our families. I had already made up my mind that my wife had taken care of the house very well while I was gone, and I would try to stay out of her hair until we got used to each other. I told my friends I intended to stay at home and enjoy some Glenmorangie Scotch, until my wife told me I could start doing my old chores.

By the afternoon of May 18, we had assembled and moved over to the airfield. By 12:30, we had loaded onto the contract airliner that would fly us home. It was a comfortable flight as we made our way to our first stop in Gander, once again for refueling. We watched some movies until we landed and waited for 45 minutes. The aircrew had informed us we would fly to Pope Air Force Base, just outside of Fort Bragg, North Carolina. There they were to refuel and change crews. We tried to convince them to fly us straight to Colorado, but it didn't work out.

As we landed at Pope Air Force Base, they announced over the loud speakers "Welcome home," but everyone yelled back, "We're not home yet!" We waited over in the marshalling area, where many of us had put on parachutes for airborne drops during our days at Fort Bragg. The waiting area, known as "Green Ramp" brought memories back for many of us. There were a lot of improvements since our days, and it wasn't a bad place to wait. After an hour and a half, we reloaded the plane and began the final leg of our journey to Colorado. It was a bumpy ride, with some turbulence as we came closer to home. We had been warned ahead of time to expect a media circus once we got back to our headquarters. What a shout went up when we touched down at Colorado Springs Airport! Everyone was happy to be finally home. I was excited to see my family again and could hardly wait to get to them. The buses were waiting for us, and there was a detail already there to off-load our bags for us. We all loaded up on the buses for the 20-minute ride back to our compound on Fort Carson.

The bus ride was relatively quiet, with most of the guys keeping their thoughts to themselves. I spent my time looking at the changes to the area south of Colorado Springs, knowing I would be driving past my house on the way to Fort Carson. The biggest thing I thought about was what I was going to do when I saw my family. How would I react when I saw them, and how they would react when they saw me? It had been a long time. What would my family look like? How much had my daughter grown? I wanted to avoid the media; I didn't want my reunion to be televised. Soon all these thoughts dissolved as we approached our unit's compound on Fort Carson. The headquarters is located on top of a hill, so we could see all of our families waiting, and we could see the lights of the television cameras. Soon we were pulling into our headquarters area, and we stopped. The doors opened, and we unloaded and fanned out to find our families.

As I stepped off the bus, I saw my wife and daughter rushing up. I turned, and soon we were all locked in a joyful embrace. We moved away from the growing crowd and the media attention. I have always tried to remain stoic and not shed tears at reunions or farewells, but this time I was so happy I couldn't stop a tear of joy from falling. My daughter had grown since I last saw her, and we stood off to the side and talked. She was upset because she had carried a "Welcome Home" balloon, but it had gotten away from her and sailed off. It didn't matter to me. I was home in one piece, and I was with my family. After waiting for our bags to arrive, and after securing them, we loaded up in my truck and went home. It was such a wonderful feeling driving my own truck again. When we got home, one of our friends had decorated our garage with Welcome Home banners. I gave their kids some Iraqi money for souvenirs and thanked them. I was home, my mission complete. (At least, for now.)

The mighty JSOTF-N JOC crew posing in front of the 21st SOS MH-53s at Irbil, Iraq. The mini-me doll is located in the front row, far right.

The day the rain came. The flooded shower foundation that was used as an improvised swimming pool.

Photo of the JSOTF-N PRCC, the author on the left, Chief McPherson center and Jim "Jimbo" Wilson on the right.

The Mini-me fan club

Unfortunate occurrence where a waste fire went out of control

CHAPTER 12

OPERATION IRAQI FREEDOM II AND THE RADWANNIYA PALACE COMPLEX

As I feared, I must have jinxed myself back at that street bazaar by saying, "I will never return to this place." After I returned home and eventually readjusted back to my home environment, I realized this wouldn't last for long. With the situation in Iraq becoming worse as guerillas began an unconventional war against the United States and the Coalition, we knew it was only a matter of time before we would be sent back. The 5th Special Forces Group, which had remained behind at the conclusion of Operation Iraqi Freedom, needed a break. Most of the other groups were busy supporting operations in other countries around the globe. Our group was pretty much available to take over their operations, because not much was happening in Europe, our normal area of operations. We would have seven months to prepare, train, and spend as much time with our families as we could. Over the years, my wife and I had become accustomed to my going away. While I was coordinating exercises, I would be gone from Colorado almost once a month on survey or coordination trips to Europe. We had both become so used to this that she would sometimes comment, "Isn't it time for you to go somewhere?"

One of the biggest things I never could understand was why most of the senior staff was reassigned right after returning from a major deployment. It had taken us several months of training to get ready for Operation Iraqi Freedom, and now our staff was a well-rehearsed, well-oiled machine. However, just about all of the command staff officers were reassigned and sent off to their new duties.

All new personnel, who had never worked with each other before, replaced the staff. I was saddled up with Major Andy Miltner, our new Group Chemical Officer, who was also covering future plans and exercises. Colonel Cleveland had received his reassignment orders, and Colonel Michael Repass would be taking us over to Iraq. Those of us in the Non-commissioned Officer Corp (NCO) were under stop loss, which meant we could not retire or leave the military. Almost all of the NCOs on the staff were new and would have to be trained. Chief McPherson was reassigned to Fort Bragg, which left me in charge of the personnel recovery program all by myself. Myself along MSG Hudgell were the only NCOs from the Group Staff who had participated in Iraqi Freedom and would be coming over for Iraqi Freedom II. For the majority of the staff, both officers and enlisted/NCOs, this would be their first time on a high-level staff in a combat theater.

As before, we began a training rotation for the staff, and SOCJF-COM came out once more to Fort Carson from Norfolk, Virginia to run the staff through training seminars and classes. I returned to Fredericksburg to attend JPRA's Non-conventional Assisted Recovery Operations Management course. Seeing that I alone would be running the full spectrum of personnel recovery for special operations forces over in Iraq, I needed this training. Staff training wasn't all we did. Our Headquarters' (HHC) First Sergeant, ISG Brad Connors, the Group Support Company's (GSC) First Sergeant, ISG Robert Irby, and I trained our support personnel in marksmanship, tactics, and convoy operations. Learning from the experiences of Jessica Lynch and what had happened to her convoy, we wanted to make sure our soldiers were ready to face such a situation. Our support personnel were going to be in harm's way, and we wanted them to be very proficient in small arms and convoy procedures, not wanting to make the same mistakes the 507th did that resulted in their capture. We already knew that one of the missions our support personnel in the group would be conducting over in Iraq would be convoys. Except for a few of us Special Forces NCOs within HHC and GSC, the majority of the soldiers were from support specialties like administration and maintenance; they were not infantrymen. This is why I always respected the Marines; all of their soldiers received basic infantry training, before specializing like being a mechanic.

The training started in the classroom, where we went over the basics of urban warfare and convoy operations. The soldiers needed to understand both, because in Iraq, most of the convoys would have to travel through an urban environment. Bringing experience, knowledge, and expertise, ISGs Connor and Irby, along with some of us old hands, developed a SOP for everyone to follow. Then the classes moved out to the training areas and the ranges. We followed the principles of crawl, walk, and run when it came to learning the new SOPs. During the crawl phase, each step was demonstrated and rehearsed. Then during the walk phase, the soldiers conducted the drill slowly, under our supervision and mentorship, with corrections as needed. The final test was the run phase, where the soldiers were put through their paces on their own. Additionally, each person was rotated through the different positions on the vehicles so they could learn each other's jobs. The same training procedure was used in the urban fighting and tactics classes.

I was amazed at how quickly these support soldiers picked it up. We then moved out to the ranges where the soldiers not only became proficient in their assigned weapons, but with the weapons they would use as part of a convoy or for base defense such as machine guns and grenade launchers. The final training occurred in early December when both HHC and GSC participated in a culminating training exercise for a week out on one of the training areas. There, everything was put into practice, including base defense, convoy operations, battle drills, and marksmanship. This exercise also worked on our camp's configuration and the procedures we would use once we arrived in Iraq.

As in the year before, the holidays came and went, and soon I was preparing myself to once again head for Iraq. All of the soldiers who had attended the training were placed into a convoy pool, so the 1SGs could draw from a trained group of soldiers for convoy duties. I was also a member of the convoy pool. I wasn't sure what I would be doing over in Iraq. I didn't believe I would be doing only personnel recovery this time. Back in Iraqi Freedom, never had so few been led by so many. We had gone in with a very large command staff, but it wouldn't be the same for this mission. We were going to be doing more jobs with less personnel not having the manpower to draw from like we had in Iraqi Freedom. Our staff would be greatly reduced in size, but not the workload.

We thought we had made a major breakthrough with the fighting in Iraq when in December 2003; the search for Saddam Hussein came to an end. Elements from the Special Operations community and the 4th Infantry Division, using information provided by informants, moved in on a farm near the outskirts of Tikrit, the region from which Saddam came. During the search of the farm, a false cover was found in the yard and was opened to reveal a small room underground. Inside, the soldiers found Saddam Hussein hiding with a pistol in his lap. He did not use the pistol. Instead, he stated, "I am Saddam Hussein, President of Iraq, and I am willing to negotiate." It always seems strange that these hard-core dictators talk a lot of talk until they are confronted directly. Then they are willing to negotiate. He had been moved around a lot to avoid capture, not to mention possible annihilation by a few well-placed 2,000-pound bombs. The running around had not done much for Saddam, who looked rather dirty with a matted grey beard. After he was secured, he was brought to Baghdad, where he was given a medical examination, to await trial. As of the time I am writing this book, he is still being held and is awaiting a full trial by the new Iraqi Government. But even though Saddam was captured, his loyal and fanatic Fadayeen fighters continued fighting, as did other radical Muslim fundamentalists who had come to Iraq to kill Americans.

By January 20, 2004, I was once more packed and ready to go. Weapons had been packed and additional equipment issued. This time I had real body armor with plates, so I felt better about my equipment. I had done all I could do, getting the unit as close to ready personnel-recovery-wise as I could, with the proper briefings and ISOPREPs checked. The group traveling to Iraq from our base this time included about 75 from both HHC and GSC support personnel.

As with my trip the year before, we all arrived at our headquarters to leave, only to find out that our plane had broken down and we would have to try again in the morning. There was a rumor that the aircraft had happened to break down on the night of a hockey game over at the Air Force Academy, but it was only a rumor. We headed over to Peterson Air Force base, which shares Colorado Springs Airport on January 25 in the early morning hours. This time, we would be flying over in the gigantic C-5 Galaxy transport instead of on a contract aircraft. After palletizing our bags and the extra bags with our body armor, helmets and chemical protection gear, we headed out to the C-5. Entering the rear of the aircraft, we climbed a small staircase suspended in the cavernous belly of the aircraft to get to the passenger section on the second deck. There, I found myself a seat and made myself comfortable as best as I could. The seats were just like the ones on commercial airlines, so it wasn't too bad.

This flight wouldn't make as many stops as we had endured on our trip to Iraq the previous year. One of the major advantages to the C-5 is that it can be refueled in mid-air. Unfortunately, there were no in-flight movies, or any entertainment for that matter, only what you brought with you. I tried to catch some sleep, not having slept well for the past two days because of the anxiety of deploying again. I snoozed for only a little bit, not wanting to take any of the sleep medication the docs had provided for us. I had decided to save it for when I really needed it. The time arrived for the aerial refuel, and we all strapped ourselves in. It was a bumpy ride as the C-5 flew through the jet wash of the tanker aircraft. The turbulence lasted for only about fifteen minutes, and then it was back to normal flying. To help pass the time, I listened to my CD player and read a book. From the few portholes we had in the aircraft, I saw that it had changed to night. In the wee hours of January 26, we landed in Moron (yes, that is how it is spelled), Spain, where the aircraft would be refueled and the crew changed. After moving into a waiting area, we all headed over to the dining facility for a good meal. One thing about the Air Force, they have the best dining facilities. If anyone who is reading this is interested in joining the military, I recommend the Air Force. If you crave excitement and want to do the "hoah" stuff, join the Army or Marines. If not, go for the Air Force, a military institution that is as close to civilian life as you will ever get.

After enjoying a good meal, we all headed over to the waiting area. The sun was up now, and we continued the tradition of hurry up and wait. What I didn't know at the time was that for our protection, we were waiting so that it would be dark when we landed in Baghdad. Unfortunately, no one told us the reason for the wait, and the hours dragged on and on. I spent the time wandering around the waiting area, reading all of the pictures and displays in the building. There was a television to watch, and I continued to read my book. At least we could enjoy the dining facility one more time, which was fine with me. Definitely better than an MRE! We spent nearly the whole day waiting before we headed out to our C-5 for the final leg of the trip. For the most part, the trip in was uneventful until we got close to our destination. The flight crew put on their armor and helmets, and all lights were turned off in the aircraft. Granted, a C-5 is a huge dark shape in the sky, even with no lights on. The crew was taking no chances, though, knowing that a C-5 and a DHL-contracted cargo plane had both been hit by SA-7 shoulder-fired, heat-seeking missiles a few months before near Baghdad Airport. Approximately twenty minutes out, we started our approach, which included some evasive maneuvers. This is impressive when you're sitting inside a giant aircraft, facing the rear in complete darkness with no sense of direction. The landing was uneventful, and I was once more back in Iraq for my final tour.

Once the C-5 shut down, we navigated down the tiny stairs to the main deck and picked up our extra bags, including our armor and helmets, which we hadn't worn on the way in. Waiting for us were two small buses that were going to take us over to our new home. We waited for about an hour as our bags were off-loaded, and then we headed into the night. I had no idea where we were going; I only knew that our camp was near the airport. The buses took us along some dirt roads, which were choked with mud and deep puddles. It had rained heavily just before our arrival, and some areas were under water. Driving around at night in an area you have never been in before can be very confusing. I was sitting in the back of the bus, so I couldn't hear what the driver was saying. After about a half hour, we arrived at the illuminated gate of our new home. The camp was located inside a walled compound, and we passed a couple of buildings before turning down a road and coming to a stop.

One of our supply sergeants, SGT Becky Ostwald, led us to a tent where we would bed for the night. We would be broken up and assigned to our respective tents in the morning, which was better then what had happened back in Irbil. The morning of January 27 arrived, and I began my six-month tour in Iraq. Luckily, we would stay in the tent we had been placed in that evening. It had electricity, heat, and air conditioning, and was shared by twelve of us. This included my old teammate Todd Sowerby who was now a CW/3 warrant officer. My old sniper partner and teammate from ODA-035 from Germany, John Reed, was with us as well. I chose a spot right next to the door, so I could be found in case of emergencies. There was a plastic table between my neighbor and myself and we would share it as a shelf. After setting up my cot, and stowing my gear, I then made my way over to the new JOC and checked it out.

The camp was located in the Radwanniya Palace Complex (RPC for short), one of Saddam's palaces surrounding the airport. It was completely surrounded by a wall, and we believed it had served as a hunting and fishing retreat. We shared the complex with a battalion from the 5th Special Forces, an element from the 82nd Airborne Division and some conventional army support personnel. My tour started off with a bang as four rockets hit the far side of the complex, near the 5th Group's battalion headquarters. No one was hurt. The rockets landed inside the area where housing units were being built, damaging some of the units. As I walked to our new JOC, I passed a small building with large iron cages. It looked like a small prison, but it was Uday's (Saddam's eldest son) cages for his pet tigers. He had kept several tigers as pets, but they were all gone now and the cages were empty.

First and foremost, I wanted to know what job I would be performing. I already knew I was running both the regular personnel recovery and the non-conventional recovery operations, and riding with convoys as needed, but the rest was rumors. The JOC was located in a large row of buildings that were administrative and support buildings for the complex. One was a dining facility, one was a theater, and two were former administration offices. I believed that Saddam's Republican Guard had used these very buildings when they protected the complex.

The JOC was set up in an open room with four rows of tables split in the middle by a central walkway. I met with the current head of personnel recovery operations that I would be replacing. He was from the National Guard, Master Sergeant Johnson, whose only PR experience was the introductory course given at Fredericksburg. He seemed very happy to pass the responsibility on to me. I stayed long enough to watch the evening changeover briefings, in which I too would be participating. The briefing was designed to keep the commander informed of the day's event and what to expect in the next twenty-four hours. This briefing was different from the ones we had used last time in Iraq, probably because it was a 5th Group creation, but we would have to learn it.

My true first day on the job began on January 28, with my going through personnel recovery paperwork and standard operating procedures, as well becoming accustomed to the battle rhythm of the JOC. I received the additional responsibility for tracking all conventional, as well as Special Forces operations in Northern Iraq. This title was known as a GOO (Ground Operations Officer). Because we were short-handed, my primary daily mission was to track the locations and activities of both the conventional as well as our special operations forces in the north, and brief the commander during his nightly briefings. I had known I wouldn't just be running the personnel recovery operations, so the new responsibility was no surprise. I was still responsible for coordinating and running any recovery mission if it happened. Until then, I was the GOO of the North! As with the first day of any deployment, I began to immerse myself into the battle rhythm and to tune my body clock to it. One of the more difficult aspects is getting your body synched with the battle rhythm so it would feel like a "normal day." In the days to come, my rhythm would consist of getting up, working out, eating, going to work, working out again, eating, and completing the twelve-hour shift on duty. 5th Special Forces had converted one of the smaller palace buildings into a rather nice gym. We were working twelve-hour shifts, and I was partnered with SFC Salvador (Sal) Cruz. Salvador normally worked in the operations section of the group staff. Basically he was a placeholder, that is, he covered my desk during the night and knew where to get me if an emergency occurred. He had no training or background in personnel recovery, so he mostly tracked what the forces were doing in the north.

I was on from noon to midnight, and he worked the graveyard, midnight to noon. Once my shift was finished and he took over, I had to return to help build the slides for the nightly briefing. During this process on the first night, I heard explosions off in the distance, another rocket or mortar attack. Two attacks already! You would think we were in a war zone or something.

On January 29, my second true day on the job, I started to help with a personnel recovery mission. An OH-58 scout helicopter had crashed into a river, and we were told that our Navy SEALs might have to help in the recovery of the pilots and their equipment. The Army engineers were assessing the site, where the debris was spread over the muddy bottom of the river and would probably need help from the SEALS to recover the bodies. I continued to monitor the situation, passing to the SEAL liaison in the JOC the information that they might get a call from the Army for assistance.

Working in the JOC that day, I could hear explosions in the distance. The Baghdad International Airport (BIAP) was being mortared. I also learned that I was being given the additional duty of serving as the liaison between our JOC (Combined, Joint Special Operations Task Force-Arabian Peninsula or CJSOTF-AP) and our 3rd Battalion Headquarters up in Mosul. One thing about a heavy workload, it helps the shift to go by faster.

Before the day was over, I also attended my first Friday Bar-B-Q in our compound. All of our sections took turns running the Bar-B-Q down at the MWR building. This was a tradition started by the 5th Special Forces and we would continue it. At least it was something different for lunch. The MWR building supposedly had been a "party hut" for Saddam's sons when they were in the complex. Now there was a small store, a room with computers and Internet access, a room with a big-screen TV and couches, and a central area with two play stations, a pool table, and a ping-pong table. This was definitely an improvement over the MWR tent we had back in Irbil.

One of my responsibilities was to update the commander's situation map in his office. He was located across the street from us in another small building that had been used by one of Saddam's sons.

In fact, his office was the bedroom, a large marble-floored room. To make our life a little easier, our procurement NCO obtained a computer, which was set up in an old bathroom next to the JOC. This was so we could check our e-mail and still be close by if something happened.

I tried to use what laundry facilities we had, but the washers and dryers were very small, and it took all day to do a load of laundry. When I experienced my first big thunderstorm, which poured down huge raindrops but didn't last long, I was relieved to see that our compound didn't go under water like our old camp in Irbil.

In the beginning, the strain of doing multiple jobs and getting used to the rhythm played havoc with my body. I was very tired and seemed to operate in a daze. Eventually everything worked out as our procedures became more fluid and the staff learned to work together.

A story we had heard prior to arriving in Iraq concerned several young soldiers, who had on patrol, discovered several bundles containing hundreds of thousand dollars (in US currency) in one of Saddam's old palace complexes. From the story, they said they had found the money in some small vacation huts. That story made me think, were they talking about the very same complex we were based on, seeing there were small, vacation-like huts on the compound. Talk about a moral dilemma! How would you act if you found nearly a half a million dollars? The soldiers took the money and tried to smuggle it out of Iraq, but one had a guilty conscience and went to the authorities. The officials were able to secure most of the booty the soldiers had taken; the rest was thrown down a sewer system outside of the complex.

After I had gotten myself settled in, which took about a week or so, I began to explore the RPC compound. We lived in the central portion of the palace complex, which was approximately three miles long by about a mile or so wide. A thick fifteen-foot wall surrounded the whole central core. Within the complex were several outbuildings as well as the palace itself. Our area was on the eastern side. The main entrance we used was actually a portion of the wall that had been blown open during the fighting for Baghdad. This allowed access to the main road on the outside of the walls. Immediately past the gate were some smaller buildings that were used by our perimeter defense forces, provided by the 82nd Airborne. Following the road in, you drove over a small canal that fed water to a man-made fishing pond. Built out in the middle of the pond on concrete stilts was a large, log-cabin-type house, which we called the "Tiki Hut." The construction of this house had not been completed, but it had marble floors and several large rooms.

Around the edge of the fishpond were several Bar-B-Q buildings and smaller huts, as well as the converted Gym, which used to be a guesthouse. Rubber mats had been placed on the marble floors to protect them from our gym equipment. The gym was broken into sections. Right off the entrance way was a room used for sit-ups and crunches, the marble floor covered with mats. The central entrance room served as our aerobics training room, the room to the immediate right held Nautilus equipment, and the main room to the left was full of free weights. The aerobics equipment consisted of two treadmills, one working and one broken stair climber, and two stationary bikes. The dumb-bells and smaller hand weights were set up in a smaller room off the main workout room. The gym over-looked the Tiki Hut and the man-made fishpond.

Continuing along the perimeter road, basically heading north, you came to the converted MWR building that sat across the canal. The canal and fishpond used to be stocked with fish, but something had happened to the water and whatever it was had killed them all. (We believed detergent had been poured into it.) The perimeter road then turned west and followed the wall for about a half a mile to its intersection with the road that led to our area on the left. Continuing west after the intersection, the road followed both the wall and a large pond for another mile or so until it came to the main entrance of the RPC. This was a large, four-way intersection with the main complex gate that opened to the outside on the right, the gate to the palace to your front, and the perimeter road to the left. The entrance gate had two gatehouses, with a main gate next to the road to the airport and a second gatehouse near our central area. There was a second perimeter road and wall that circled the whole complex as an outer ring.

The main palace itself sat on top of what I believe was a man-made hill that rose about 400 feet into the air. It was rumored that Saddam had built the palace for his wife, but we never really found out if that was true. There was an arched gatehouse flanked by a tower on each side that guarded the palace entrance. Just inside was a smaller complex of buildings that included a swimming pool. The road went up around the hill to the palace itself. Compared to Saddam's other palaces, this one was small, but it was very ornate on the inside. The palace had been occupied by one of 5th Group's battalions, and it served as their JOC. As part of getting to know everyone, I made a trip up there and was given the ten-cent tour by one of the 5th Group guys. Nice place, for a small retreat next to the airport. Gold fixtures in the bathrooms, gilded woodwork along the walls, marble floors and staircases, and large chandeliers in the central rooms. To coin a phrase from Mel Brooks in *History of the World, Part 1*, "It's good to be the king!" 5th Group even used a small pool that Saddam had built, which had recently been repaired after being hit by a rocket.

From the top of this hill, you could see for miles around the complex, depending on how clear or how smoggy the air was. The view included the airport off to the northeast and one of Saddam's palaces (Abu Gharib Palace) under construction to the southeast. For me, this hill was not only a good place to look at the surrounding area, but also, if you walked up and down the hill, a good spot for physical training. This had to have been a man-made hill, seeing the surrounding area for miles was flat, and this hill was just too perfectly situated and formed.

Continuing south on the perimeter road, which still followed the pond for the most part, you came to a large hotel, which we called the "Eagles Nest." This was probably where dignitaries and VIPs stayed when they came to visit Saddam. It was a large structure, about five stories tall with a corner tower. It was now being used to house an air defense unit and some other American support units.

The perimeter road turned back toward the east and continued toward our entrance. Along this part of the road, there was another swimming pool mini-complex that was being used as a headquarters for one of the perimeter defense companies. They had occupied the pool house and used it as a makeshift barracks and headquarters. The pool itself was used for storage. On the right side were some abandoned quad 14.5mm anti-aircraft guns, which were rusting peacefully. 5th Special Forces Group had built a small range complex where we could conduct marksmanship drills and rehearsals for all of the units on RPC. The road came to the pond once more and then reached our JOC area. Just past our area was another, smaller crossroad where our support center and supply points were established. In between our JOC and the support area, there had once been a large vineyard, but it had been badly neglected. Finally, the perimeter road intersected with the entrance road, completing the loop.

The thing that I found most amazing within our compound was how green everything was. There were palm trees, other trees, and thick bushes that nearly covered the whole central crossroad near our sleeping area. At night when you walked down the road, the arched branches made it look as if you were inside a tunnel. With the water and irrigation canals, this place was probably one of the most fertile spots in the city of Baghdad. Seeing the palace and the new construction, I began to understand where all of the country's money had gone, and it wasn't to the Iraqi people.

As for the personnel on the staff, we became accustomed to our battle rhythm, and everything began to flow. Though we had a dining hall, locals cooked and prepared our meals. Most of our food was local fare, just like the food we had eaten up in Irbil. Dinner was beef or chicken kebobs, some of it either burned or undercooked. Diced vegetable salad was made mostly with cucumbers and tomatoes in a type of vinegary sauce. There were three televisions in the dining hall so we could watch the news and sports while we ate. The locals only cooked breakfast and dinner, while lunch was the trusted MRE, which I normally avoided, sticking to fruit instead.

The small hunting palace occupied by the 5th SFG
on the RPC complex.

The lion cage which held Uday's pet tigers on the RPC complex.

The "Tiki Hut" on the RPC complex, one of many
elaborate buildings used by Saddam and his sons.

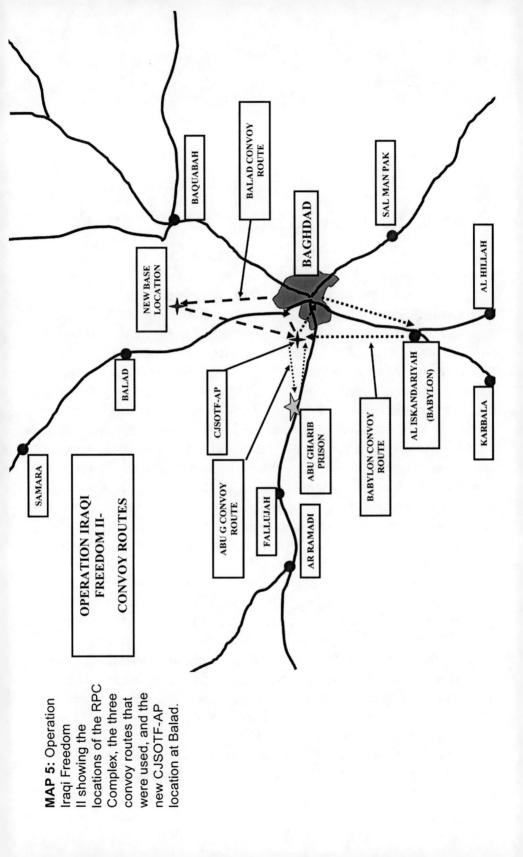

MAP 5: Operation Iraqi Freedom II showing the locations of the RPC Complex, the three convoy routes that were used, and the new CJSOTF-AP location at Balad.

OPERATION IRAQI FREEDOM II-CONVOY ROUTES

SAMARA

BALAD

NEW BASE LOCATION

BAQUABAH

BALAD CONVOY ROUTE

BAGHDAD

SAL MAN PAK

AL HILLAH

CJSOTF-AP

ABU G CONVOY ROUTE

FALLUJAH

ABU GHARIB PRISON

AR RAMADI

BABYLON CONVOY ROUTE

AL ISKANDARIYAH (BABYLON)

KARBALA

CHAPTER 13

MULTI-TASKED AND CONVOY OPERATIONS

During Operation Iraqi Freedom, never had so few been led by so many. This time it was the other way around, and staff members had to become multi-tasked experts. I had to juggle the personnel recovery and non-conventional assisted recovery operations, as well as being a liaison to the 3rd battalion up north and ground operations officer. In early February, I added another hat to my growing responsibilities. With the frequent mortar and rocket attacks against us and the Baghdad Airport, we had to be prepared for causalities. Sometimes our camp was attacked directly, and other times we were hit because the intended target was the airport, and the rockets fell short. With my medical background, I became one of the few triage officers assigned to respond to an attack site to assist our limited medical personnel in evaluating and treating causalities. I was issued a small medical bag with enough bandages so that I could render first aid if something went bad.

We not only rehearsed our battle drills for events within the JOC, but we also had to rehearse what to do if ground forces or indirect fire either attacked the camp. We kept our helmets and body armor on a "coat rack" we had built in our radio/break room. If we were attacked, we would grab and put on our gear, and then return to our workstations. If insurgents trying to enter the complex attacked us, we had a bunker at one end of the building and a defensive wall on the other side, which us old gunfighters would man.

Over on the Baghdad Airfield was a dining facility called the "Bob Hope" in honor of that legendary comedian and supporter of the American military. This was one of the best dining facilities in the region, while our dining facility was considered one of the worst. To help alleviate some of the stress of normal day-to-day activities, some of the guys would drive over to the Bob Hope and bring us back real food, especially real vegetables. Now and then, I tried to get over there myself and eat in the dining facility, then bring back several meals for the staff on duty. Food is always important to a soldier, and this place was the best. There, I could enjoy salad with a bowl of clam chowder soup, dishes that were never seen in our dining facility.

In addition to the challenge of getting better food, showering was also a problem. In the section of the camp where we lived, there were only two working showers. These shower buildings had only four showers in each, and one was reserved strictly for the female soldiers. So there were a total of six shower stalls for the males and two for the females supporting roughly three hundred people. Depending on when you decided to take your shower, there might or might not be any hot water. This was especially difficult for us working the night shift, because our morning shower was the rest of the camp's evening shower. Half of the time, I took cold showers. Being from upstate New York, I'm used to dealing with the cold, except when it comes to showers. We also had to conserve the limited water. So you got into the shower, stripped down, got wet, turned off the water and soaped up, and then turned the water back on to rinse off. There was not enough water for a long shower; we had perhaps three minutes at most.

During the first week of February, I was getting up early to help train the headquarters personnel on the local range. Baghdad Airport received another rocket attack, but most of the younger soldiers just thought it was a drill and didn't take it seriously. The airfield would be hit two more times during the week. I felt bad for the folks stationed over there, but in a self-centered sort of way, figured better them then me.

For the most part, nothing really exciting was happening in the JOC. The Army and our SEALS were able to recover most of the crashed helicopter and its equipment, but they were still looking for the remains of the pilots. I coordinated with our units, as well as partnering with other units to develop courses of action to find these pilots. One way or another, they would be found and returned to our control.

The situation in the JOC continued to be stressful. Without a major crisis to work on, some of the senior officers seemed to go out of their way to find or cause a crisis. I had been briefing the commander on operations in northern Iraq for several days, when they noticed that the slides that I was using were designed differently from those used by the others. So I was ordered to change my slides in order to match everyone else's. Power Point can be a great tool, but it shouldn't be the driving force behind the briefings.

On February 5, our headquarters troops went to a training range away from camp. I remained back in the JOC since there was no one to cover my position. During the day, we received radio updates on their status, and then we received a situation report and a SALUTE (Size, Activity, Location, Uniform/Unit, Time and Equipment) report as well. During the range firing, our troops went to investigate a nearby explosion. They found two Iraqis with explosives and detained them on suspicion of planting improvised explosive devices. The two were turned over to the military police, and later found that they were using the explosives to knock bricks out of old buildings so they could use them to build their house. They were released and allowed to go back home.

About this time, I was moved from the noon-to-midnight shift to the graveyard. Once again, I had to go through the rhythm change and get my body used to the new time schedule. This proved to be difficult, with sleep being the greatest challenge. I am a light sleeper, and the simplest of noises will wake me. With the enemy rocket attacks, I slept with "one ear open" for the sound of a rocket or a warning siren. Added to this were the constant over-flights of aircraft, the Explosive Ordinance Disposal (EOD) technicians blowing up captured munitions, and the continuing construction of the camp. The other thing about sleeping when deployed is a situation I call, "Field Dreams." These are strange dreams you have while in the field. Mostly brought on by the exhaustion, stress, and the events of the day and combined with our anti-malaria medication, can be quite vivid. For me, most of these dreams involved battles or fighting, and sometimes they repeated what had happened in the JOC during the day.

Situated right next to our JOC was a small room that serves as our radio room, break room, and coat rack. There was a small area with some toilets right off of this small room. Now and then when I went in to get some coffee, I talked with our radio operators. One day as I was sipping my coffee, I was listening to a young soldier shooting his mouth off about how he was going to go out on convoys, going to kill some Iraqis, real "hooah-hooah" talk. I understand the exuberance of youth, the hyped-up look at the world. I was the same way as a young Ranger, ready to prove myself in battle. However, these were our communication soldiers, not infantry or any other combat arms skilled troops. If he was supposed to engage the enemy, something had gone very wrong. I didn't say anything, but just listened for a bit before returning to my desk.

As our staff came from different branches and groups, from time to time I ran into officers who had been my students back in the qualification course at Fort Bragg. Now they were majors in the Special Forces, and we were all working together.

The high point of my day was talking to my wife via the Internet. Using MSN Messenger, we were able to talk back and forth in real time. It always amazes me how far we have come technologically. Now I can communicate with my wife in Colorado from Iraq in real time, typing messages and answering one another. It helped to close the distance between us and ease the burden of loneliness.

Even though it was nice having dull days, which meant no one was getting hurt, the calm wasn't going to last for much longer. A sandstorm hit while I was trying to sleep, and the tent slapping against my head awakened me. Sleeping in a corner can be nice, except for when the tent hits you from two sides. Just as I had seen before, the sky turned to orange as the strong winds and sand hit. After making sure the tent was secured, I moved my cot as far from the sides as I could and went back to sleep.

The insurgents were becoming bolder in their attacks. Baghdad Airport continued to be hit by rockets, and a patrol near our camp was attacked. On February 15, the insurgents launched a well-executed attack on a police station, which included blocking and support positions and assault teams. Some of us speculated that this may have been a "confidence target," and we should expect to see more enemy activity soon. Little did I realize how true that would become.

It didn't take much to make one happy in Iraq. A warm shower was considered a good day; speaking to my wife and daughter via the Internet was a great day. And it seemed that things were going to get better. We were told that the engineers were going to construct two-man trailers for us to live in, no more living in open bay tents. Additionally, we were going to switch to three eight-hour shifts because Salvador and I would have a third person to work with us.

Excitement broke up our dull routine on the night of February 20, when a call for a medic was received in our radio room. A soldier had been shot in the foot at the entrance to the guard shack. I grabbed my aid bag and ran down to the gate as he was being loaded into a waiting truck. The kid was sitting there, shivering from the shock with his bandaged foot up in the air. His eyes were a mixture of shock and fear, and no one was directly attending to him. One of his medics was already there so there was no need for me to get in the way. Come to find out, the sergeant of the watch had somehow accidentally discharged his M16 as he walked past the kid in the guard shack. I guess his trigger caught on something, and unfortunately the safety was off on his rifle. The bullet barely nicked this kid's big toe, but they were making a big deal out of it. The kid probably received a purple heart for the wound.

The understanding that everyone who was working in the Iraqi theater of operations was undermanned and over tasked didn't fully sink in until I had a meeting with some of the other Personnel Recovery planners. I found out that of the approximately twenty-seven different rescue coordination cells stretched across Iraq, there were only two of us who had gone through all of the JPRA's training courses to be operations managers. All of the soldiers manning the Special Operations Rescue Coordination Center (SOCRCC) at this time were part-timers. The main officer was primarily the flight safety officer, and his two assistants were life support/survival specialists.

On February 26, I helped the Army RCC when another OH-58 scout helicopter crashed into a river. I believe the pilots were using the river as a guide to help them navigate, and unfortunately they crashed into the water this time with no survivors. Our SEALs were heading out to give them a hand in searching the river bottom for wreckage and the bodies.

My first convoy operation was with our Civil Affairs personnel, who were driving to the main CPA (Coalition Provisional Authority) complex where the United Nations was working with the Iraqis to form a new government. On this mission, I served as a machine gunner, bringing an M249 Squad Automatic Weapon (SAW). I rode in the rear Hummer, providing the rear security for our small convoy. We drove out of our compound and followed the main road toward the city. The convoy moved as fast as the Hummers could go to make it difficult for an improvised explosive devise (IED), or homemade bomb, to hit us. The road we followed headed east and ran next to another palace that Saddam had been building. The only civilians I saw were on the rooftops of the houses on the other side of the wall that ran next to our camp for about a mile. Then the ground opened up, and you could see on either side of the road. This palace, known as the Abu Gharib Palace, was located about five miles from our camp. It was abandoned, the heavy construction equipment sitting idle and gathering dust. After the palace, the road headed north toward the airfield, which was on the left side and protected by a high wall. Our road finally connected with the main highway that ran from the airport to the city of Baghdad.

Once we reached the main highway, we stopped our trucks and loaded our weapons. The road we had just driven was considered relatively safe, but now we were heading into a high-threat area. After making sure my weapon was on safe, I found a comfortable sitting position and began scanning the six-lane highway, which had three lanes on each side divided by an open median. There had been trees and bushes in the median, but they had been destroyed or burned to make it difficult for the insurgents to hide IEDs. The road was very busy, especially after we merged with the regular civilian traffic. I stayed alert, because there were a lot of places to scan, from bridges to civilian vehicles heading toward us. The hardest part of fighting insurgents is that you never know who is a bad guy and who is simply a civilian going about his or her business. It only took us about fifteen minutes to reach the outskirts of the city, and more buildings were crowding the road. Now, not only did I have to scan to my left, right, and rear, but up as well. When you are wearing body armor and a helmet, scanning can be a challenge, a complication known as turtle syndrome. There wasn't a lot of space between the bottom of my helmet and my armor vest, so I had to swivel my head and shoulders a lot to cover my area of responsibility.

Our convoy arrived at a major checkpoint leading into the "Green Zone," an area, which was believed to be safe, where all of the U.N. delegates worked. We cleared our weapons, which meant we were supposed to remove our ammunition and make sure there were no bullets in the chamber. I didn't feel comfortable doing this, but it was the rule. The convoy proceeded into the Green Zone and passed a monument to the Iraqi Military as we drove into the CPA complex. The complex was located in one of Saddam's large palaces and government buildings in the center of the city near the river. After parking our vehicles in a large lot, we walked into the main CPA compound. After U.S. Marines screened us, checked our identities, and had our weapons inspected to be sure they were clear, we entered the compound. There were a lot of people here, including contractors, U.N. workers, and soldiers. Our convoy transported a Colonel back over to his area, and he allowed us to store our armor and equipment in his room while we waited, although we kept our weapons with us. After he attended to some meetings, we were to return him to the RPC compound. He lived in a three-man trailer that was very nice. As we walked to the main building, we passed a swimming pool. Boy did these guys have it made! We ate in the CPA building, and I enjoyed a real cheeseburger and a hot dog.

We divided up into smaller teams, and I went with the group who had to change out their cell phones. Instead of taking our truck, we rode in a contracted SUV to the conference center next to the Al Rashid Hotel. The Green Zone was completely enclosed by a wall, but I still didn't feel safe, especially looking up into the tall apartment buildings next to the zone. As the group conducted their business, I stood off to the side and observed the comings and goings of people.

There were a wide variety of cultures represented here. A group of Sheiks went by in their traditional robes and turbans, talking with Iraqi men in business suits and ties. Some of the women were in the traditional flowing robes while others wore western-style clothing. The conference center was very modern, and the cell phones were being contracted from MCI. Once the cell phone exchange was completed, we returned to the CPA complex where a surprise was waiting for us. The Colonel we had escorted here was going to take us over to see Uday's palace, which was just down the road.

We walked for about a quarter mile to the palace entrance. Across from the entrance was a corner store and Internet cafe, and we went inside for a soda break. The temperatures were now in the low 80s, so I enjoyed a Pepsi.

The palace itself was huge, towering five stories up and topped with a large dome that stood another five stories. The colonel led us into a side entryway, and we made our way through the corridors. The halls were now musty and choked with dust, with rubble piled everywhere. There wasn't much left inside. The majority of the furniture had been looted right after the fall of the city the year before. I recall watching the news show Iraqis carting everything off following the fall of Baghdad, including a grand piano! We looked inside a couple of the large rooms, which had murals painted on the walls. The murals reminded me of the castles I had visited in Germany, stretching from the floor to the ceiling.

We looked out into the main entrance at a large chandelier, which had to have been about twenty feet tall and twenty feet wide. It was hanging at an odd angle from the top of the carport arch. The colonel then led us to a corner of the building that had been heavily damaged by the bombing. We had to be careful for there was no electricity or lights inside this palace. Most of the top floor had collapsed down to the bottom floor where we were standing. Then the colonel shocked me by telling us this was nothing but a facade. The whole palace, costing roughly twenty million dollars and taking about ten years to build, was erected solely to hide the bunker complex underneath!

The colonel led us to a stairway that led down under the palace, where it was very dark and musty smelling. He told us to make sure the large, metal doors stayed open so we wouldn't become locked inside. The bunker was very large and went down for about three stories underground. We had to use our flashlights to see. Water was dripping from the ceilings into the hallways and the carpets were soaked, giving off a humid and mildewed smell. This bunker was similar to the cold war bunkers that had been built in the United States. Saddam could run his government and the war from down there, safe from any conventional bombing attack. We looked into a large conference room furnished with a large, U-shaped oak table where the government would have held meetings. The power plant to run the bunker was from Siemens in Germany. All of the equipment appeared to be in perfect working order, and it wouldn't have taken much to get it to work. I wondered why we didn't occupy it and use this place to run our operations. We checked out some of the living apartments, which were certainly better than our tents. It was an impressive thing to have seen, looking like something from Germany at the end of the Second World War.

The colonel then led us up another stairwell, and we climbed up into the large dome on top of the palace. The dome was constructed out of wood, as was most of the palace. Instead of thick blocks of stone and marble, the sides of the palace were wood with a thin layer of brick and marble made to look like thick blocks. The palace construction began in 1984 and had been completed in 2001. It hadn't been up long before we helped to renovate it during one of our night strikes. Up in the dome, you could see two holes, one on top of the other, just off center by a little bit. These were the entrance holes for two JDAMs (Joint Directed Attack Munitions, a GPS Guided Bomb), which had entered the dome and passed through to the floor below. There the bombs detonated and caused all of the destruction we had seen. It was still a sight to see, the large wooden dome and the damage caused by those bombs. There were still looters taking items out of the palace, and we didn't interfere with them as we returned to the CPA complex.

The trip back to camp was uneventful, and I finished my shift and went to sleep. However, I wasn't destined to sleep well that night. Every time I got close to drifting off, someone opened the door and looked inside, the light streaming in from the outside. They were trying to find someone, but I didn't know which tent he was in. Then the insurgents fired a rocket at our camp. They were close enough that I heard the "pop" of the rocket being fired and then the large explosion that shook the tent when it hit. The rocket had landed about 800 feet from my tent. I looked outside in time to see the black plume of smoke from the explosion rolling over our wall. Fortunately, the rocket had landed just outside of the perimeter wall, causing no damage.

Visiting the contracted barber who had set up shop in one of the small buildings on the edge of the pond was an adventure. He was of Hindu descent and a good barber. It was his massage afterward that everyone talked about. He massaged your head and neck, doing some pounding on your head. He also cracked your ears, and then to my horror, cracked your neck! I have a rather thick neck to begin with, and having some stranger crack it made me very nervous. I survived, but made a note never to allow him to do that again.

One night, we were alerted that we might have had a vehicle bomb arrive at our camp entrance. The security dogs that sniffed for bombs had detected explosives, and the driver and his truck was secured. After a thorough check, the truck was found to be clean and the driver was released. Better safe then sorry.

I began to feel like a yo-yo when on March 1, I was moved once more to the day shift. The promised third person had not arrived yet, so it was still just Sal and myself. Due to my briefing skills, they wanted me for the main CUB (Commander's Update Brief). In order for me to make the switch, I had to stay up and run an eighteen-hour shift instead of my normal twelve. However on the plus side, I moved into the new trailer that I would be sharing with Sal. It was a small, prefab box that was about eight feet wide by twenty feet long. It had a single air conditioner. I chose to sleep on the side next to it. We had a wooden slat bed with a foam mattress. This was great, seeing that the air mattress that I had brought with me had developed a leak. We both had a small wall locker, about a foot wide, in which we could store our things. I brought the white plastic table with me, and set it up next to my bed, which nearly fit completely across the width of the trailer. The trailers reminded me of a prison, with rows of these living quarters in our compound. But despite this, the move was a big improvement because the trailer was nearly soundproof.

Perhaps I could finally catch some sleep without being disturbed by outside noises.

Every night there was a commander's call at which every commander in Iraq spoke to the CJTF-7 commander on the radio and briefed him on what his unit had done and what it expected to do. Our Commander, Colonel Repass, who left our JOC and went to his office to brief General Sanchez or his operations officer on the CJSOTF's situation for the past twenty-fours hours and what we expected to do in the next twenty-four hours, conducted the large conference call over the radio just after our Update Brief. I normally listened in on my radio headset. This way, I was able to stay abreast of what was going on with the other units across Iraq. The Briefing involved Brigade and Division-level commanders, including coalition forces. They briefed on how many patrols they had conducted, how many engagements there had been, and how many detainees and equipment had been captured. Because we had just arrived in sector, our JOC briefings were rather short.

Laundry continued to be a challenge for me. There were some washers and dryers next door to the JOC building. I would bring my laundry with me, but these were small washers, so it wasn't a large load. The challenge was not knowing if you would be shocked getting your laundry out of the washer. I guess the machines had grounding problems. Now and then when I grabbed my wet laundry, I would receive shock that tingled my arm!

On March 2, I participated in a convoy escort mission with the headquarters troops I had been training. We were going to escort the commander, Colonel Repass, to the CPA complex, and escort him back to the camp after his meeting. We would be using two modified HWMMV (Humvees) with all of the doors removed and extra gun mounts in the passenger door spaces. These were regular Hummers and were not armored in any way. I would man the large, M2 .50-caliber machine gun in the rear vehicle. The two passenger positions were armed with the M240 machine guns. Basically, we looked like a porcupine, with two machine gun barrels poking out of the sides and my machine gun on top. We all attended the convoy briefing, going over the route, the threat, and our procedures. The radio frequencies and call signs were reviewed, and then we did a final check of the vehicle and all of its equipment.

After getting my armor vest on, I climbed up on top of the vehicle and climbed inside my turret. I first checked my machine gun, making sure the headspace and timing were set correctly. I then checked my ammunition and the other cans of ammunition stored next to me. Additionally, I checked the hand grenade and smoke grenade taped to the weapons mount inside of their cans. I also checked to see if the turret moved smoothly and didn't stick. The last thing I put on was my helmet, and I did this only as we were starting our engines. It gets rather warm up in the turret. To help with comfort and to keep the sweat out of my eyes, I had a handkerchief tied over my head, with my helmet sitting on top of it. Once everyone was ready, we moved over to pick up the commander in his vehicle. We took the same route as I had traveled earlier with the civil affairs folks. One of the challenges of manning the M2 machine gun is that it has no safety other than your finger. It has a butterfly trigger in between its two grips. I rotated my hand behind the trigger so it wouldn't depress and fire by mistake. Since a round fired by this machine gun can travel nearly five miles, I was extra careful to make sure it stayed safe.

I explained to some of the other guys that we practiced "peace through superior intimidation" to insure our safety. Granted we had no extra armor protection, but without it, we could travel fast. Anyone looking at our convoy would see at least two large and four medium-sized machine guns scanning their sectors. The M2 is an intimidating-looking weapon, being so big. As the rear gunner, I made sure that our rear sector was safe and that no vehicle came too close. We tried to keep a safety buffer of twenty-five feet around our vehicles. If an Iraqi came too close, I oriented toward him and gave him a hand gesture. If the driver failed to heed my warning, I then lowered the barrel so it was pointing at him. Normally, this conveyed that I meant business, and he would back off. Later we were told we shouldn't aim our weapons at people, because we might be hurting their feelings. Personally, I was more concerned with keeping my troops and myself safe than with worrying about their feelings. Iraqis understand power, and we exercised our force projection by using our weapons.

With the ever-increasing temperatures, the cool breeze on top of the turret was refreshing. The colonel arrived at the CPA compound without incident. We went back to our compound and then returned a few hours later. We were warned to be on the alert, the intelligence folks believing that because it was an Iraqi holiday, there might be some bombing attacks. While waiting for the commander to finish up, we heard a car bomb going off nearby. Other than that explosion, all was quiet, and we got our commander back to the camp safe and sound.

As we drove back to our camp on the airport highway, I saw an SUV speeding up toward us. Calling out that we had a fast mover coming up behind us, I oriented my turret toward them. They kept coming toward me, so I gave them the hand gesture to back off, which they ignored. The truck had closed to within fifteen feet of my vehicle when I lowered the machine gun toward them. That seemed to get their attention as every piece of U.N. identification, flag, and orange marking panel came out to identify themselves as friendlies. These were contract workers who hadn't been briefed on how to approach U.S. convoys, and they received a quick lesson from me. After making sure everything was cleared, I waved them to pass us, and they waved back with a relieved look on their faces.

On March 5, I went on a convoy to escort our supply personnel up to the main camp on the Balad airfield, about a two-hour drive north of Baghdad. We went through our pre-convoy checks and briefings, then mounted up and prepared to move. I would be riding in the rear vehicle. I guess they liked the way I kept the traffic away. Our convoy took the normal route toward the CPA, then turned left at the monument and headed out of the Green Zone. What an impressive site to see! Two M1A1 Abrams tanks were sitting in the road, watching over the gate. We waited our turn to exit, and I kept a watchful eye with my machine gun safely pointed skyward. I watched the soldiers manning the gate go through the security checks of all of the people walking into the zone, as well as all of the drivers. When we pulled out, my senses picked up a notch as we were now completely on our own and out in potentially hostile territory. We had to follow the main road through the city to reach the highway that ran north. For the most part, the city of Baghdad looked to be in OK shape, although some of the government buildings had been destroyed. As we passed the Baghdad Train Station, we saw another palace that had been under construction. Even the "Mad King" of Bavaria, King Ludwig II, built only four castles/palaces and didn't spend that much time in them. There were at least thirteen palaces around Baghdad alone. Saddam must have spent little to no time in most of them, but he built them anyway.

Driving through the city of Baghdad was a challenge, more because of the local drivers than any real threat. There was no traffic control, and all of the cars zoomed around without a care. There was no way we could maintain a buffer zone around our vehicles, so we did the best we could, keeping a sharp lookout. I scanned every vehicle, and looked into everyone's eyes to see if I could detect any hostile intent. For the most part, these were regular Iraqi civilians just trying to drive their vehicles through the city traffic. Driving through Baghdad compared to driving in Naples, Italy, during rush hour. Sometimes we were forced to stop, but we tried to go around obstructions and to keep moving. I had seen a CNN report from Christine Amapour in which she criticized how the military drove in the city. I guess she didn't realize that if we were to sit in traffic without moving, we would be sitting ducks. Our security was in moving and never being caught sitting still.

After braving the city, we drove under an arch and out on to the main highway that ran toward the north. Just outside of the city had to be the foulest smelling section of the country I had passed through. On one side of the road was a refinery, and across the road from it was a garbage dump that was almost three miles long by a mile deep. I was glad that we drove quickly through this section. Once past the dump, the terrain was mostly open, flat land, with some houses now and then. There were small refreshment, fuel, and cooking stands on the sides of the road.

After traveling for about twenty minutes, we passed Baji, which was also a military camp. It had once been a military complex for the Iraqi Army, but now it was under our control. As we drove by, I looked inside the complex to see row upon row of Soviet-made tanks and armored personnel carriers. This was a collection point for military weapons and vehicles that would eventually be turned over to the new Iraqi Army. I found it impressive to see all of these tanks and vehicles lined up in neat rows.

Along the side of the road from time to time were the burned and rusted hulks of destroyed tanks and fighting vehicles. Now and then, you saw an artillery piece with no wheels or a missile with no launcher. Even on a bright sunny day, there was a lot of dust. For the most part, the terrain was flat with very little change in elevation and no hills to speak of. We passed a major fueling area, and the ground in and around it was covered in black oily residue. From my perch on top of the truck, I had a good view of the area as I swung back and forth, keeping an eye on my sector. The majority of the Iraqis who drove on the roads had already learned to keep their distance from convoys, so my job was fairly easy. Every time we passed a large truck, I scanned its back for any sign of a threat. There is never a dull moment on a convoy; you're always scanning and looking. As we got closer to Balad, the sky became overcast and the temperature dropped to a more comfortable level.

We finally arrived at the main camp, known as LSA Anaconda, on the Balad airfield. This was a major logistical support base for the northern region of Iraq. We drove over to where the supply people would conduct their business, and we took a little break. But soon 1SG Brad Conner, the convoy commander this day did a quick after-action review with us so we could improve our convoy procedures. As we hung out for a while, I was amazed by all of the civilian vehicles I saw. Over in the CPA, all major officers or other important persons had their own vehicles, usually high-end SUVs. As we sat there on Balad, we even watched a civilian Hummer pull in. It always completely amazes me how much money the U.S. dumps into an operation, while we the war fighters have to make do.

We drove over to a dining facility to have lunch. I am still amazed at the difference in mentality between conventional personnel and us in special operations. There was a soldier standing outside to make sure our weapons were clear and there was no dust on our desert boots. I understood the need for cleanliness; however sometimes this just seemed a little silly to me. Weapon safety I strongly believed in, but dusty boots? We received our normal funny looks for our sterile uniforms and different hats. The food was good, and we took a group photo before we left.

After waiting for five hours, we drove over to where the new camp would be located on Balad. With the drawing down of forces, our current compound was to be turned over to the Iraqis and we'd have to move the whole CJSOTF up here to Balad. On the way over, we passed a line of seven rusting Mig-27 fighter-bombers that had been dragged off the airfield into this empty lot. The once mighty Iraqi Air Force had been reduced to a couple of rusting aircraft that were being used for birds' nests. There is not much to say about our new camp location. It was in a large open area next to some aircraft hangar/bunkers that had been hit during the bombing campaign. These were large structures, each capable of holding two to four fighters inside a reinforced concrete dome with steel doors. They took a punishment though, and a few had large gaping holes through the top.

We switched out for the return trip, with me riding in the lead truck this time. As we drove along the very rutted and bumpy road, a rock bounced up and struck my face. Luckily I was wearing ballistic glasses that protected my eyes, and the rock struck just below my glasses on my cheek. I thought I had been shot from the force of the impact. I checked my face to see that everything was where it was suppose to be and there was no blood. Lucky for me I have a tough face. I think I only bruised my cheek. The rest of the trip was uneventful, and I finished out my day in the JOC.

The convoy crew in Balad after eating lunch and getting ready to return to Baghdad.

Conducting the first convoy to the CPA complex in Baghdad.

Uday's Palace complex next to the CPA Complex. The command bunker was built underneath it.

Inside of the dome to Uday's palace, showing the destruction caused by US bombings.

Another view, looking out of the dome at the
destruction of Uday's Palace.

Conducting pre-mission checks prior to departing on a
convoy operation.

CHAPTER 14

ABU GHARIB PRISON, THE CONFERENCE, AND THE CONVOY TO BABYLON

Ask the average person on the street for the one thing he or she remembers from the military operations in Iraq, most would cite the scandal that occurred at the Abu Gharib Prison. The prison, which we referred to as "Abu G," was notorious from its use under Saddam's regime by his personal secret police. I saw this place on March 6 when we escorted a detainee over to the prison and turned him over to the military police. We went through our normal pre-convoy briefing and checks, and then mounted up and headed over to our holding facility. There, the detainee was escorted out by two of our soldiers who would ride with him to the prison as guards. They carried his paperwork and personal effects, and we loaded him into a Hummer and secured him. I was in the rear vehicle as our convoy moved out. This time, we took a different route, exiting through the camp's main gate. We passed through our inner perimeter wall and stopped just before the outer gate. Here, we loaded our weapons and took up our sectors of responsibility. The outer gate was manned by local Iraqi security forces who watched us drive through. We followed another two-lane road that ran from the airport to the main east-west highway, which we took.

The hunting palace sat majestically on its hill, overlooking the whole area bordering the RPC. We passed several farms where families were working in the fields or bringing in their livestock for the night. There was little or no traffic on our road, so we had an easy drive until we reached the main highway. Once there, we had to contend with the extra volume of traffic that was common on highways. The terrain over here was flat with farms dotting the landscape. We had to be careful with bridges, and there were more of them along this route. Normally, as we drove under a bridge, we quickly changed lanes in case someone tried to drop a grenade. As we passed underneath, I scanned the top of the bridge to look for any possible troublemakers. Everything was going fine until we passed under the last bridge, just before the prison complex. American vehicles were stopped on the opposite side, and traffic was starting to back up. I hoped the traffic would be cleared by the time we finished at the prison.

The prison itself is an impressive sight. As we passed under the last bridge and were getting ready to leave the highway, Abu Gharib stretched out before us on the right. Large white plastered walls, which were about twenty feet high and very thick, ringed the main part of the prison. Every hundred feet or so was a guard tower occupied by military guards with heavy weapons, either M2 machine guns or MK-19s, 40mm automatic grenade launchers. Our convoy pulled off the highway and turned onto the dirt road leading to the prison. In order not to aim at our troops, I rotated my turret away and oriented my weapon toward the highway. The road ran alongside of the wall as it towered over us for about a quarter mile, and then we came to the prison complex's entrance. This road moved through an open field, between the walls and a stretch of new holding areas that were under construction. Our convoy traveled along the wall for another quarter mile, and then turned into the main compound area. We stopped in a parking area just inside the walls where the military police (MPs) had their in-processing station. The two escorts took charge of their detainee and walked him over to the station. As we waited, we cleared our weapons and took off our armor and helmets. I sat on top of the hummer and looked around the prison complex.

The MPs came out and took charge of the detainee, with one of the escorts going inside the tent to do the paperwork and hand over the detainee's personal effects. I watched a line of detainees walk by, being guarded by two MPs. Except for the lead detainee; each had his hands on the man's shoulders in front of him. It reminded me of SERE training, except they were not yelling "boots….boots…boots" in unison. Across from where we were parked was a large fenced-in area that served as an exercise yard. The perimeter had an inner and an outer fence line, and had guard towers looking over the area. Inside were about a thousand detainees, some playing soccer, some appearing to be reading their Korans in small groups. Behind the recreation area were lines of tents where the detainees must have slept. There were definitely a lot of them in there.

We didn't have to wait long before the escort came out, and we loaded up for our return trip. Our convoy proceeded out just as a Blackhawk helicopter took off from the helipad. We went through the gate and once more got onto the highway. The traffic jam was still there as we drove across to the other side and made our way through the traffic. We reached the first stopped American Hummer and asked what was going on. The soldier told us they had found an IED composed of two 155mm artillery shells hanging from the guardrail. This was the very bridge we had just driven under less than a half hour earlier! Breathing a sigh of relief that it hadn't gone off when we went under it, we found a dirt road that ran parallel the highway. I kept scanning, not knowing if the insurgents had planted the IED to force a convoy off the highway and onto this side road. We followed the road past the danger area and were able to get back onto the highway and make it back to our compound without incident. That was about as close to an IED as I wanted to get. Unfortunately it wouldn't be my last.

One thing about being deployed on combat operations is that you become more superstitious than normal. I guess this is from all of the stress and from knowing that something could go wrong at any time. The most difficult part of conducting operations is that you have little control over things that can harm you. That is why you keep your senses super-tuned and take every precaution you can. I became a little spooked on March 9, when I couldn't find my dog tags while getting ready for another convoy to Balad. On my dog chain, I have my ID tags, along with a Celtic cross that I have carried since Desert Storm and a Saint Michael (the patron saint of paratroopers) medallion, all taped together to keep them quiet. I am not an overly religious person and would not normally become superstitious, but I wasn't going to take any chances. Since I started

193

wearing the cross and the medallion, I hadn't been seriously injured during airborne jumps or on any of the multiple contingency I operations I had participated in around the world.

The trip up to Balad was uneventful for the most part, except when we were about halfway there just above Baji. A van was following our convoy, which didn't really bother me. As the van got closer, I saw the occupants had small camcorders filming us. The passenger held one out of his window, and even the driver had a camcorder he was holding out the window while driving. This caused my "spider senses" to tingle. They never approached closer than fifty feet, but I kept my turret turned toward them. Then they were stopped at an Iraqi police checkpoint, and I didn't see them again. I told Brad Conner about it, and he said we should have stopped and confiscated their cameras. Who knows what they were really up to? They could have been working for the insurgents and taping our convoy procedures, or they could have just been stupid tourists.

While we waited for the supply personnel we had escorted up there to finish with their meeting, we drove over to the new CJSOTF compound area. There was a lot of construction going on, and we moved over to where our section would be built. While we waited, we put up a tent that would be used by our support personnel, who would eventually move up there. Instead of the old green canvas tents, known as "GP (General Purpose) Mediums," these were the new dome tents. The first step was to build the rigid metal frame that was marked by corresponding colored ends and pieces. Anything that is used by soldiers in the American military has easy-to-follow instructions with pictures. We were able to get the base frame up and had started to put the sides up when we noticed we didn't have anything to use as a ladder. We improvised by having a few troops stand on my or another tall guy's shoulders as we put the frames up. To make it more interesting, a strong wind and dust began to blow through Balad. Fighting the wind, we were able to get the tent up just as the meeting was over, and we got back on the road.

On the way back, one of the tires blew on a Hummer, and we had to pull over. We had actually rehearsed something for this, and the designated team members quickly fanned out and took up security positions around the trucks. The rest parked in supporting positions as I scanned with my heavy machine gun. We drew some curious on-lookers, but they kept their distance from us. This was a potentially bad situation for us, but luckily the insurgents didn't strike. The tire was changed in less than ten minutes, and we were on our way once more. When I got back to camp, I found my dog tags, which had been with me all along inside my trousers' cargo pocket. The next day we escorted six more detainees over to Abu G without incident.

Despite the danger on convoys, I really enjoyed going out on them. This was not only because I missed being a "gunfighter," but also because of the closeness that comes from being on a team. For the last four years, I had been on a staff, no longer a member of a team. I enjoyed the closeness and trust you develop when working with a team.

One day about this time, I went over to the MWR hut to try using a video feed with the computers. I have a video feed for my computer at home, so I was going to try and conduct an Internet chat with my wife in which we could see each other. It worked! It still never fails to amaze me how far we have advanced. My wife and I were able to watch each other as we communicated over the Internet. I had come a long way since "snail mail." Now, I could see my family and talk real-time with them from around the world.

By the middle of March, the temperatures were beginning to rise, which meant more bugs were coming out. We all had our uniforms treated with insecticide to protect us from the bugs, and living inside our new "hooches" made it better as well. Our battalion up in Mosul sent Chief Warrant Officer Bill Eustis, the promised third guy who would act as the liaison to his battalion up north. I was surprised to learn he was from Ticonderoga, just a little way north of Glens Falls. I began to train him on the briefings and on how the staff wanted them done.

On March 16, I once again celebrated my birthday overseas and away from my family. The insurgents helped out by firing five rockets that evening. It's too bad they didn't realize an AC-130 gunship was up overhead. I heard the sound of the rockets firing, boom... boom...boom, and knew they weren't too far away. It was very rhythmic, until a new sound reached us. The gunship had spotted the insurgents and flew over as they were firing and getting ready to run. The AC-130 is armed with a 25mm cannon, a 40mm cannon, and a 105mm howitzer. The crew fired the 105 at them, and the big boom of the shell hitting them quickly replaced the smaller booms of the rockets.

I made the same mistake I had up in Irbil on the night of March 17. Once again I failed to allow my eyes to adjust to the darkness before walking to the bathroom. This time, I ran into a pile of sandbags instead of falling into a trench. Unfortunately as I fell, I drove my knee into the crushed rocks we use as a roadway and tore it open. Since it was dark, I didn't realize how badly I was bleeding until I returned to my hooch. After cleaning myself up and bandaging my knee, I took my light with me and checked out the port-o-john, which had blood all over inside it. Not wanting to freak anyone out, I cleaned up my blood and returned to bed.

The next day was spent arranging a flight down to Qatar so I could attend a meeting with the personnel recovery planners at CENTCOM. That evening, I called my daughter, Samantha on one of the morale lines, and wished her a Happy Birthday. My other deployments hadn't been hard on her for she was younger then. Now she understood what was going on, and it was difficult for her, so I made sure I contacted her whenever I could.

My odyssey began on March 19 when I was dropped off at the terminal for space available flights. Basically, if a plane was heading to your destination and it had room, you could get on. I had made the arrangements the day before and thought everything was good to go. Boy was I wrong! Unfortunately for me, the next three airplanes heading to Qatar canceled, and I had to wait for a fourth. I spent the day hanging out in the waiting area, reading my book and watching TV. The next airplane was not due to arrive until around 1:20 a.m., so I made myself as comfortable as I could. A whole bunch of Marines arrived and were waiting for transports to drive them to their new camp. It was very crowded, and I wasn't able to get any rest. Their trucks arrived, and the Marines all filed out, leaving a huge mess behind which disgusted me. I went around and cleaned up their MRE wrappers, wondering what happened to self-discipline. I ended up sleeping there in the terminal because the 1:30 a.m. flight didn't work out, and I would have to catch one in the morning. The morning of March 20 found me finally aboard a C-130 on its way to Qatar, and I was met at the airfield by one of the survival specialists. He drove me over to the Air Force compound where they lived and worked.

From what I saw, Qatar was nothing but a bright white, very hot desert. This would have been a pretty place, if it had been an ocean beach instead of a desert. This base, which was called Al Udied, was north of the main city of Qatar. I had a good meeting with my counterparts who were running the SOC RCC. Then, one of the Air Force Survival guys took me over to their hooch where I would be staying, and I caught up on some sleep. I woke up to a strong wind-storm, but they didn't have dust there like we had in Iraq.

I went over to the JSRC and met with my counterparts there. Talk about a small world! One of the officers working there was Major "Hoss" Feathers, a man I had worked with before when he was with the 352nd SOG planning group. We talked for a bit, and I watched their operations for a while. I was impressed by the way they had their JOC set up. The whole room was dark, and everyone worked in "pits" below walkways. Huge screens were to the front where the digital situation maps, BFTs, and TV were displayed. After finishing with them, I returned over to the SOC RCC and spent time observing their operations. They too had a nice layout, with three huge screens in the front and everyone working on tiered rows. I have to admit, when the Air Force puts something together, they really do a good job and take care of their people.

I was trying to arrange to meet with CENTCOM's Non-conventional Assisted Recovery representative, but it didn't work out. The morning was pleasant though. I found their gym inside a large hangar tent and did a morning work out. Later I met with Major Jim Ledbetter, CENTCOM's planner and with the JPRA representative. We had a productive meeting, and I came away with some good ideas.

The next challenge was finding a ride back to Iraq. The two SERE specialists were coming with me because they going to tour around, check out the other camps, and meet with their counterparts. The three of us went over to the space available terminal and found that there were no spaces available. I would have to spend another night there, which wasn't too bad. I had a room with a TV and a VCR, a gym, an Air Force dining facility -- everything a wayward Special Forces soldier would need. That night I stood on top of their "hooch" or building where they had built themselves a patio and watched the aircraft fly by. Everything from transports, to fighters, and even B-1 bombers was taking off. In the night sky, you could see the afterburners as they climbed up to altitude. I thought how much my daughter would have loved to have been there. She likes watching jets.

I was still there waiting for a ride on March 23. We had been the top three for a flight when we were bounced by a delegation of civilians heading to the CPA in Baghdad. It wouldn't have been too bad, except for the smirk on the guy who knew we been bumped by his party. I actually had begun to miss the JOC and wanted to get back to work. The Air Force commander of the Special Operations folks, where the SOC RCC was located, must have taken pity on us and arranged for an MC-130 to pick us up. Never was there a more wonderful sight than one of our own special operations MC-130s taxiing up to us. We weren't the only passengers; there were a couple of others heading to Ali el Salem in Kuwait, where we were going. The flight was uneventful, and we caught up on some sleep. It was nearly midnight when we landed in Kuwait. We thanked the flight crew, and I followed the SERE specialists over to one of their hangars to get with people they knew. We were driven over to the tents where we would be staying and dropped off. It may have been a tent, but inside were real wall lockers and a real bed. After dropping off our gear, we headed over to the dining facility for midnight chow. There I had a real omelet, which was the best thing I had tasted in a long time.

After sleeping until noon, I found the main gym and worked out. We wouldn't be leaving until that evening so I had the rest of the day to kill. The gym was great, and after showering, I went exploring. I visited their store, and then stopped to get a real Subway sandwich. Here I was in Kuwait and I was having a Subway seafood sandwich! Who would have ever thought it? Kuwait is just like Qatar, a large, open desert with chalky white sand and stone. There was nothing around this base, except for sand and scrub brush. When it was time for us to go, we walked to the hangar and linked up with the rest of the passengers flying to Baghdad. At least this flight was certain, and I was finally on my way back to Baghdad on March 24. It had taken five days for an hour-long conference and a couple of meetings. After we arrived in Baghdad, I walked the SERE guys over to where the other Air Force survival guys stayed, and they drove me back to our compound. I gave them a brief tour of our operations and wished them luck.

I jumped right back into action. I learned I would be on a convoy on March 26, except this time, I would be a vehicle commander instead of a gunner. The convoy was composed of six trucks taking supplies up to our new compound in Balad. The only problem was that I became "geographically challenged," or in other words lost, and missed one of the turns in Baghdad. I had seen what the Baghdad streets looked like along our route from the rear and never from the front. So I missed the turn and quickly altered our route to get us back on track. We were able to correct the problem and got the convoy up to Balad with no more problems. We said good-bye to the supply and support folks who would be staying behind to work on the new compound and the rest of us returned to Baghdad.

On the morning of March 28, the insurgents sent a wake up call of four 120mm mortars and rockets. Three of them landed in the fishpond, and one hit the road about 300 feet from my hooch. I was outside when it struck, the explosion rattling everything, and I watched the smoke roll overhead. Right after the explosion, we heard the fourth rocket whistle overhead. It sounded just like it does in the movies, and I yelled out "Incoming!" We took cover, but heard no explosion. Either it had been one of the rockets that went into the pond, or it was a dud. No one was injured. I checked out the small crater in the road when I did my morning workout. The area smelled of burnt powder and asphalt, the trees and bushes nearby peppered with fragments.

We weren't so lucky the night of March 30, when I learned that MSG Richard Ferguson, a friend of mine, had been killed when his Hummer rolled over while he was up in the turret. He was killed instantly. There wouldn't have been anything the medics could have done for him. We had known each other for a long time, going back to Germany and Bad Tolz. I had been working with him in Special Activities during the Iraqi Freedom push in the north. He was going to retire but had decided to stay in and deploy with a team once more. I had just spoken to him before I had gone to Qatar, when his convoy had stopped at our compound before heading back up north. I had commented earlier that I thought smoking would kill Ferg, as we knew him. He had smoked a lot, but he had stopped smoking and cut back on his drinking, getting his life in order.

I have lost other friends during my military career. Tony Hernandez, who I had been with through Desert Storm and Provide Comfort, was killed in a skiing accident during our weather environmental training in 1992. Another friend of mine, Mike Delaney, was killed in North Carolina by carbon monoxide that came from a malfunctioning space heater, and Bill McNeil died from a heart attack after he had retired.

You try to prepare yourself for losing a teammate or a friend, especially in this line of work. However, when it happens, you are never fully ready. I guess the hardest thing was the fact that Ferg was killed not in battle with an enemy, but returning to his base after a mission. The Hummer went off the road a little and the embankment gave away, flipping the vehicle. He was a great guy and will be sorely missed by all. We held a memorial service for him in our theater on the compound. Rick Johns, who was over in Iraq as a contractor, came to the service. I knew Rick as a weapons instructor over at the qualification course in Fort Bragg, and when he was with 10th Group.

It may have been awful, but I had to get back to work. On April Fool's Day, I was going on convoy to one of the 5th Group's small compounds in the ancient city of Babylon where ISG Brad Conner would have a meeting. We met in the early morning to go over our briefings and check our equipment. Along with our normal crew, two SEALs would be coming along, one in each truck. I am always glad to have them with us, because they're very good to have in a scrap. The route would be new to us, heading south instead of our usual north. Also, the populace in the region was not as friendly to Americans as they were in the north, so we had to be on our guard.

Once again I would be manning the rear vehicle's heavy machine gun turret. We went out the main entrance and took the road over to the highway that led to Abu G, but went east instead of west. The highway curved south and entered the southern part of the city of Baghdad. This was a very tense area for us as we headed into a heavily congested urban sprawl. The traffic was bumper-to-bumper and moving at a snail's pace. I was very busy scanning the area, focusing on the buildings, which came right up to the side of the road. There was no way to bypass this congested area, and we had to crawl along with the rest of the traffic. I kept searching the rooftops and down the alleys. As we drove by a school, the play yard was full of kids in the same type of school uniform as I had seen Media wear up in Zahko. The kids were smiling and waving at us, just as a rock came flying over their wall and hit me in the shoulder. It bounced off my armor for the most part, and I couldn't see who threw it. I yelled out, "Good arm kid!" as we continued slowly along the road. I wondered if these kids really knew what was going on, or if they were imitating the rock throwers they saw on TV.

I felt better once we reached the open road and headed south. Scrap metal was big business in Iraq, and everyone was collecting it. Along the roadside, you found numerous scrap-metal collection points. I watched a small Toyota pickup truck with its bed loaded with 500- and 1,000-pound bomb casings. It was nearly doing a "wheelie" from all of the weight in the back. At another collection point, there were piles of artillery shells, stacked like cordwood along the side of the road. I assumed these were no longer armed or filled with explosives, but it was clear where the insurgents were getting their IED materials. We passed more burned-out tanks and armored fighting vehicles as we continued southward. As we approached an open stretch, we saw Iraqi police cars blocking the road. We stopped and asked what was going on. The Iraqi police officers made a gesture of an explosion with their hands, and we believed it meant that they had found an IED. This was confirmed when we saw an officer rolling up some yellow wire. I was scanning the tree line when one of the SEALs spotted a dead dog with red wires coming out of it. The insurgents had been placing explosives inside dead animals along roadsides to serve as IEDs. Believing we had found one, we got out of the area as soon as we could. The insurgents sometimes set up a series of IEDs, and we wanted to be safe.

Our convoy drove through a small, residential area where some of the Iraqi men yelled, "No America, no!". We smiled, I blew them a kiss and muttered under my breath to go get bent, and we continued on our mission. The city of Babylon was soon before us, but we turned off on another road before getting close to the ancient ruins. I did see some ruins in the distance, but we were here for a mission and not sightseeing. Our convoy pulled into a 5th Group compound, and we hung out for an hour or so as a meeting was taking place. We watched two young puppies play with the gate guard while we waited. Once the meeting was over, we were back on the road again, taking a different route back from the way we had come. We had passed on to the 5th Group folks the information about the possible IED and its location before we left. The trip back was uneventful. The only unique thing I saw was a salt marsh and a body of water. The area south of the city is just like the north, all flat and open country except for the marsh we passed. After we returned to base, we also told our intelligence folks about the possible dead dog IED and its location.

The next couple of days were fairly uneventful. However, this would end April 3 as the insurgents launched a series of attacks we called the "April Offensives."

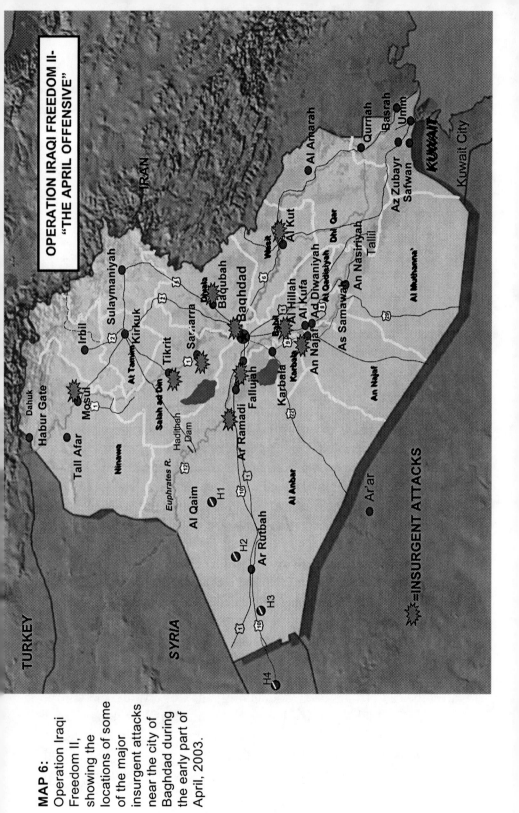

MAP 6:
Operation Iraqi
Freedom II,
showing the
locations of some
of the major
insurgent attacks
near the city of
Baghdad during
the early part of
April, 2003.

OPERATION IRAQI FREEDOM II-
"THE APRIL OFFENSIVE"

TURKEY

SYRIA

IRAN

KUWAIT

Kuwait City

Dahuk
Habur Gate
Tall Afar
Ninawa
Euphrates R.
Hadithah
Dam
Al Qaim
Ar Rutbah
H1
H2
H3
H4
Ar Ramadi
Al Anbar
Fallujah
Mosul
Salah ad Din
Tikrit
Al Tamim
Kirkuk
Irbil
Sulaymaniyah
Samarra
Baghdad
Baqubah
Diyala
Al Kut
Wasit
Babil
Al Hillah
Al Kufa
Al Najaf
Karbala
An Najaf
As Samawah
Ad Diwaniyah
Al Qadisiyah
An Nasiriyah
Talili
Dhi Qar
Al Muthanna'
Ar'ar
Al Amarah
Qurnah
Basrah
Umm
Az Zubayr
Safwan

= INSURGENT ATTACKS

CHAPTER 15

THE APRIL OFFENSIVE AND BEGINNING TO ROTATE HOME

"April Offensive" was a name we in the CJSOTF coined for the period of time from the end of March through the beginning of May. No name was officially given to this period by the military, but we called it the April Offensive for our own purposes. Insurgent activity had been steadily increasing throughout Iraq, with more and more rocket and IED attacks occurring. On the last day of March, four civilian contractors with Blackwater had been ambushed and killed by insurgents in the city of Fallujah. Their dead bodies were dragged through the streets and hung from one of the bridges in the city. This reminded us of the events that had occurred in Mogadishu, Somalia. Perhaps the insurgents believed that if we saw our dead treated like they had been in Somalia, we would lose our resolve. Seeing what happened to these contractors, however, only stiffened our resolve instead of eroding it.

On April 4, all hell broke loose south of Baghdad in a town called Najaf where the Spanish compound was under attack by insurgents. Additionally, the insurgents captured the bridges in the city of Nasariah, and the personal army of the radical cleric al-Sadar, the Mahdi Army, was making trouble in the slums located in the northeast corner of Baghdad, known as Sadar City. This section of the city was once called Saddam's City, but the name was changed to Sadar City after the fall of Baghdad. Moqtada-al-Sadr was a young cleric, who wasn't very high up in the hierarchy of the Muslim religious leaders, but his father was a high-ranking cleric, and he was using his father's name to further his own goals. Though he was not of high rank, Sadar had a large following of supporters. We had been keeping an eye on him and watching his radical supporters, who came from the poor and uneducated citizenry. One of the radio broadcasts from an American compound in the region that was under attack showed some of the desperation felt by our forces on the ground. A commander was calling for air support, and the Air Force was having a hard time clearing the aircraft to attack. The commander was becoming very desperate, and we heard, "If you don't drop right now, we are all screwed! He got his air strike, which stopped the insurgent attack. There had been at least 60 causalities reported by the coalition during this outbreak of attacks, and it was only the beginning.

As we monitored the situation around Iraq, explosions rocked our compound, with bombs or rockets detonating outside. As night fell, the enemy activity continued to grow. Our team in the city of Tuz reported being fired upon by Rocket Propelled Grenades (RPG). Camp Golf, one of the U.S. compounds in Najaf was coming under frequent rocket attacks. A number of our folks came into the JOC to watch what was going on, staying until early morning when the activity seemed to quiet down some. The attacks were not as frequent the following day, but now the insurgents were firing on the Abu-G prison, which didn't make sense to me. Either they thought it was just another U.S. base, or they were trying to blowholes in the walls to allow the prisoners to escape. In either case, it was the prisoners who were being injured in the attacks, not the American guards.

On April 6, the insurgents conducted an all-out attack against the CPA compound in Al Kut. The main ground commander over at Camp Victory (TF-7) tried to get reinforcements and air support down there. We had an element stationed with the Ukrainians in the area, but the Ukrainian Commander would not let them leave his compound! Instead of fighting the insurgents, all of the Ukrainians returned to their base and stayed inside. With the Ukrainian Commander in charge of the sector, no air strikes were allowed against the insurgents. Monitoring the situation, I became more and more frustrated and angry as politics once more interfered with military operations. In a way, I could understand their situation. For the most part, the Ukrainians were there for the money and not to fight. Still, it was very upsetting to see a coalition partner refuse to put up any resistance while the insurgents took over a government installation. It was a terrible situation in the city as the insurgents ran free, and no one stopped them. The CJTF-7 Commander even wanted to drop bombs near the compound to "inspire" the Ukrainians, but it didn't happen. One of our AC-130 gunships was overhead, ready to lay waste the compound, but once more the Ukrainian Commander said no.

The Mahdi Army was making moves toward the holy city of Karbala, and Fallujah was still a major hotbed of insurgent activity. As the situation began to deteriorate in Fallujah, we were preparing a convoy of ammunition and medical supplies to be brought to the 5th Group's detachments there. Most of the people selected for the convoy were SF series, including myself, instead of a normal convoy crew due to the good chance of making enemy contact. The convoy was canceled, and we remained in our compound. For the next couple of nights, the insurgent activity remained high around the central portion of Iraq. We monitored the situation by observing the live video feed from Predator, an unmanned aerial reconnaissance platform that flew over the country, guided by remote control. On the aircraft were various sensors and video equipment so the ground commanders could get real-time information. Our commander was going to take some of our detachments that were not busy in the north and use them to reinforce the detachments under attack in Fallujah and Karbala.

While I was monitoring the air traffic over the radio on April 7, I listened to the conversation between a Marine commander and the Air Force as they discussed air support. A Marine company was under fire from a Mosque and needed air support. The enemy was using our own rules of engagement against us. Normally, we avoided mosques, unless they were being used by the enemy, which in this case they were. Unfortunately, the Air Force didn't want to drop explosives, because it was a mosque, and dropping bombs violated the rules of engagement. But this Marine Company was receiving automatic weapons fire from the mosque. After arguing back and forth in what I called the "Air Force Follies," fighters were finally cleared to attack. A single fighter fired a rocket at a minaret (a tall tower in a mosque where the faithful are called to prayers), where several shooters were located. The missile impacted next to the minaret, but did not topple it. The aircraft were once more called off. I believe the company commander had had enough. He called his own artillery on top of the mosque. Later that day, a platoon cleared it and made a video record of what they found inside the mosque. This included enemy fighting positions built into the walls with clear fields of fire on the road. Though no bodies were found, there were a lot of spent ammunition casings and blood trails. Unfortunately, the press reported that we attacked a mosque, but they left out the part about the enemy positions being built in it, which violated the rules of land warfare and made it a legitimate target.

Enemy activity was beginning to increase around our area as well, and the Baghdad Airport was coming under more frequent rocket attacks. Now, insurgents were firing on our patrols and compounds with small arms fire, mostly AK-47s and light machine guns. A convoy was hit near us and stopped at our compound to drop off two wounded soldiers. Our medical staff took care of them and evacuated them over to the main hospital.

It still was amazing to see how far we have advanced in the use of technology. During some of the fighting in and around An Najaf, we were able to watch real-time from a Predator unmanned aerial vehicle (UAV) that was filming from over the fighting. During one of the morning flights, we witnessed a bizarre event. The enemy had been using the Mosques to hide weapons and equipment in, a complete violation of the rules of war. One morning, the Predator observed a fire from inside one of the insurgent occupied Mosques. As the Predator zoomed in, we could see fires and what appeared to be small explosions coming from a shack inside of the Mosque's courtyard. My guess, one of the insurgents flicked a cigarette and started the fire on one of their caches.

As the drama continued, fire trucks approached the mosque and were fired upon by the insurgents. Then a vehicle that appeared to be an ambulance arrived and backed into the area near the burning shack. The insurgents were scurrying like rats to load boxes from the shack into the ambulance. I may not be the smartest intelligence analyst, but I could figure out they were moving weapons. The ambulance made several trips as the fire grew until they moved everything they needed to. Then the fire trucks were allowed in, but by then most of the shacks along the wall in the compound were burnt to the ground.

The hardest thing about being caught in a rocket attack is that there is nothing you can do about it. At least in a regular gunfight, you can shoot back at the enemy. During a rocket attack, you can only sit there and hope for the best. The local workers were placing sandbags around our sleeping hooches, but that didn't completely protect them. The sandbag wall only came about half way up the sides, which meant the top of the protective materials was about even with my chest as I lay inside on my bunk. Most rockets plunged from above, however, and there was nothing you could do to stop them. At night, I listened for the pop of a rocket launch. By the time the siren went off and you ran to the bunker, the rockets would have already landed. Every night I faced the fear of being caught in a rocket attack. Since there was nothing I could do about it, I tried to get as much sleep as I could. It still bothered me, but I pushed it to the side and tried not to let it interfere with my mission.

We received intelligence reports that enemy activity would increase around Baghdad in the next couple of days. There was also a report that the insurgents had acquired five Hummers and American uniforms in an attempt to make a VBIED (Vehicle Born Improvised Explosive Device) and attack a US target in or around Baghdad. Our guards were placed on extra alert because of these reports. We also received reports that Mujahadien were in our area, which gave us some concern. These were experienced fighters from Afghanistan who knew how to handle themselves. On April 9, a fuel convoy was hit just northwest of our compound by a well-coordinated attack. We saw the columns of black smoke from the convoy from the palace hill. This was the convoy from which two U.S. service members and the insurgents reportedly took seven contractors.

Our guards engaged around ten insurgents near our wall, killing one and capturing a couple of others who were wounded. From their distinctive black clothing and red headband, we could tell they were Mahdis. These were the fighters that followed the radical cleric Mughtada al Sadar, and were known as the Mahdi Army. For the most part, they were thugs and gangsters, not really fighting for a cause.

The morning of April 10 started with a bang as a rocket around 4:30 a.m hit our compound. We received intelligence that our compound might be attacked that day, so we kept our gear and weapons close by. Around midday, two rockets impacted right outside of the civilian gate of our compound (the gate we used to go to Abu-G). More reports were coming in about sightings of the black-pajama and red-headband Mahdis near our compound. Later that afternoon, a rocket landed near the fishpond and the barber shop, causing a small fire. As darkness fell, reports of enemy activity near the walls were enough for us on the Quick Reaction Force (QRF) to kit up and man the vehicles. We pulled our Hummers out of the garage and stood by. We later found that this was a false report, and we stood down and returned to our normal duties.

Fighting had increased in the city of Baqubah, north of Baghdad. One of our Special Forces detachments from 10th Group was stationed there in the city, helping to defend the city's government building and police station from repeated enemy attacks. Those guys did a great job even though the insurgents outnumbered them.

As the evening continued, I was working on some course of action development and early planning for a possible rescue of missing personnel. We had received reports about a possible location of hostages, and I began to plan in case we confirmed their location and had to recover them. I was coordinating with my various personnel recovery assets to get times and capabilities to develop my course of action. Unfortunately, when I brought this info to the JSRC, somehow it was misunderstood as a definite recovery rather than a course of action development for the possibility of a recovery. Normally we get all of our info together to present a plan or develop a plan in case something was to occur. A colonel got the info and then went to General Herril, the CFSOCC Commander, who in turn called my boss Colonel Repass demanding to know what was going on. I found out about it when I was called into our Operations Officers office to receive a very vocal reprimand, also known as a royal butt chewing. This was known in the military as a snowball effect. As the situation becomes bad, it rolls down hill like a snowball, gathering speed and getting bigger. By the time it got down to me, it was a huge boulder that broke on top of my head. I attempted to explain what had happened, but my boss, who didn't understand the PR infrastructure, continued to voice his displeasure. To make the situation worse, I had told him that I had in fact briefed our watch officer about what I was doing, but the watch officer also didn't understand the PR infrastructure.

After receiving my final chewing out and a threat of having to write of an official letter of apology to a general officer, I returned to my workstation. The watch officer left with me, saying "thanks for diming me out" as he walked to his desk. I couldn't believe it. Here was a captain who I had told what I was doing, and he was so concerned about getting into trouble that he wouldn't admit I had told him what I was doing. If he hadn't understood what I was doing, why didn't he ask me? At that moment my morale was at its lowest, and I was seriously thinking of asking to be reassigned to something or somewhere else. Working with a staff that was more worried with their personal lives than with getting the job done was the final straw for me. But then I realized that I was the only person here who knew how to run a recovery operation. I couldn't leave my guys to the care of some untrained staff officer, so I decided to suck it up, deal with the problem, and continued to do my job.

I went outside to get a breath of cool, night air and to clear my head. Off in the distance, you could hear the staccato burst of automatic weapons fire. It sounded like it was coming from the other side of the airport perimeter. I guess the insurgents were probing the defensive lines, trying to find weak points. After finishing my shift, I went back to my hooch and tried to get some sleep. I kept going over in my mind what I had done wrong concerning the course of action development. I also felt like I had let my commander, Colonel Repass, down, which was a bad feeling. Needless to say, I didn't sleep well and woke up on May 11 not feeling my best. However, this would not last long as a few rounds impacted inside our compound. Go figure. Who knew it would be enemy fire that pulled me out of my funk and got my morale back up.

Around noon, enemy activity increased as more rockets impacted in and around our compound. Soon reports that they were under small-arms fire came in from the civilian gate. The whole compound went on alert as we all manned our stations in full "battle rattle."

From additional reports, it sounded like insurgents were hitting all around the airport area, as well as in the city of Baghdad. One of our Marine Majors took up one of the SAW machine guns and began to load the weapon. He and I had become friends, with him calling me "gunny" instead of sergeant. A gunny was a Marine E-7, so I just ran with it. As I watched him put a belt of ammunition into the weapon, I advised him to keep the belt out for safety reasons. I was concerned about an accidental discharge, but I knew I could trust this Marine Major. The situation became bad enough that we of the Quick Reaction Force were called to man our vehicles. Leaving the SAW in the care of a friend of mine, Master Sergeant Mike Leehan, I ran to the vehicles.

Because I was next to the garage, I was one of the first ones there as we pulled out our vehicles and prepared them. Originally, I was going to use one of the SAWs, but I took up my normal position in the turret with the .50-caliber machine gun due to the experience I had with this weapon. We had some extra folks with us this time, including an old C Company medic I knew as "Face." We were ordered to head over to the perimeter defense command post. Our perimeter defense force had been changed out from the 82nd to a National Guard Multiple Rocket Launch System (MRLS) battery from the Midwest. As we waited at their command post, their vehicles were lined up as well. The orders came in for us to move over to the civilian gate to see what the situation was. As we took up our positions and loaded our weapons, we heard the "rebel yell" and "go get some" from our MRLS brothers. Giving them big thumbs up, we rolled out towards the gate.

Our vehicles rolled along our perimeter road, and we passed some of our JOC folks manning a ditch near the corner by the MWR hut, including my friend Mike Leehan. We rolled by and headed out the first gate towards the main gate. In the distance you could see smoke from some civilian buildings rising from across the street. Off in the distance was the sound of AKs popping and being answered by our weapons. What a feeling! Your senses are overloaded with the smell of smoke, the sound of gunfire, the feel of the wooden grips of the machine gun. Every sense is highly tuned to your surroundings as you scan for enemy activity. We stopped at the main gate and could see we were not needed. There was a small army there, between the Iraqi National Guardsmen, soldiers from the 82nd, our SEALs, and more 5th Group folks. 1SG Brad Conner ran over to talk with the on-site commander as we took up watch positions. I turned my turret and machine gun towards the gate. A car was speeding toward the gate with at least forty weapons tracking it, including mine as I shouted out the vehicle's approach to my teammates. It was more of the Iraqi National Guardsmen coming to the compound.

The enemy had moved through the small civilian housing area across the road from the main gate, but then had moved away as we concentrated forces there. There had been no activity in the last fifteen minutes, so we were advised to move to a position back in the corner near the MWR hut and to wait for further guidance. We backed our vehicles onto an old bridge that crossed the canal, but the bridge had been secured with several rolls of concertina wire blocking the middle. We dismounted, but stayed near our vehicles and talked with some of the other folks in the area. The "All Clear" was finally sounded, and we returned to the garage and put the vehicles away. After stowing my kit, I settled back down to a normal shift. What I referred to as "The Great Battle for RPC" came to a quiet end, just another day and another insurgent attack among all the others across Iraq.

The following day was quiet for us, but the rest of the country was still in turmoil. The insurgents released eight of the Kellogg Brown and Root (KBR) contract drivers from the ambushed fuel convoy. The two American servicemen were still missing as well as a few of the civilian drivers. The eight were not American or Western employees, and perhaps that is why they were freed.

During my shift, a patrol from 5th Group had been repeatedly ambushed south of Baghdad. I wore my radio headset so I could monitor the radio traffic closely, in case we had to run a recovery mission. The patrol had been hit hard and had causalities. The insurgents pursued and continued to fire on the patrol until they evaded and hid in some low ground. The radio traffic was so clear; I could hear the sound of frogs chirping in the background while the patrol remained silent to avoid detection near a swamp. This was difficult, wanting to help but being able to do nothing about it. A Marine company was dispatched to link up with and assist the patrol, but it was going to take time to get to them. Unfortunately, one of the causalities died before the Marines arrived, which everyone took hard. The Marines had to fight to them, but they eventually linked up and assisted the patrol to return to base.

Late that evening, we dispatched a flight of two MH-53 Pave Lows to recover the body of a soldier recently killed in action and bring it back for processing. I was briefing Sal before going off shift when a call came in that our flight, call sign Mongoose 33, was under fire. As the lead aircraft approached the SF compound, the insurgents, who had been waiting for it, fired a Rocket Propelled Grenade at the aircraft. The rocket struck the front of the helicopter just above the crew compartment, bringing the craft down. The pilot's wingman flew over and provided suppressive fire with the aircraft's rear-mounted .50-caliber machine gun and its side miniguns. After the insurgents fell back, the second MH-53 landed and recovered the crew of the downed helicopter. As they were being loaded onto the second helicopter, I was busy working the coordination piece back in the JOC. I had to keep the spectators and everyone who wanted to help away so I could do my job. It was the only action we had had, and everyone wanted to become involved, even though they didn't know the procedures.

The second helicopter lifted off with the crew and flew back to Baghdad Airport. The rocket fragments injured the flight engineer and the two pilots, and some of the crew in the back of the aircraft suffered minor injuries. I was still working the coordinating piece to secure the aircraft when they arrived at the airport, and I was able to confirm the recovery was complete. We were coordinating with a nearby Marine company to secure the crash site so we could recover the aircraft, but the insurgents had other plans. The Marines were ambushed along the way and were caught up in the fight. Unfortunately, we had no choice but to shell the aircraft with artillery, and then finish it off with an air strike to deny the equipment to the enemy. It's always hard to loose a multi-million-dollar aircraft that way, and we didn't have very many MH-53s left.

The weather was turning hot as we began to close in on the Iraqi summer. Insurgent activities lessened to some degree around us, but the insurgents continued to intimidate the locals. They were sending out leaflets as part of their own propaganda campaign, telling the people that our area would become a "war zone" and they must leave the area or become caught up in the fighting. This was the standard practice for the Mahdi Army, who tried to intimidate the local populace. With the increase of activity, I was assigned a new role as a Mark-19 gunner with our QRF, because I was the only experienced gunner available. The Mark-19 is a machine gun that fires 40mm grenades. Because our compound was coming under mortar and some small-arms fire, I was to ride up to the top of the big palace hill and watch from there. If I spotted the enemy, I was to engage them with the Mark-19.

The temperatures continued to stay in the 90s, going down to the 60s at night. The 60s may not sound that bad, but when you are living in a desert climate, it is quite cold because of the huge temperature variance from day to night. For the next couple of days, it remained quiet. Everyone seemed to be holding their breath, waiting to see what the insurgents would do next. I continued to follow leads and conflicting reports on possible hostage locations. Nothing was solid, so I combed the reports for more concrete proof of their locations. Most of the action was around Fallujah. Politics was becoming involved once more, and we were on hold as negotiations between the Iraqi Interim Government and Sadar continued. The Marines were poised to go in and squash them, but now they were on hold once more. All that these negotiations accomplished was to allow the enemy to reequip and catch their breath.

On April 20, the Abu-G prison was hit hard by an insurgent rocket attack, which killed 22 detainees and wounded some 90 others. It still amazed me. They must have known that there were Iraqis there and at least half of the detainees were their own insurgent fighters. Yet, they still attacked the compound and killed their own people. I believe the attackers were mostly foreign fighters, so it didn't bother them to kill Iraqi detainees.

With the continued lull in the fighting, I went over to the Camp Victory compound where CJTF-7 Headquarters was located. The compound had been another of Saddam's palaces, this one on the main road between the airport and the city. We drove quickly over to it because of the chance of coming under enemy small arms fire, and we arrived without incident. It was a nice compound, with a large Base Exchange (BX-military store) which was called the Mother of All BXs (MOAB). We hadn't gone there for the store, but to be issued new equipment as part of the Rapid Fielding Initiative. All of the soldiers would be issued new desert boots, camel backs, and warm clothing, enough to fill a duffel bag. I accepted my new gear and loaded back up in our truck. It was now night and very dark, and we had to negotiate the obstacle course of getting out of the front gate with no lights on. It was a challenge, but we made it out in one piece and returned to our camp.

For errands like this and to go over to the dining facility at the airport, we had a small, rather beat-up Toyota pickup truck that had seen better days. Instead of a driver's side rearview mirror, it had a signal mirror that had been tied on to the old broken mirror. Yet, when we went to the CPA compound, most of all of the "important people" had new SUVs. I would have loved to get .001 percent of the money that was being spent on rentals and SUVs so the "important people" could have their own transportation. We, the gunfighters, were stuck with hand-me-down, barely running vehicles to support our missions.

With the changing weather, more wind and sandstorms were popping up. These storms normally knocked out our power, so we had to change over to generator power. This had happened so frequently that we could do the switchover in a matter of minutes.

On April 24, we witnessed a new means of insurgent attacks, suicide boats! The insurgents attacked the oil platforms off of the coastal city of Basra. Once again I couldn't begin to fathom the thinking process of the insurgents who were attacking their own infrastructure.

Even though the Marines were holding their positions around Fallujah, the fighting continued. The insurgents fired on the Marines from the mosques, and then faded into the city when the Marines advanced. Once the Marines pulled back, the insurgents returned to the Mosques and once again began to fire on the Marines. It looked like they were trying to get us to destroy the mosques so the other

Muslims would attack us. It must have been very frustrating for the Marines.

Receiving intelligence reports of a possible chemical attack on Baghdad Airport, we positioned our Nuclear, Biological, and Chemical protective gear close, just in case. I once again was having difficulties sleeping, because I am a light sleeper and I was listening for warning sirens. I went for days on limited sleep, until my body was so tired that I would finally get one good night's rest. Then the cycle would repeat itself. To make it more difficult, the senior CJSOTF staff decided to change the shift hours once more. To help relieve some of the stress, I continued to work out and go for walks around the compound. I had purchased a CD player and a belt to carry it. I walked the perimeter, as well as climbing up the palace hill, and then finished at the gym with a workout. In addition to relieving stress, it was a way to get some fresh air before the temperatures got really hot.

Our Explosive Ordinance Disposal techs were sent to disarm a van that turned out to be a VBIED, and they had to detonate it instead. The resulting explosion was large enough to shake our building and break some windows up in the hunting palace on the hill. This van was about three miles away, thank goodness, and it was stopped before it hit a target in our area.

The negotiations concerning Fallujah ended on April 28, and the Marines were released to go do what they do best! Even though I am in the Army, I have always been impressed with the training and dedication of our Marines. Now we had "released the dogs of war" into Fallujah. Early reports showed heavy fighting, which was not surprising since the enemy had had time to build defensive positions during the negotiations. Our aircraft dropped some twenty-one 500-pound bombs on various targets in the city. The most disturbing thing I heard about didn't concern any of the fighting in Iraq, but was in the news from the United States. Jesse Jackson had stated we should have sanctions placed on the United States for killing Iraqis. I couldn't believe what I heard. Isn't this guy an American? I guess he felt it was better to smother the insurgents with hugs and kisses than to fight them. This just demonstrates how ignorant some people back in the United States were about the situation in Iraq. We were not dealing with "cold war" conventional fighting, but with a hard-core, fanatical insurgency that was killing both Iraqis and coalition soldiers. I understood that this was a political season and he was trying to sway the pacifist votes, but he needed to at least get a grip on what was going on.

Politics even made it into my own family when I found out my stepbrother John was going to run for a Congressional seat as a Democrat. No credible candidate was going to run in his district, so he decided to run himself, which I supported 100 percent. He asked me if he could use me as an example in his platform, saying how I was away from my family and unable to coach my daughter's Little League team. I said I didn't mind if he used me in his platform, but he needed to understand that I wanted to be where I was. This was a job we had to do, and it should have been done earlier. Even though I am a Republican, I wished him the best of luck because he is my brother. Eventually another candidate with more money jumped into the race for the same seat, and John withdrew. At least he got the ball rolling and someone eventually stepped up to the plate.

As quickly as it started, the offensive in Fallujah was stopped, once more due to politics. When politics become involved, it's like the clowns are trying to give the whole circus away.

On April 30, I celebrated my wedding anniversary once more in the field on a convoy to Balad. Before leaving our compound, we test fired our weapons, so at least I could say I fired my machine gun in Iraq! The original convoy of seven trucks with ammunition was reduced to a single dump truck to be escorted by our two Hummers, which didn't bother me. I was glad we weren't escorting ammunition trucks. The trip up was uneventful, but we were told we were going to spend the night because the meeting our supply personnel were in was going to run late. By now we had three tents up, including the one we had helped to set up on a previous trip. After securing my cot, I went out and dusted off and did a quick clean of my machine guns. Old habits die hard. Afterwards, I hung out and read a book that I had brought with me. I believe an alert was called. I could hear the siren and see people manning bunkers, but we were not informed as to what was going on. It must have been nothing for the "all clear" was soon sounded. A few of us drove over to check out the BX on the compound, which looked like any BX back in the states. After we returned to our tent, I was laying on my cot reading when I looked over a saw a small scorpion crawling toward my gear. It was a clear, tannish color instead of black, meaning it was one of the more poisonous scorpions. I picked it up with my leatherman's tool and gave a quick class about it to my teammates. After they took a couple of photos of it, like hunters holding up their trophies, I released it outside.

That night, a large thunderstorm and sandstorm hit the camp. The sandstorm hit first, and then the thunderstorm. I went outside to watch the light show. On one side of the valley was the dust wall, and on the other were the thunderclouds with lightning. In the center was clear, star-filled sky. What a unique weather pattern this was!

The following morning was rather interesting. We followed our procedures, doing our equipment checks and loading our weapons. As we arrived at the gate, the guards would not let us depart because our weapons were loaded. Due to a recent increase in accidental discharges on the compound, the commander had issued a directive that all weapons would be cleared on post, which I understood. However, we were departing the compound, and they wouldn't let us leave until we cleared our weapons. I guess they thought that we would do a timeout once we were outside of the gate in possibly hostile territory so we could load. It is standard tactics taught in all the schools that the most likely place an enemy will attack you is when you depart your lines. I guess these guards hadn't gone to those schools, so we left the gate with cleared weapons, and we had to stop out in the open to load them.

It was a grey and foggy morning as we drove down the highway back to Baghdad. We passed a civilian truck on fire that had been hit just before we arrived, so I was extra cautious scanning my sector. The fog worked both ways, making it hard for the enemy to see us, but also making it hard for us to spot them or any IEDs. About halfway back, I encountered an impressive sight: two M1A1 Abrams tanks rolled down the opposite side of the highway on patrol. Boy is that a monster coming out of the fog! I'm glad we have them, and the enemy doesn't. The fog burned off by the time we reached the outskirts of Baghdad, and we decided to cut through the Green

Zone instead of taking our normal route. As we drove through the zone, we picked up radio traffic from a convoy under fire on the route we would have normally taken. The convoy had stopped to repair a truck and was in the process of deciding what to do with the disabled truck. This allowed the insurgents to encircle them and get close enough to lob mortar shells at them. They should have just abandoned the truck and not spent so much time sitting there, which made them a juicy target. If we had stayed on our original route, we could have come to their aid, but we were now too far away, and we returned to our base.

On May 2, Thomas Hamil, one of the civilian hostages from the ambushed fuel convoy was recovered. After the ambush, the insurgents moved him around from house to house, but they hadn't guarded him well. In fact, he had escaped earlier but had no idea where he was and didn't have much in the way of supplies, so he returned. This time, he heard the sound of American trucks and made a run for it. Even though he had no formal survival training, he was able to be smart and take advantage of the insurgents' lack of attention. The Americans were conducting a roadside patrol looking for IEDs. Mr. Hamil, not wanting to be shot by accident because he was dressed in local Iraqi clothes, pulled off his long looking "man dress" and waved it. Along with his bright white abdomen and yelling in English, the American soldiers quickly helped him in to their trucks and removed him from the area. I was on duty when the news arrived through the personnel recovery coordination cells. We were quite happy to learn of his recovery, it was some good news on a rather bleak day. He was quickly loaded on to a C-17 transport bound for Germany and was on his way home.

The news about the Abu-G scandal hit the airwaves that day, and everyone was making a big issue about it. The Muslims were having a field day through the Al Jazeera network, condemning the actions. Even our own politicians, mostly Democrats and the Anti-War movement, were using it to further their own cause. Granted, I strongly feel these soldiers were wrong and should be punished to the fullest extent of the law. However, some of the "techniques" they use to soften up prisoners had been included in our resistance training to face interrogation. However, it was made into a big deal, once more due to it being a political and election year.

The rest of the first week of May was quiet, which was both good and bad for us in the JOC. Good in the sense that no one was getting hurt, but bad because now the shifts were boringly quiet. Our temperatures during the day were in the low hundreds, making it difficult to do anything outdoors. May 8 signaled the beginning of the end for our tour. The first advance party aircraft of the staff from 5th Group headquarters, which was to replace us, arrived, and we had begun shuttling equipment and non-essential personnel back to Colorado. On May 9, a headless corpse was found just north of the city of Baghdad, hung from a bridge that I had frequently passed under on convoys to Balad. Being the personnel recovery guy, I was shown the photos of the head in order to see if it was one of our missing servicemen from the fuel convoy. It wasn't. It turned out to be Nicolas Berg, an American contractor who had come over to Iraq to help work on their power grid. I first thought it might have been PFC (now sergeant) Keith Matthew "Matt" Maupin, the one serviceman from the convoy who had been shown on Al Jazeera television.

Members of the staff, mostly the senior officers, were beginning to rotate out and head back home. The news continued to show the Abu-G scandal. I guess there was nothing else to report about. Perhaps now back in the states, the people could see what kind of animals we were dealing with as the news reported about Nicolas Berg. Perhaps they could see that the radical and hardcore Muslims extremists could not be treated peacefully; they respect force and that is what is needed to stop them.

By mid-May, the focus had shifted to changing over and heading home. Our new complex was being constructed up in Balad and would be finished soon. We were going to shut down operations and move up there around the end of the month. My convoy operations came to an end on May 15, as Chief Eustis returned to his battalion up north so he could go home. No one would be able to cover my desk and give the nightly briefing when I was gone, so there were no more missions for me. This was both a blessing and a curse, just another factor I had to deal with. To add to this, I was informed I would be on the third (and final) aircraft out of here for home. I knew my wife and daughter were going to travel to see her family in Germany, and with my luck, we would pass each other in the air going in opposite directions.

Our food situation became better on May 20 when four trailers of supplies finally arrived with real food. All of the supply convoys were halted after the fuel convoy was shot up. Not many drivers wanted to risk being captured. I can't say I blamed them, but if you came to Iraq to work, you should have understood the risks involved. Sometimes the lure of easy money clouds the eyes of common sense.

We were getting ready to conduct missions in Karbala against the Mahdi Army when Ambassador Bremmer said no. Again, politics and military operations don't mix. I guess they were trying to reach a deal with Sadar, so no military operations were allowed. Perhaps there were things going on which we down at our level didn't know about, but it was still very frustrating.

It stayed quiet for the next couple of days. I thought they might have canceled the war and not told us. I had been working a deal so I could get home sooner so I could spend some time with my family before they left to visit my wife's family. I also asked if I could purchase a ticket and take leave so I could be with them in Germany. At the moment, it wasn't looking too good in my favor.

The news media continued to hound the President and push their anti-war message, mostly the *LA Times* and the *Washington Post*. The *LA Times* was pushing an article about a wedding party that had been attacked by our AC-130 gunships. First of all, who would hold a wedding party some 250 miles out in the desert? The *LA Times* claimed the party came from one of the cities and drove out there for the celebration. There was more to the story, but due to the sensitive nature of the operation I cannot say more, other than it was a smugglers' camp that was providing aid to the insurgents who were coming into the country. The *LA Times* would much rather believe the "victims" than their own people. Granted it is difficult when some of the truth couldn't be revealed due to the classified nature of our business. But they would believe an Iraqi over an American to further their own agenda, and I thought that really sucked! Our own media was helping the enemy by causing dissension back in the

United States, when we should be supporting each other. The insurgents didn't need to have a propaganda mechanism; our own media was doing the job for them.

Enemy focus had shifted away from Fallujah and was now centered on Karbala. The situation in Fallujah was turned over to the Iraqi Civilian Defense Force (ICDC) known as the Fallujah Brigade, commanded by a former Republican Guard commander. I thought the brigade was rather fishy, and there were no longer any actions against the insurgents. Karbala was now the center of interest as Sadar supporters were holing up in the holy shrines. Once again confusion reigned as politics and who was in charge of the area were debated. Our gunships overhead saw enemy ambushes and heavy weapons but were not allowed to fire upon them. With the increasing threat against the Interim Iraqi Government, CJSOTF received the new mission of protecting the new officials. So instead of conducting missions against the insurgents, the SEALs had been pulled off to be bodyguards. That's a rough job, because it is not a matter of if you will be attacked, but rather when. The insurgents wanted chaos to reign and would do everything in their power to disrupt the new government.

Now the daily temperatures were at 110 degrees, making it extremely difficult to work outside. Our battalion began starting to send its people back on the night of May 27. It was becoming more and more difficult to watch the news from back in the states. All of this badmouthing the President and the statements some of our people were making made me very angry. The ACLU was going after the Los Angles City symbol because there was a small cross in it. Then Al Gore got up and stated that what happened at Abu-G was the President's fault. Then there were the Dixie Chicks who made their statement while performing a concert in England. These folks were trying everything to swing votes their way by badmouthing the President and using events here in Iraq to further their own political agenda. As a soldier, I am the one who fights for their freedom of speech, which allows them to say this kind of trash. It's hard for me to sit there and watch them abuse these freedoms. I sometimes feel we have too many freedoms in the United States and the people don't realize how good they really have it. There would be no way they would get away with this in another country, and yet they sit there and say how bad the Americans are. If you don't like it, leave, and see how far you will get without the freedoms we in the military protect for you.

Convoy where PFC Keith "Matt" Maupin and Thomas Hamil were captured, seen from the top of the Hunting Palace hill.

CHAPTER 16

JUNE AND MOVING TO CAMP ANACONDA

June arrived quietly. The new Iraqi Interim President, Vice President, and Cabinet had been chosen. Now our security folks were going to have a busy time keeping them safe. This was my final month in Iraq, and my bags were packed and ready to be moved to Camp Anaconda, our new camp up in Balad. For the most part, it was still quiet around us, and our compound was beginning to pack up its equipment as well. The MWR hut had packed their computers, so no more conversations with my wife were possible except through our computers in the shop. We learned that the reason why it had been so quiet around here was that the security forces had captured the man responsible for planning the attacks against our compound and the airport. It was a contract employee who had been working with Kellogg Brown and Root! I guess they received a tip and went to this guy's place where they found bomb-making materials and charts. He had been arrested earlier and sent to Abu-G prison. Due to all of the flak over the scandal, most of the detainees had been released. Sure enough, about a week after his release, attacks against the airport began again. Some of the detainees, I'm sure, were innocent, but some of them were insurgents and now they were back on the street trying to kill Americans.

It was still hot, Africa hot. Tarzan couldn't have handled this heat! At least it was a dry heat. It would have been a lot worse if there were some humidity involved. We had been reduced to half strength as more of the staff was sent up to the new camp. Our food situation was back to where it had been before the resupply. With the unit packing up most of the equipment, we had Burger King every day for lunch, which became old fast. I like Burger King, but not every day. Our staff was working through the flight schedule to get us back to the United States. It was like waiting for the lottery results to see if your number comes up. So far, only the first two flights had been confirmed, but not the one I was to be on. It was a long procedure of going through the scheduling and assigning the aircraft to support the mission, especially with the heavy demand on our transport aircraft. The insurgents continued with their terror and intimidation campaign against the locals, and now they were firing more on Camp Victory, the other compound located on the southern side of Baghdad International Airport, than on us. On June 16, the insurgents did fire rockets at Camp Anaconda on Balad and hit the BX area. Unfortunately, Major Paul Syverson, who had been working with us, was killed in the attack. Major Paul Syverson was a volunteer from the 5th Special Forces who was working with our staff. He was a great guy. I had gotten to know him working in the JOC. He was like Fergie; he didn't need to be here, but did it anyway and was dedicated to his job.

Our team from 10th Group stationed in the city of Samara was coming under frequent insurgent attacks. As with the April Offensive, there were problems between our forces and the conventional forces (2nd Brigade of the 1st Infantry Division) that controlled the area. The team was requesting close air support, but the conventional JOC wouldn't clear it. Even though our team could observe the insurgents and I could hear the sound of gunfire over the radio that I was monitoring, the conventional folks wouldn't allow the air strike. Luckily for us, our team was able to hold its position, and the insurgents withdrew.

To add to this pressure of watching our team under fire, I received word from my wife that her mother had been diagnosed with cancer. I knew this would be hard on my wife, especially with my being over in Iraq and not able to directly give her my support. The cancer was operable, and she would go into surgery sometime in July. This was another one of those hard things soldiers have to face when deployed. Sure I missed my daughter's birthday, my anniversary, and special events, but it was especially hard when family issues arose and I couldn't do anything about it. My mother-in-law is a strong woman, however, and I had complete confidence she would pull through.

On the night of June 21, the last official Commander's Update Brief was given in our JOC. After the briefing, everything was shut down, and the new JOC up in Balad would assume the duties as we moved ourselves up there. We spent the day of June 22 tearing apart the JOC and removing all of the wood and structures we had built inside. The compound was going to be turned over to the new Iraqi military so we had to return it in its original configuration. The original plan had the first bunch of the staff flying up in a CH-47 helicopter, but our ride was changed to a C-130 transport plane. I thought this would be a nicer trip, but boy was I in for a surprise. We took off and went through the normal jinking to avoid possible enemy tracking.

Somehow, the crew had the heat turned on inside the aircraft, and it was very uncomfortable. As we approached Balad, we started violently turning left and right, because we were receiving some ground fire. We were not hit, and we soon landed at our new home. After grabbing our gear, we loaded onto some buses and headed over to the new compound. Where once our three tents had stood, there was now a large complex surrounded by a protective barrier. It was late at night when we arrived, and we were taken to a half-completed tent. There were lights, and I found a cot to call my own. Then we waited for our gear to arrive. After grabbing my things, I tried to catch some sleep to be ready to begin my job in the new JOC the following morning.

After only a few hours of sleep, I got up and headed over to the compound. Even though this was the new CJSOTF compound, we still had to follow the rules imposed on everyone by the conventional commander of Camp Anaconda. This meant helmet and armor every time you walked out of your tent. I made my way over to the new JOC, which was in a large domed tent, about 200 feet long. The JOC itself was located on one end, and the rest of the tent contained offices. I was surprised when I saw our new working area. Normally, our rows are slightly tiered above each other so you can see over the person's head in front of you, but the local workers misunderstood the blueprints when they built it. The tiers were only supposed to be one foot high; they thought it was one meter high! So each tiered row was three feet higher than the next instead of the usual one. Luckily for me, I still sat in the front row and didn't have to perch up so high. The JOC was not fully operational. Computers were not working, and neither was the air conditioning. I sat at my station and sweated, using a towel I had brought with me to wipe my hands and face. We had no dining facility. You had to walk about a mile to the closest one, or wait to catch the bus over to the bigger dining facility a couple of miles away.

I always enjoyed walking so I could stretch my legs a bit after sitting at my workstation for so long. The problem was you had to do the walk in your armor and helmet. It was very hot and very bright in Balad, the almost white sand reflecting the sun's glare. The sand was like talcum powder, making little "poofs" of dust as you walked through it. The food was good and made the walk worth it, but then there was the mile walk back to the compound. There is absolutely no shade on Balad. At least back on RPC, we had had some shade to keep the sun off us. Not here. The sun pounded down on us, which made wearing armor and the Kevlar helmet an anything-but-enjoyable experience.

On the other side of the compound from us was the ever-burning garbage fire. Like in the TV show, "The Simpsons" and their ever burning tire fire, there was a constant garbage fire and a steady column of black smoke that arose from the other side of the camp.

My sleeping didn't get any better here. I shared a tent with about ten other men who worked different shifts. There was the constant sound of generators just outside of the tent. It was a low hum that you could both hear and feel, which made sleeping a challenge for me. The engineers continued to have problems getting the air conditioner to work, so the JOC was much like a sauna as the 100-degree temperatures baked the tent. Air conditioning for our sleeping tent was less than adequate. We believed that the temperature control was fixed so it couldn't be changed, and we couldn't seem to find anyone who could fix it. It was always warm in the tent. I had to sleep on top of my covers, which meant I had to keep applying bug spray to keep off the sand flies. To add to the misery, there were no laundry facilities to wash our clothes, and with the constant sweating, my uniform was starting to get rather rank. We were told that we could man our stations and be up and running in no time. Unfortunately this was not the case. There were a lot of glitches in the system that needed to be worked out. The compound had only one contract worker for the computers, for example, and he was just overwhelmed.

We later found out that the air conditioning repairman, who was a local contract worker, had been ambushed and killed while he was heading into work. So we had no idea when the air conditioner would be fixed in the JOC. The outside temperatures were around 111 degrees, and the inside temperature was around 96. I was looking forward to going home -- no more sweating, no more sand, and no more sleepless nights. If and when I went on leave, I planned to spend the first couple of days just sleeping and the next few days soaking in a hot tub or pool to get the sand out of my pores. Adding to this working environment was the constant pressure of not knowing when I would be rotating home. It was difficult knowing that my family would be in Germany more than likely by the time I reached home. This trip to Germany wasn't anything new. My wife had already planned to see her family at this time, and it would have been nice to see my wife and daughter before they left.

Most of the month of June was spent getting used to the extreme working conditions in the new JOC. As bad as we thought our old JOC was back in RPC, it was never as bad as the one we now had in Balad. Then to make things more difficult, the insurgents fired three mortar rounds at the compound around 5:30 a.m. June 25. Ironically, the insurgents fired another set of rockets at the compound, and two of our guys were wounded while attending the memorial service for Major Paul Syverson, who had been killed in the June 16 insurgent rocket attack.

I was told that I probably would be in Iraq until July 1 or 2. I knew that my family would be in Germany by then, so I asked permission to take leave en route, seeing that we would be stopping in Germany enroute back to Fort Carson.

One night after shift, I went and took a shower and was making my way over to the porta-johns when I heard the distinct pop...pop... pop of enemy rockets being fired at us. The rounds landed just on the other side of our protective wall, about three hundred feet away.

There was a loud explosion and the ground shook. I went back to my tent, grabbed my gear and headed to the bunker, which was already full of the new personnel just arriving in country. I watched the scout helicopters fly over in the direction that the rockets had come from, and soon we could hear the sound of our own compound's mortars firing back.

I was more concerned about the new personnel running around the camp than about the enemy fire. There were a few kids in the bunker who were wondering when they were supposed to lock and load. Just great! We didn't need some young, jacked-up kid with a loaded weapon running the compound in the dark. I told them not to do anything but to wait for the all clear. I guess they hadn't done a train-up before coming over, seeing this was the same unit we had replaced six months before. Perhaps they had gone through a large turnover and most of these guys were new to Iraq. I continued to be concerned as I watched the most heavily armed intelligence kids walking into the JOC where their section was located. Grenades were hanging off them, and they looked more like they were going off on a mission instead of manning their computers. If these guys had to fight, then more than likely we would all be dead. The insurgents could launch rocket and mortar attacks against Balad, but it would take all of the insurgents combined to take the base because it was so large. I continued to hope my replacement would be here soon so I could begin the transition and become an advisor while my replacement assumed my role. Until I was official transitioned, I was not going anywhere.

My morale took a big boost when on June 26 my leave request was granted. I would be allowed to take leave in Germany with my family. Besides the fact that I would have time in Germany with my family, I would save almost $1,700 dollars in airfare by being dropped off there by the Air Force.

The total number of us in our sleeping tent continued to dwindle as more and more left to go home. Now there were only six of us in a tent that had once held about twenty. A laundry service was now provided, but I decided to play it safe and stretch it out as best as I could, not wanting to leave there without my clothes. The camp was still being rocketed every night, but most of the rockets were landing on the other side of the base, away from us.

At the BX, I tried to purchase some civilian clothes and a box or bag to put my battle gear into, but I had no luck with either. I began to process out on June 27 by turning in my trusty pistol and ammunition. The base was hit again that evening, again away from us. Superstition was beginning to worm itself into my head, as I got closer to my departure date. I wasn't worried about not getting the transition done; I was more worried that I would be wounded in a rocket attack before I was able to get out of Iraq. One of our National Guard officers, Major Paul, was wounded in the neck during one of these rocket attacks. The wound wasn't bad, but he was still evacuated to Germany so he could heal in a clean environment.

Because of the changeover, we were becoming more short-handed, so I was assigned to two hours as door guard after my shift was completed. I sat in front of the door to check on the badges of those who entered the JOC. At least, this assignment allowed me some quality reading time. Happiness came on June 28 when my replacement arrived and I began to run him through the transition process. Basically, I briefed him on how to set up the slide presentation and when it all had to be done. I wrote a timeline for him telling when reports were due, and I showed him the different links on the computer that I checked daily to track current situations in the north. I felt bad for him. After overwhelming him with so much information, I was afraid his head would explode. I made a book with all of my contacts, computer links, and everything else he needed to know in order to run the station.

Meanwhile, the insurgents were following their own timeline. More rockets fell onto the base around 9:30 p.m. Once more, the scouts were up tracking the enemy, and we fired our base's mortars back at them. They dropped a couple more rockets that night, which landed close to our compound. I kept thinking: I just have to make it two more nights, and then I am out of here.

I found out in the morning that the rocket that landed close to us had impacted inside the new living area for our compound. Because space was becoming scarce, the living CORIMEXs, the two-man sleeping trailers, had been moved next to the perimeter fence. The rocket landed in and amongst the CORIMEXs, shredding a couple of them with fragments. Luckily no one was living in them yet. June 29 was supposed to be the hands-on day for my replacement, but I would do the briefing once more so he could see how I did it and follow suit. In between, I was packing my gear, trying to get everything I needed into a duffel bag and my rucksack, including my armor, helmet, and battle gear. I threw out some of my old T-shirts and underwear to make room. I was told there was a possibility we would be landing in Stuttgart rather than in our normal Frankfurt. This didn't bother me any. Having been stationed there for several years, I knew my way around the city and especially how to get to the train station where I could catch a train to Bavaria and my family.

June 30, my last day in Iraq, arrived in normal fashion with a morning rocket attack that landed on the other side of the base. The 5th Special Forces Group was to assume command of the CJSOTF that day, and the rest of us would return home. I spent the day going around and out-processing at the different sections of the CJSOTF. My replacement had the ball, and it was now all his.

As with all good military operations, our aircraft was delayed. We would be on a later flight, arriving around midnight or so. In a way I didn't mind. Being here technically on July 1 meant another month of tax-free and combat pay. Around 11 p.m., those of us who hadn't already left boarded the buses and headed over to the airfield. We had heard reports of a possible rocket attack that night, and after the last several nights' attacks, we were not surprised. Many of us were thinking, "As long as they do it after we leave so they don't delay us any longer."

We were moved over to a holding area where we were to wait to be processed through customs. There were a lot of other soldiers waiting to catch flights out of there so we found some chairs and made ourselves as comfortable as we could. We did a quick huddle so Colonel Repass could give us some parting words, and after a little while we were moved over to the customs area. We dumped our gear, and the inspectors went through it looking for contraband. Once everything was checked, we were moved to another set of tents to wait for the aircraft, which was scheduled to depart around 4 a.m.

I found a cot and was able to snooze for a little bit. Then the call came for us to line up and move out to the aircraft. All of our bags had been loaded onto a pallet after being inspected so they could be moved out to the waiting aircraft. We formed a column of twos and walked out to the C-17 transport. Slowly we made our way to the airplane and found a place to sit along the side. There was no cargo on board except for our baggage pallet. We wore our helmets and armor as we taxied out to the runway. The engines roared, and we shot down the runway and climbed into the dark skies.

It was finally over. I was on my way home, and I was in one piece. After we reached our cruising altitude, I took off my helmet and body armor, grabbed my poncho liner (a camouflage blanket), and found an open space on the floor. Using my armor as a pillow, I curled up and went to sleep. It was only a couple of hours to Germany, so I was going to catch up on what sleep I could. It was some of the best sleeping I had done in a long time, but soon we were awakened to take our seats for landing. What a wonderful feeling to touch down once more in Frankfurt, Germany! After taxiing up and shutting down, we climbed down the stairs and headed for the terminal to wait for our bags. As would happen in a regular airport, our bags came on a luggage carrousel. I grabbed my duffel and pulled out some shorts and a T-shirt, along with my running shoes. They were the only civilian clothes I had. Now dressed in a T-shirt and tan shorts, I said my good-byes as the rest of the folks, who went over to the holding tents to await their civilian flights back to the states the following day.

I walked across the street to the Welcome Center to catch the bus over to the civilian side of the airport, where a train station was located. This was the same Welcome Center that my family and I had passed through when we had returned to Germany from Fort Bragg back in 1996. I didn't have to wait long until the bus arrived, and soon I was shuttled over to the main airport. With a rucksack with my armor and battle gear strapped to the outside on my back and a duffel bag in my hands, I must have made an interesting sight as I made my way to the train station. I was able to purchase my ticket, and I made my way to the track. After about a half hour, the train arrived and I boarded the car that would take me to Bad Tolz. I had spent the extra money for a first-class ticket, knowing I would need the extra room for my gear. First class was rather nice, with big seats and a lot of space. I did receive some funny looks from the other passengers, but it made no difference to me. I settled in and enjoyed looking at all of the green trees whiz by as we traveled into southern Germany. I made my connection with some effort just outside of Munich and continued on my way to Bad Tolz. It's strange how the world and fate travels in a circle. My adventures in Iraq had begun back in 1991 when I was stationed in Bad Tolz. Now I was arriving after my fourth time to the country, back to where it had all begun. I walked over to the taxi stand and took a cab down to my in-laws' house. At the house, my father- and mother-in-law warmly greeted me. My family was scheduled to arrive the following day.

I spent time speaking to my in-laws, using my rusty German. It soon came back, and I was able to hold a pleasant conversation while I enjoyed a good Bavarian beer. I was soon off to bed and in the morning, we were on way our up to Munich airport to pick up my wife and daughter. I still didn't know what to expect when I meet my wife after being away for over six months. I was trying to figure out what I would do when I saw them coming out of customs. As I walked up, I asked my wife why we always do things backwards. Wasn't she supposed to meet me at the airport, and not the other way around? It didn't matter. I was reunited with my family, and my time in Iraq had finally come to an end.

The author during a stop during a convoy operation between Baghdad and Balad.

The last day in the JOC in Baghdad, a parting picture of some of the CJSOTF staff before moving up to Balad.

CHAPTER 17

FINAL THOUGHTS

As I am typing this book, my computer is sitting on a tough old box that used to hold my clothes and gear in Iraq. Not only is this the conclusion of my tale, it is the final chapter of my twenty-year military career. My house is empty. All of our furniture and belongings have been shipped, moving us into the future. My career in the military may be coming to a close, but my new career is about to begin. I have seen the best and the worst that humanity can dish out, from Africa through Bosnia and across Iraq. I look forward to my new life as an instructor, passing on my knowledge and experience, a lot of which I learned in Iraq. It is with mixed feelings that I move on, knowing that the job is still being done over in Iraq. My Group returned for another six-month tour, and it was hard for me to sit here and watch them go. I have always been there with them, in the thick of the fight. Now my focus is on my family and my new career.

When I was younger, I had always wondered why I had this desire to be in the military, and never really understanding the reason behind it. Now having served for the last twenty years and still serving as a government contractor, I now understand why. It was to make a difference, and hopefully I had made a difference with the different people I had helped. The Iraqi Kurds in the north, both during the humanitarian effort following Operation Desert Storm and returning to liberate them from Saddam Hussein during Operation Iraqi Freedom. The happiness I saw in their faces, as well as in the faces of the citizens of Baghdad, as they waved when I rode or walked by.

Iraq continued in the news as the people responsible for the Abu G abuse went on trial and were given their sentences. The Iraqis held their first free elections in a long time, one of the major goals we were striving for over there. Now, the country has a new government, and Saddam sits in prison and is on trial. However, the insurgency is not over, and the insurgents are killing more Iraqis. Perhaps one of these days, they will say, "enough is enough" and will do something about it. Until then, the United States and the men and women of the Special Forces, along with the other services and with our Allies will be there to help them continue the fight and bring democracy to this war-torn land. I would only ask the people of the United States and the world to be patient; it took our nation nearly seventeen years following the American Revolution to get their new government organized.

I have to admit, I never thought I would make it this far in my military career. I always thought that I would be dead before I reached my twenty-year mark. There have been several times when that almost came to pass, but I survived and made it to the end. I hope that what is contained in this book dispels some of the rumors and allows you, the reader, to see Iraq as I saw it. I attempted to provide this information in as unbiased manner as possible, allowing you to form your own opinion. A lot of what went on and the deeds performed by the many went unnoticed because it wasn't news material. There are a lot of unsung heroes over there fighting the fight, and in the end, this book is a testament to them so that some of the story can be told and history can be passed on to the next generations.

CHAPTER 18

A MOTHER'S POINT OF VIEW

I would like to show this tale from more than one point of view. Having told how I saw the war, now I would like to present another voice concerning the military operations in Iraq. During the summer I was to start my senior year in high school, I moved in with my father and his new family. They had been married for a while before I moved in, and I had developed a good relationship with my stepmother, stepsister and stepbrothers. We were a large family that lived in one house, between my father Richard, stepmother Sheila, stepbrothers John and Michael, my twin sister Katrina, and my stepsister Susan. At the time, my younger brother, Bob, still lived with our mother. We weren't just a large family due to our numbers, but due to our size as well, all of us brothers being athletes and playing scholastic football, wrestling, track, and power lifting. When I moved in with my father, Sheila was a reporter for our local newspaper, *The Post Star*.

She wrote her own column concerning the goings-on in our family, which everyone in our community seemed to really enjoy. Most of the time, people would ask how she could feed all of us, how us kids didn't drive her and my father crazy, and other day-to-day facts about our family. Though we became well known, the drawback was that if you messed up really bad in my family and my stepmother wrote about it, everyone in three counties would know you screwed up. Needless to say, we tried to stay on our best behavior around the house. But sometimes you just couldn't help yourself.

Here is an example of what I mean. This article was from the Glens Falls *Post Star* around April or May 1985. At the time of the article, my stepbrothers and I were participating in the Sectional

Championship track meet. The article was titled, "Phone calls can cheer or upset parents." For the most part of the article, Sheila wrote about the trials and tribulations of being a parent and receiving the dreaded phone calls from school. To show some of the frustration us kids caused, she wrote, "I don't like to admit that my six aren't perfect, but there have been a few moments in their careers when I would rather not have acknowledged any relationship." Yes, I am one of those reasons, which probably added a few grey hairs to Sheila's head. My contribution is as follows:

"But after all of this sad experience, I was still amazingly off-guard the other day when sports editor Greg Luckenbaugh walked up and said he wanted to congratulate me on Erick's performance. I knew Erick, Katrina's twin brother, had been competing in shot put that day so I looked up eagerly to hear how he had done. I learned later that Erick had won his event with a 49-foot, 8-inch throw, but that wasn't the performance Greg wanted to talk about. He had been covering the baseball game, not the track meet, and as members of the track team finished their events, they apparently wandered over to watch the championship game between Glens Falls and Ballston Spa. My helpful coworker had walked over to my desk to discuss Erick's performance as a spectator. "He ate a spider. A live spider," Greg said in disbelief. Does a mother need to hear news like that?"

I had indeed eaten a spider while sitting in the stands with my teammates. It was a dare, and I did it. I had become a spider eater before becoming a snake eater. This story was printed, and it soon faded from my memory until I was conducting an airborne training jump with the 1st Special Forces when I was a Ranger out at Fort Lewis. One of the support soldiers from 1st Group who was jumping with us was from upstate New York. He and I sat there and talked about places we knew. He kept looking at me as we talked and finally came out and said, "You're the guy who ate the spider!" Here I was on the other side of the country and I ran into someone who knew my past.

Sheila was probably just like the majority of the mothers out there across the United States, even if we were a rather "unique" family. Like any other parent, she was looking out for our best interests, supportive and concerned when things were going bad. For

Sheila, this situation became very bad in January 1991 when news came that Operation Desert Storm had begun. Her article from the Moreau Sun is titled "The war in the Middle East: A mother's view."

"The radio played quietly all day on the window ledge near my desk as I waited for the news. It was hours past the deadline, and the President's words echoed: 'Sooner rather than later.' As the children and I worked in the kitchen, the first bulletins came over the television. The rolls I had placed in the toaster oven were forgotten until black smoke filled the kitchen. Fighting tears, I listened for clues as to what was happening halfway around the world. Now my head was filled with the old public service announcement: 'Do you know where your children are?' 'Where are you Erick?' I wondered. 'What are you doing tonight?'

"Our son is a staff sergeant with Army Special Forces. He had flown from Germany for what he would call only 'some interesting assignments.' Where he was going and what he would be doing was, as usual, classified. His unit has been training for months, disappearing for weeks at a time and then reappearing, unable to tell wives or parents where they had gone or what they had done. Now war had come and the training was over. His wife remained alone in Germany, and we waited in Glens Falls. Hoping for news from him. Hoping not to get a call from the Army. Like many Americans, my feelings about this war are divided. I am angry that we aided and armed a dictator like Saddam Hussein, just as we have aided and armed so many dictators that have turned out to be more foes than friends. I am angry that for 10 years we have abandoned any pretense of an energy policy, thereby encouraging the greedy and the arrogant. But I cannot ignore the Amnesty International reports about what has been happening in Kuwait. And I hope this really is the beginning of a new world order in which such aggression will not be tolerated.

"I am glad a vote was taken in Congress. Whatever the flaws of our system of government, it has given us freedoms unprecedented in world history. I am a believer in the Constitution, which gives Congress the power to declare war. The vote has been taken, and I respect the results. But I don't spend much energy anymore thinking about such generalized concerns. Most of all, I am terribly, personally, selfishly afraid. Like family members all across the country, I want my son to be safe. And now there is nothing left that I can do but listen to the news and pray."

Back during Operation Desert Storm, the only way I could communicate with my family was through the regular mail system. It would take weeks, sometimes months for a letter from me to reach my family in Glens Falls, N.Y. Compared to the technology of today, with cell phones and e-mail, it took a long time for my family to hear from me and learn how I was doing. They had to face every military parent's worse nightmare, the lack of information. You wanted some news, but you also dreaded to hear the news. The not knowing what was going on was perhaps the greatest burden that the military families had to face during Operation Desert Storm. However, this wouldn't be my only time over there as I headed back for Operation Provide Comfort. Sheila wrote the following commentary on April 14, 1991 titled, "A mother's disappointment with our leaders," for the *Moreau Sun*:

"There is a sour taste in my mouth. My stepson Erick called last weekend from Germany to say he was returning to the Middle East. A staff sergeant with the Army Special Forces, Erick was sent from Germany to somewhere in the Persian Gulf area a few days before American bombing began. Since most of what he does is secret, we don't know where he was in the weeks that followed or what he was doing. But at the end of the war, he returned to Germany. Now he is going back, this time, he tells us, for humanitarian reasons. Erick has medic training, and he will be working with the desperate Kurd refugees, trying to ease some of their suffering.

"I watch television and read the papers and I am appalled at our national leadership. They took our sons and daughters, our husbands and wives, and put them at risk in the desert. They dropped enough bombs on Iraq to throw the country back into the pre-industrial dark ages, killing and maiming more people then we can count. They made speeches about right and duty and honor. And then, with Saddam Hussein still in power, they said it was not our problem as helicopter gunships rained bullets and napalm on the rebels we had encouraged to resist. Now, embarrassed and clearly unsure about what to do, they offer too little help too late. I do not understand why the arms dealers are already back in business, using the recent battle as a demonstration of the potency of their products. I do not understand why we support policies that aid the Khmer Rouge in Cambodia, surely one of the most immoral regimes in history.

"I do not understand why we reward the Chinese leadership for mowing down its own students by immediately offering trade advantages. Our leaders talk about right and wrong, but too often they ignore both, patterning their actions on what they perceive as the best short-term strategic opportunity for profit. They use terms like 'realpolitic' or 'geopolitical reality.' We need a strong, unpartitioned Iraq to counter Iran, we are told. We can't offend Turkey or the Soviet Union, and both have large, unhappy Kurdish populations. Twenty-four years ago, I sat in my rocking chair, nursing my oldest son, and watching televised images of Vietnam. 'I am not raising you for cannon fodder,' I vowed. But sometimes it does not seem as if we have much ability to control events. I am not a total pacifist. I know there are times when nations have to fight. But I want to trust the people who are making the decisions. I want to believe that we are standing up for things I believe in, consistently and intelligently. I want to believe that all of our actions seek peace and that we resort to war only when we have run out of choices.

"I do not want my sons and stepsons putting their lives on the line because we have no clear energy policy or because we need to improve our trade balance by selling weapons. I am glad that Erick will be able to use his training, his skills, and his natural compassion to bring relief to a few of the fleeing refugees. But I wish I did not have this bitter taste in my mouth, this feeling that decisions made by political leaders here in the United States contributed to their desperate plight."

This is definitely one of those articles where Sheila and I are both in agreement. I was disappointed by what our government did to the Kurds, by encouraging them to rise up, only to fail to show up with help when they really needed it. I have never been a big fan of politics or politicians for that matter, especially when they interfere with combat or military operations. My instructions prior to infiltrating the camps were not to instruct the Kurds in weapons

241

and/or tactics. I am a Special Forces soldier, trained to organize, train, and lead guerrillas and partisans in overthrowing oppressive governments. This was perhaps the best time to do this, and it would have saved us so much time and money to have helped the Kurds and Shiites to overthrow Saddam Hussein then. I hated having my hands tied, but I am a professional soldier, and I obeyed my instructions. Pity though, from what I observed of the Peshmerga, they wouldn't have needed much training and only assistance with anti-armor or anti-aircraft weaponry. They were a very well trained and organized fighting force. Sheila would write a follow up article in her "My House" column titled "A Mideast snapshot from Maine" in the *Moreau Sun*:

"On a Memorial Day trip to visit my mother-in-law in Maine, we enjoyed yet another demonstration of how technology has shrunk the world. Sitting in her rural home talking by phone to our son in Germany, we heard details about the tragic conditions endured by the Kurds in Northern Iraq. Erick, a sergeant with the Special Forces, had been sent to the Persian Gulf during the conflict there, but he had returned to his base in Germany at war's end. Almost immediately, his unit was rushed back to Turkey to assist the Kurds who had fled from Saddam Hussein's murderous attacks. Erick and his unit have now returned once again to Germany. We received two letters from Erick that were written during his time with Operation Provide Comfort. At the time he wrote, his unit was sitting in a small camp near the Iraqi border, unable to reach the refugees they had come to help. Erick now speaks angrily about the difficulties placed in the American Army's way by Turkey, a NATO ally, but a country that has its own problems with the Kurds.

"But finally, his unit arrived at a camp in northern Iraq. In our phone conversation, we heard details about the valiant struggle of the Special Forces against the massive medical problems facing the refugees. Erick has been interested in medical work since high school, when he served as a volunteer with the Moreau Emergency Squad. In the Army, he has received further training, but he is not a doctor. Nonetheless, he treated between 200 and 300 patients a day, mainly for malnutrition and dehydration. Working in a temporary facility set up in a tent, Erick even did some simple surgery. In one case, he cut out a badly infected ingrown toenail. And at times, he put on his dentist's cap – filling teeth as needed. Languages have always fascinated Erick, who studied both beginning German and Russian at Queensbury High School. The leader of this particular refugee camp was an English teacher, and his children were college students. They served as translators and taught Erick enough simple Kurdish to get by.

"Soon, he reports, he was making 'house calls,' visiting tents and using his new language skills to talk to patients. During the time they served this camp, Erick reports proudly, only three patients died: two elderly men and a badly dehydrated child who didn't live through a Medevac flight to a hospital. Erick returned from the Persian Gulf with six new medals. Perhaps more importantly, he returned with a new commitment to a medical career. He is now talking about attending college to become a physician's assistant. Whatever the political questions we might have about the decisions that caused the flight of the Kurds from the Iraqi Army, I believe all Americans can be proud of the job the Special Forces did in restoring hope to the refugee camps. I know we are very proud of Erick."

I myself wrote a quick letter to the editor expressing my thanks to the people of my hometown who supported us during the war. It was printed in the Glens Falls *Post Star* on April 8, 1991, and went as follows: "Thanks to all for their mail and moral support. This letter is mostly to the people of the Glens Falls area. I was deployed to the Gulf with the 10th Special Forces. My parents put an article in the paper requesting mail be sent to me. I received a lot of mail from the Glens Falls area people who were showing their support. I received mail from church groups, a fifth and sixth grade Sunday school class, two seventh graders from Argyle, and a whole bunch from people around Glens Falls. It made me proud to see all the support and patriotism coming from my hometown. We soldiers in the Gulf needed the support to keep going. The Glens Falls people showed it strongly, and it made me proud to be from Glens Falls. Thank you to all the people who showed support from the Glens Falls area."

I found it rather interesting that on the day my letter to the editor was printed, so was an article from Mike Royko, a syndicated columnist, titled "Turning our backs on the Kurds."

These articles that were written by Sheila were clipped from the paper by my mother and made into a scrapbook, which she gave me later. The town of Glens Falls even produced a video filmed in the Glens Falls Civic Center during an Adirondack Red Wings hockey match. The video was titled, "Hurry Home, to our service men and women in Saudia Arabia from the families in Warren County, NY." During half-time, the film crew panned around the center as all of the people in the stands held up yellow ribbons and signs supporting the troops, and applauding and yelling loudly. I still have the video, as well as all of the letters that I received from the various folks around Glens Falls during Desert Storm. I thought it would be appropriate to include Sheila's columns so the readers of this book can get a sense of what the families were experiencing while we were at war. To fully understand what happened during that time, you need to see it from two points of view.

GLOSSARY

AC-130 H/U Gunship: Modified C-130 Hercules transport aircraft equipped for close air support, air interdiction and force protection. "H" models are known as Specter, "U" models are known as Spooky. Aircraft are armed with side mounted 105-mm howitzer, 40mm and 25mm cannons.

Army Airborne School: Located at Fort Benning Georgia, a three-week course that trains and certifies military personnel in military static-line parachuting. Upon graduation the student earns his Airborne Wings and Maroon Beret.

Army Infantry School: Located on Fort Benning, Georgia and responsible for taking fresh recruits through a six-week basic training routine, then a seven-week advanced individual training course in infantry skills.

"Assaulter": Specially trained personnel in advanced urban warfare and breaching who have attended SFARTAEC, which is comparable to police Special Weapons and Tactics Team (S.W.A.T.).

C-130 Hercules: Standard Air Force military transport aircraft responsible for performing the tactical portion of the airlift mission. The aircraft can is capable of operating off of rough landing strips, and is the prime transport for air dropping personnel and equipment into hostile areas

C-17 Globemaster III: Newest and most flexible cargo aircraft capable of rapid strategic delivery of troops and all types of cargo to main operating bases or forward deployed bases. Powered by four powerful jet engines, it can carry up to 102 troops/paratroopers and equipment.

C-5 Galaxy: Largest air transport aircraft in the Air Force inventory, capable of deploying personnel and equipment, including the M1A1 Abrams tanks, anywhere in the world.

C-9 Nightingale: Air Force version of the McDonald-Douglas DC-9 passenger jet.

CH-46 Sea Knight: Twin-rotor helicopter with a rotor in the front and one in the rear. This is a medium-lift assault helicopter used to provide all-weather, day/night, and night vision goggle assault transport of combat troops, supplies, and equipment.

CH-47 Chinook: Twin-rotor medium-lift helicopter used by the Army. It is similar to the CH-46, except it is slightly larger and can carry up to 44 personnel or 46,000 pounds of equipment.

CH-53 Super Stallion: Marine Corps heavy-lift helicopter designed for the transportation of material and supplies, as well as combat troops between ships and ship-to-shore operations. It can carry up to 16 tons of equipment or 38 fully equipped combat troops.

Combat Search and Rescue (CSAR): The process in which a military force conducts a limited search for an isolated person in a hostile environment in an effort to return them to friendly control.

CPA, Civilian Provisional Authority: Organization assisted by the US State Department, the US military, and NATO to organize and build an Iraqi Civilian Government.

F-15E Strike Eagle: A two-seat, dual-role version of the F-15 Eagle fighter used for conducting strike/bombing missions with improved accuracy at low altitude, day or night, and in all weather.

The Green Zone: An area in the center of Baghdad that is completely enclosed by a wall and security forces. It is the location of the CPA as well as humanitarian aid organizations and their quarters.

HK-21: German-made 7.62mm (.308) machine gun that can be either belt-fed or magazine fed with a quick change barrel. Used by special operations units.

"Hooch": Military slang for an improvised shelter, as well as living quarters for soldiers.

HRC, High Risk of Capture: Any personnel that due to their mission potentially may be captured by a hostile force is considered High Risk of Capture.

IED, Improvised Explosive Device: Homemade bomb used by Iraqi insurgents to attack coalition convoys and personnel.

JFKSWC, John F. Kennedy Special Warfare Center and School: Primary school for Army Special Forces, from the Qualification Course, to specialty schools such as HALO, SFARTEAC, and SOT-IC, located at Fort Bragg, North Carolina.

JOC, Joint Operations Center: Primary command post of a joint staff that monitors and executes missions.

JPRA, Joint Personnel Recovery Agency: Primary Department of Defense organization responsible for the training and education of military and civilian personnel in personnel recovery matters.

MC-130H Combat Talon II: Modified C-130 Hercules aircraft with advanced avionics, terrain avoidance, and threat detection equipment used to infiltrate and support Special Operations forces into hostile or denied areas. Aircraft can carry 77 troops, 52 paratroopers or 57 litter patients.

MC-130P Combat Shadow: Modified C-130 aircraft which conducts clandestine or low visibility, single, or multi-ship missions intruding politically sensitive or hostile territory to provide air refueling for special operations helicopters, normally during periods of darkness.

MH-53M Pavelow IV: Heavy-lift helicopter, the largest, most powerful, and most technologically advanced helicopter in the Air Force inventory. Aircraft is a modified version of the CH-53 Super Sea Stallion designed for long-range infiltration, exfiltration and resupply of special operations forces in day, night, or marginal weather.

M24: Standard military sniper rifle, normally a Remington Model 700, bolt-action 7.62mm/.308 caliber rifle with a ten-power Leopold scope.

M249 Squad Automatic Weapon (SAW): 5.56mm gas operated, magazine or belt-fed light machine gun with fixed headspace and quick change barrel feature.

M203: 40-mm grenade launcher that is normally attached under the barrel of M4 or M16 rifles. The weapon is a lightweight, combat, breech-loading, pump-action, single- shot system.

M4 Carbine: Standard issue military carbine which fires the NATO 5.56mm (.223) bullet. Smaller then the M16, it is equipped with a telescoping stock and is modular for specialized equipment.

M60: Standard military issue 7.62mm/.308 caliber, gas-operated, belt-fed, air-cooled, and general purpose machine gun. Currently, this weapon is being replaced by the M240 Machine Gun.

M67 90-mm Recoilless Rifle: Breach-loaded anti-armor weapon that fires a 90-mm High Explosive Anti-Tank (HEAT) projectile as well as anti-personnel ammunition.

M79: Vietnam era 40-mm grenade launcher which looked like a large shotgun.

M82A1: Gas-operated, magazine-fed, .50 caliber sniper rifle used by Special Operations and Conventional forces. This rifle can effectively engage targets up to a mile in distance.

M9: Standard issue military side arm, based on the 9mm Berretta 92F. It is a light-weight, semi-automatic pistol, which replaced the M1911A1 .45 caliber pistol. It uses a 15-round box magazine.

Military Free Fall: known as HALO for High Altitude Low Opening, is a specialized school ran by the John F. Kennedy Special Warfare Center and School at Fort Bragg, North Carolina and Yuma Proving Ground, Utah. Students learn the skills to conduct free fall parachuting from 30,000 feet while under oxygen and opening their own parachutes.

Military Occupation Specialties (MOS): A numbered code to indicate an individual's specialty in the service. For example an infantrymen is 11B, a Special Forces Weapons Sergeant is an 18B.

MRE, Meals, Ready to Eat: Standard military ration used by the United States armed forces. It is designed to have a long shelf life.

Peshmerga: "Those willing to die," Kurdish freedom fighters normally from Northern Iraq who fought against Saddam Hussein.

Rangers: The 75th Ranger Regiment, composed of three Ranger battalions, is the premier light-infantry unit of the United States Army. Headquartered at Fort Benning, Georgia, the 75th Ranger regiment's mission is to plan and conduct special missions in support of U.S. policies and objectives.

Ranger Indoctrination Program (RIP): Three-week program administered by the 75th Ranger Regiment to take new volunteers and introduce them to ranger tactics before being assigned to a ranger battalion.

Ranger School: Eight-week course designed to include ranger, reconnaissance and surveillance leader courses to further develop the combat arms skills of officers and enlisted volunteers. The course is broken down into different phases to include mountaineering and desert and jungle operations.

RC-135 V/W RIVET JOINT: Modified Boeing 707 reconnaissance aircraft that supports theater and national level consumers with near real-time, on-scene intelligence collection, analysis, and dissemination capabilities.

SA-2 Guideline: Soviet built, medium-to-high-altitude, surface-to-air, anti-aircraft, two-stage missile.

SA-8 Gecko: Soviet-built, low-altitude, single-stage, surface-to-air, anti-aircraft missile.

SCUD: Soviet built SS-1c is a single-stage, short-range tactical ballistic missile that can be armed with either conventional or chemical warheads with a range of 300 kilometers.

SFARTAEC: Special Forces Advanced Reconnaissance, Target Analysis and Exploitation Course: Eight-week Special Operations course which teaches advanced urban warfare and breaching techniques at Fort Bragg, North Carolina.

SEALs: (Sea Air and Land) Navy Special Warfare Unit members who specialize in conducting special operations along coasts and rivers, and against enemy ships and vessels.

SERE: Survival, Escape, Resistance and Evasion: Specialized training that teaches personnel how to survive, escape from capture, resist interrogation techniques, and evade enemy personnel.

Sniper: A specially trained soldier in field craft and advanced marksmanship who can use a scoped, high-power rifle to surgically remove enemy personnel. Schools include the Army Sniper School, the Special Forces Special Operation Target Interdiction Course, and the Marine Corps Scout Sniper Course.

SOP, Standard Operating Procedures: A well rehearsed plan of action that becomes second nature and requires little or no thinking to execute.

Special Forces (SF): An elite Army unit referred to by their distinct headgear, the Green Beret, which specializes in unconventional warfare, direct action, strategic reconnaissance, foreign internal defense, and counter-terrorism.

"Strip Alert": This occurs when an alert crew, which has been designated for a special purpose, such as personnel recovery, is located next to the runway or taxiway where its helicopters/aircraft are located.

Thermite Grenade: A grenade that looks like a standard smoke grenade, but is painted red and filled with magnesium. It is used to destroy large weapons or metal blocks.

VBIED, Vehicle Born Improvised Explosive Device: A homemade bomb that is built into a vehicle to be driven into a convoy or installation by insurgents in Iraq.

Printed in the United States
113947LV00003B/70-87/A